THESE HOUSES ARE OURS

THESE HOUSES ARE OURS

Co-operative and community-led housing alternatives, 1870-1919

Andrew Bibby

GRITSTONE
SOCIAL HISTORY

"... The tenants are all landlords as well as tenants.
None of them can say 'This house is mine'; they can all say
'These houses are ours' ..."
- J.S. Nettlefold, 1914

Published in 2023 by

Gritstone Publishing Co-operative Ltd,
Birchcliffe Centre,
Hebden Bridge HX7 8DG.

www.gritstonecoop.co.uk

ISBN 978-1-913625-08-5

CONTENTS

Author's Introduction: the view from Keswick 1

1. Housing and the co-operative movement 10
2. "Thinking over the dwellings question": Ben Jones and the Tenant Co-operators 18
3. Co-partnership in Housing: enter Henry Vivian 31
4. With the Garden City movement 39
5. Scaling up: a national infrastructure 50
6. Finding the money 65
7. 'Full of comradeship': life as it was lived in the estates 77
8. The movement in 1911 87
9. The trouble with tenants? 100
10. 'Housing is a women's issue' 110
11. The eve of war 118
12. Housing and the First World War 127
13. Afterwards 138
14. Conclusion 152

Gazetteer 160
Abbreviations 171
Acknowledgements 172
Bibliography 173
Endnotes 184
Index 198

THE VIEW FROM KESWICK

Few English towns can boast such attractive surroundings as Keswick, in the Lake District. To the north is Skiddaw, the country's fourth highest mountain. To the south are the waters of Derwentwater. West and south-west lies the Newlands Valley and the high fells that enclose it. Over to the east is the distinctive shape of another high Lakeland mountain, Blencathra.

Not surprisingly, therefore, Keswick is enormously popular with visitors. Throughout the year the town's streets are packed with holiday-makers. Much of the local economy is focused on the tourism industry, and many local people depend on this for their living. There are jobs of all kinds to be had servicing the various different needs of the visitors, though jobs in the tourist sector can be notoriously poorly paid.

So not surprisingly, Keswick also has a housing issue. A local paper reported recently that nearly half of the properties in the Keswick area have become either holiday lets or second homes. Drawing on council tax data the paper noted that there were now 1,271 of these, out of the 2,600 or so houses and flats in the Keswick postcode area. The trend in this direction seems to be increasing rapidly.[1]

The key problem is the absence of housing to rent, at prices which local people can afford. "Many people who work in Keswick are having to move out," Bill Bewley told me, when I met him and his wife Wendy in the upstairs room of a café in the centre of the town one sunny summer Sunday. "Or they live in appalling apartments, renting damp properties and paying a fortune. It quite breaks your heart."

It is a serious problem which is well-known locally. Even estate agents have advised the local council that affordability is the key issue for the town's property market.[2]

For the past decade, however, some in the Keswick community have been trying to take practical steps, in a hands-on, bottom-up sort of way, to begin to make a difference. Keswick Community Housing Trust (KCHT) is a local charitable body (technically a 'community benefit society') which was set up following a series of meetings in the town in 2009. "At all the meetings people were raising the issue of affordable housing," Wendy said. "So at the last meeting, some of us said to each other, 'well, shall we do something?'" Might it even be possible perhaps to look towards buying a house to rent out?

KCHT has done rather a lot better than acquiring simply a single house. In the summer of 2021 its fourth development, an award-winning set of houses in vernacular architecture complete with triple-glazed windows and high energy efficiency design welcomed their first tenants. (Given the number of applications, the Trust could have let these houses more than five times over.) Southey Court's four houses bring the current total number of affordable homes that KCHT has created for local people in housing need to over forty. Already the talk is turning to where the fifth and sixth developments will be built.[3]

Bill and Wendy Bewley have both been on the committee since the start of the Trust, Bill serving as the organisation's chair during this time. They moved to the town in 1998 from Liverpool for Bill's work (he worked in bakery production management) and – after a few years when Bill worked abroad – returned back to Keswick in 2007 for retirement. It was Bill who had chaired the meetings in 2009, which had been called under the auspices of the town's Churches Together group. Bill is a Quaker from a very long-established Quaker family.

I had arranged to meet them to hear the story of how they, together with their fellow KCHT trustees, had managed to achieve so much in such a relatively short period of time. Of course, they told me, there were all sorts of problems to overcome. Right at the start, for example, they wasted a year trying in vain to negotiate a sensible price for a sliver of land for a roadway which in the end turned out not to be needed anyway. But nevertheless by 2013 they had started their first development, which they named The Hopes, and which consisted of eleven three-bedroomed houses. The land, alongside the parish church, had originally been earmarked for a possible extension of the graveyard but it turned out to be too wet and rocky to accommodate the dead. Instead the church sold it to KCHT at a very reasonable price, for the living to enjoy. Funding for the build came partly from a mortgage loan from the Cumberland Building Society and partly from a grant from the government's Affordable Homes programme via what is now Homes

England (five of the houses are also affordable shared-ownership, so that their occupants contributed some of the capital needed, and one was sold outright – a mixture of tenures on estates is considered good housing practice). However part of the overall capital which KCHT needed came from investments put in by local individuals who liked the idea of what KCHT was trying to achieve and thought their savings could perhaps make a difference.

As a community benefit society, KCHT has the legal ability to issue what are known as 'community shares', a form of equity investment which is also increasingly being employed by community groups trying to save their village shops or village pubs or perhaps trying to set up small-scale community-based energy generation schemes. KCHT's business plan for The Hopes had set a target of £50,000 in community shares; in the end they raised £60,000. The minimum investment was £250, the maximum was £5,000 and Bill Bewley says that around sixty investors contributed to the share issue.

Between The Hopes (completed in late 2013) and 2021's Southey Court came two other projects, including the rather unlikely initiative to convert a former public toilet block in the centre of Keswick (given to the trust by the council for a nominal £1) into four one-bedroom flats. (You would never now guess the flats' provenance....)

It's an inspiring story. But it must be said that there are many other places where I could have gone instead of Keswick to start this book. Keswick Community Housing Trust is simply one of a growing number of community-led housing initiatives which have come about through voluntary efforts in recent years.

I could have checked out the view from, oh let's say, Lyme Regis, or perhaps from one of the West Country villages where community land trusts (CLTs) have been set up to provide affordable rental housing for local people squeezed out by an increasingly unaffordable housing market – villages like Powerstock or Worth Matravers in Dorset or Broadhempston in Devon. Further south in Cornwall, I could have started in, say, St Ives where the active community land trust has as in Keswick looked to local people to provide investment capital through a community share issue.

Alternatively, I could have started this book by going north to the Northumberland town of Wooler where a community trust is regenerating a small market town once struggling to stay afloat. I could have travelled to Wales, choosing perhaps to go to the Gower peninsula in south Wales to see what the Gŵyr CLT is trying to do. Or (declaring an interest, because for several years I acted as secretary of my own local CLT) I could have stayed at home in the Calder Valley in West Yorkshire.

I could certainly have gone to several areas of London, or to inner-city Leeds, or to Toxteth and Anfield in Liverpool. In all these places, and many more, community land trusts are trying to directly address the housing crises they face through bottom-up effort. The Community Land Trust Network is keen to point out that CLTs are an urban as well as a rural phenomenon: the Network now claims over 500 CLTs just in England and Wales (Scotland also has a host of community initiatives focused on land and housing issues).[4]

But I had not gone to Wooler, or St Ives, or Toxteth, or to anywhere else where I could have found CLTs at work. I had chosen Keswick for a deliberate purpose.

As I hope is clear from its sub-title, this is a work of history. It looks at what was done a century or more ago to meet the housing crisis that was being faced by people then. There are, however, extraordinary points of similarity with our present day.

I went to Keswick because, remarkably, the town offers the very best example of then and now. In 1909, exactly a hundred years before Bill and Wendy Bewley and their colleagues were establishing KCHT in 2009, another group of local community-minded people were setting up Derwentwater Tenants Ltd. The twenty-five houses that make up what was called Greta Hamlet (Keswick's river Greta is close at hand) were opening their doors to their first tenants a year later.

Greta Hamlet is still there today, only perhaps a ten minute stroll through the centre of Keswick from KCHT's The Hopes, Southey Court and their other developments. Close to the shops but very tucked away (no Lake District tourist would be likely to stumble on it by accident), Greta Hamlet has perhaps the very best views in a town where fine views are not difficult to find. The houses are built in blocks around three sides of a small grassy central area (the 'Green'), and from the seats which have been placed here today's tenants, just like their antecedents, can look across and enjoy the sight of almost all the mountains and fells that encompass Keswick.

Greta Hamlet looks today little changed from when the development was completed, at a cost of £7,000, in 1910. What has also not changed (and this is the particular surprise) is that it remains today a tenant-run society, still operating very much under the rules which were drawn up by its first committee in 1909. It is one of only a handful of similar 'co-operative' societies (I have identified ten, although I am not ruling out that there may be a small number of others which I have failed to uncover) which have continued to operate for more than a century through a time of enormous changes both in society and in terms of housing policies. Following the First World War (and in particular after 1945) council housing became the dominant form of social housing in Britain. The private rental market, once the mainstay for working-class housing, shrank dramatically during the twentieth century but then more recently has expanded again as the buy-to-let market has taken off. Owner occupation was promoted as an aspiration for all during the Thatcher years but has become increasingly unaffordable to many since then as house prices have accelerated far away from income levels. And meanwhile Derwentwater Tenants has continued in its own quiet corner of England, providing twenty-five homes for local people to rent – just as its founders wanted it.

Needless to say, on the same Sunday when I was in Keswick to visit Bill and Wendy Bewley I also made a point of arranging to meet one of Greta Hamlet's residents, Philip Pridmore. Philip acts (in a voluntary capacity) as the secretary of Derwentwater Tenants, making sure that the gardens are well maintained, the exterior of the houses regularly painted, and any little maintenance problems addressed. He is one of the nine tenants who comprise the current management committee of the society, who meet every twelve weeks or so, and who also take on the task of choosing the local people who will join them in Greta Hamlet as neighbours on the relatively rare occasions when vacancies arise.

Philip took me to the garden seats on the Green so I too could enjoy the views as we discussed the early history of his society. Like KCHT, Derwentwater Tenants is registered legally as a community benefit society. Like KCHT, it was an individual local Quaker (in this case the philanthropically-minded mine-owner Anthony Wilson) who was instrumental in its establishment and became their first chairman. Again like KCHT, the Greta Hamlet development was funded partly through share investments from local people with money who supported the idea. And again, in the same way as KCHT started with a small group discussing what they could do after a meeting in the town, Derwentwater Tenants also came about after a meeting.

(Having pointed out the similarities, it needs to be said that KCHT and Derwentwater Tenants, while they are aware of each other, do not have any close links. As we shall see later, most of the remaining societies from the early 1900s tend to maintain a very low profile.)

The meeting which led to Greta Hamlet being built was held in December 1908, at a Mission Hall just outside Keswick in Portinscale, on what was reportedly a very stormy night.[5] The speaker was a committed co-operative activist called Crossley Greenwood who had come up from Letchworth, the planned 'garden city' inspired by Ebenezer Howard's celebrated 1898 book expounding the idea. Crossley Greenwood came from a co-operative background: he had grown up in Hebden Bridge in Yorkshire where his father Joseph had led a pioneering worker-run co-operative mill.[6] He had moved south in his early thirties shortly after Letchworth had been established in 1903 and was in 1908 working as the paid organiser of a body called the Co-partnership Tenants Housing Council.

Greenwood would have been able to share with his Keswick audience the experience in Letchworth where a 'co-partnership housing' society called Garden City Tenants had been established in 1905 and had become the primary way that workers in Letchworth were able to find housing they could afford. But no doubt Crossley Greenwood also talked of the other similar tenants' societies which were federated members of his Council: ventures in places such as Ealing, Leicester, Sevenoaks, Birmingham, Manchester, Oldham and elsewhere. He would have described how ideas from the increasingly influential Garden City movement (or more precisely, the garden suburb and garden village movement associated with the architect Raymond Unwin) were influencing the design of the estates these societies built. He would have urged his audience in Keswick to build accordingly: to avoid densely packed streets of terraces; to build only ten or twelve houses to the acre; to create green open spaces where neighbours could foregather; to provide allotments; to give each house a generous-sized garden.

Greta Hamlet, when it came to be built, did indeed follow this prescription. Philip Pridmore showed me the ample-sized gardens and the allotments (the latter now also made available to others in the town who want to grow their own vegetables). Unlike several other co-partnership societies, the community was too small to merit other communal facilities which were often a feature of the design: a meeting hall or institute, a bowling green, tennis courts, and children's playgrounds. But like the other societies of its time, the houses were well built. They were and are delightful homes.

As I've suggested, what is happening today in terms of grassroots efforts to tackle housing issues echoes sometimes uncannily what was taking place in the later nineteenth century and early twentieth century, when community-minded groups of people (often local worthies but sometimes workers themselves in housing need) were taking steps to address chronic local housing problems. Their history is a valuable one and has the right to be recorded and acknowledged in its own right, and this is what this book sets out to do: it would be wrong to try to distort or shoehorn their story simply to reflect our own interests and concerns today.

Nevertheless, inevitably their history has lessons to offer us. I have been encouraged to pursue this line of research partly to enable those working in the community-led housing world to have a sense of their roots, and I will be delighted if my friends in the CLT movement have the same responses as I have done to the tales of the early pioneers. I hope too that this account will also appeal to those interested in wider co-operative history: it is certainly the case that, unlike several other countries in the developed world, co-operative housing has played only a small part in total housing provision in Britain for much of the past hundred years – and yet, perhaps, the story could have been very different. More generally, as the country tries to tackle what is recognised today as yet another crisis in the provision of affordable housing for its people, it feels an appropriate time to offer a new contribution to the work already undertaken by historians looking at the wider development of social housing in Britain.

The 'Addison Act' – the Housing, Town Planning, &c Act 1919, promoted by the Minister of Health Christopher Addison – has often been seen as the legislation that introduced the concept of local authority owned housing to Britain. This is a somewhat simplistic view: there was council housing created by the London County Council and several other local authorities long before 1919, and the Addison Act itself quickly fell foul of political realities, and especially of Treasury constraints, and its radical measures to promote house-building were for a time effectively squashed. Nevertheless it is true that the First World War marks a watershed in the story of social housing in Britain. Before August 1914 there was an active movement developing what we would now call community-led housing. After 1918, this movement became much weaker. Some of the pre-1914 vision disappeared from sight as increasingly a focus on business realism and profitability took over. Those societies which did develop new housing estates in the years immediately after the First World War often found themselves facing financial difficulties and up against an unsympathetic civil service when they tried to ask for help.

It seems apposite therefore to make 1919 the formal date for ending this account, even though, as will become apparent, I do carry the story forward beyond 1919 in the last chapters of the book.

As for my starting point, 1870 seems an appropriate date to choose. The national Co-operative Congress, which was held in Albert Square in Manchester for four days at the start of June that year, can be seen as a highly significant moment in the development of Britain's co-operative movement. Although this was the second rather than the first 'modern' Co-operative Congress (there had been a similar event the year before, in London[7]), 1870 was the first time that a national event had attracted widespread support from the co-operative heartlands of Lancashire and Yorkshire. It was also the moment when the decision was taken to put the development of the movement on a firmer footing by creating a central body with two staff – or in other words it was here that what would become known as the Co-operative Union (now Co-operatives UK) was agreed upon.

I am not the first to research this area. A number of academic writers have explored some of the themes in this book, mostly focusing in particular on the co-partnership societies associated with Co-partnership Tenants Ltd.[8] There is also interest outside academia: those living today in what were originally pioneering co-operative estates and 'garden suburbs' tend to take a keen interest in their history, even when the original co-operative element has long disappeared and all the houses have become owner-occupied, and this interest is reflected in a significant number of community websites and Facebook groups. There have also been some excellent local histories published of individual tenant societies, of which perhaps the best is Aileen Reid's lavishly illustrated volume on the Ealing Tenants.[9] Local authorities, too, have understood the value of these estates, many of which have now been awarded Conservation Area status or equivalent. The garden suburbs have not been forgotten, even if the impulse which led to them is little understood.

On the other hand, the engagement of the mainstream co-operative movement in housing issues in the period I am considering has been rather less covered. The British co-operative movement by the time of the 1870 Congress in Manchester had developed into a powerful social and commercial force, particularly in the heartlands of the north of England. It was, as we shall see, a live issue in the movement at the time as to whether co-operative societies should be doing more to meet working-class housing needs, and indeed whether those initiatives which were taking place were creating anything that could be considered distinctively 'co-operative housing'. This is the story which needs to be unravelled first.

CHAPTER I

HOUSING AND THE CO-OPERATIVE MOVEMENT

For those who know to decode the signs, the evidence of early co-operative interest in house-building is all around, in street names the breadth of Britain.

There are streets of houses, mainly dating from the end of the nineteenth and turn of the twentieth centuries, which make it clear that the local co-operative society was the original developer. You can live in a Co-operative Street in Keighley, Coventry, Derby, Leeds, Chester-le-Street or Barnoldswick, to give just a few examples. You can find a Co-operative Terrace in Pontypool, Maryport, Houghton le Springs, Burnhope, Heptonstall or (again) Chester-le-Street. There are Co-operative Avenues in Hucknall (Notts) and Mauchline (Ayrshire), and a Co-operative Road in Middleton, Manchester.

There are also street names which, not necessarily quite so obviously, almost certainly point to co-operative provenance. 'Industrial Street' is one example. Today the term 'industrial' may conjure up images of factories and northern grime, but in its nineteenth century usage 'industrial' was almost a synonym for 'industrious' – the idea that, by commitment and working together, ordinary working people could improve their lot in life and their surroundings. Those living today in Industry Streets in (again to give some examples) Bolton, Derby, Huddersfield, Cleckheaton, Brighouse, Todmorden and Wakefield should hold firm to the original hope which was there when their street name was bestowed in the first place.

Unity Street (Barnoldswick, Keighley, Bristol, Aberdare …) is another name which strongly suggests co-operative involvement. Less obviously, there are those streets which take their name from leading figures in the co-operative movement, the names usually being given as a form of memorial very shortly after their deaths. Roads named in memory of George Jacob Holyoake (1817-1906), a tireless campaigner for co-operation for almost all his adult life, crop up, for example, in Bingley, Blackpool, Burnley, Ferryhill, Leicester, Droylsden, Todmorden and Wellington. There were other pioneers who were remembered in this way: Hebden Bridge's co-operative society named the two next-door streets which it constructed in the 1890s after J.T.W. Mitchell (1828-1895), chairman of the Co-operative Wholesale Society, and Edward Vansittart Neale (1810-1892), the Co-operative Union's general secretary. (Both Mitchell Street and Neale Street are there to this day.)

Nevertheless, it has to be admitted that there are more street names from that period named after eminent Conservative politicians or Dukes or landowners or stately homes or colonial victories than there are celebrating co-operative house-building. It was a regular complaint that the co-operative movement was not as active as it should have been in throwing its weight behind building decent homes for the working classes. Here, for example, is one writer to *Co-operative News* in 1894 discussing house-building: "It is a matter of wonder, considering the enormous capital in the co-operative movement, and the difficulty in finding satisfactory investment for it, and knowing the security and usefulness of this means of so doing, that so few societies have entered into this subject".[10] Another writer, this time from 1902, complained that co-op societies' endeavours to house their members "have been mostly of a desultory and piecemeal character".[11]

The 1870 Co-operative Congress was more than a quarter of a century on from the event which has been widely regarded as the symbolic start of the modern co-op movement, the opening of the first small store by the Rochdale Pioneers Equitable Society in December 1844. There had been many attempts at running co-op stores and co-op factories before the Pioneers (some more successful than others) but Rochdale's success, at a time when the working-class Chartist movement was also mobilising large numbers behind the call for democracy and universal male suffrage, quickly attracted attention. Rochdale's example was followed within a few years by the creation of new co-operative societies in several of the nearby towns in the textile areas of Lancashire and Yorkshire. Then, in 1857, further momentum came from the publication of George Jacob Holyoake's widely-read book promoting the Rochdale Pioneers and their model, *Self-help by the People.*

The 1860s saw rapid growth in the number of new societies, so that by 1864 there were 395 independent co-op societies in England and Wales with 129,000 members. Three years on, in 1867, the numbers had reached 577 and 171,000 members. Data for 1870 itself are not available, but by 1873 the numbers had grown again, to 790 societies and 340,000 individual members.[12] Meanwhile societies had banded together to create, in 1863, a jointly owned wholesaling operation which, as the Co-operative Wholesale Society, would grow into what today would be called a multinational enterprise, building international supply chains to source the goods needed for the co-op stores. By 1870 the 'Wholesale' was already turning over more than half a million pounds a year.[13]

At the same time active steps were being taken to create a newspaper of and for the movement. *Co-operative News* was to appear for the first time in the Autumn of 1871, offering each week an extremely comprehensive account of all that was happening around the country in terms of the development of co-operation.

One of the stories covered in the very first issue of *Co-operative News* was a report on the passing by Parliament of a new version of the Industrial and Provident Societies Act, the legislative framework under which co-operative societies were incorporated and operated. The new Act made it easier for societies to buy and sell land and to erect their own houses, and it also permitted them to lend money to their members for house-purchase.[14]

For all these reasons, 1870 serves as a good starting point for this book. It should be said, however, that there had been previous engagement by co-operative societies in house-building. The Rochdale Pioneers themselves had in their original rules included (as their second of six objectives) the "building, purchasing, or erecting a number of houses, in which those members, desiring to assist each other in improving their domestic and social conditions, may reside".[15] The Pioneers did indeed go on to put this objective into practice. G.D.H. Cole in his classic history of the British co-operative movement describes how the Pioneers established in 1861 a separate legal body, the Rochdale Co-operative Land and Building Company, which built at least twenty-five houses.[16] Separately, the main Pioneers society engaged directly in house-building in the years after 1868, investing the significant sum of £40,000 and building an estate of over eighty houses.[17]

There were other early forays by co-operative societies into housing. For instance, Chartists and radicals in Bacup, a mill town in Lancashire a little to the north of Rochdale, had been inspired by the Pioneers' example to open their own store in 1847. According to a later *Co-operative News* report, the Bacup society also began building work in 1868.[18] Their houses were built for onward sale to their members.

Other co-operative societies who had undertaken housing developments by the mid-1870s included Leeds, Oldham, Todmorden, Sowerby Bridge and Mytholmroyd and there were undoubtedly many more.[19]

The fact that, after little more than twenty years of trading, societies such as Rochdale and Bacup were able to contemplate housing developments of some scale reflects the way that they had already accumulated significant free reserves which they struggled on occasions to know how to use. Co-op societies' funds came not only from trading profits but also, particularly, from the role which they very quickly took on as savings banks for their members' spare money. Although the run of bank failures which had been a feature of the early nineteenth century had begun to diminish, and although the Post Office Savings Bank had been available since 1861 for small savings, nevertheless many co-op members preferred to keep their money local, in a society where they elected the committee and which supplied them with their regular shopping. What's more, co-operative societies generally paid significantly more in interest than the Post Office scheme offered.

Sometimes, to cope with excessive reserves, societies (usually reluctantly) returned money to their members or closed their doors to further deposits. Sometimes societies reinvested the money unwisely: the large Halifax Industrial society had, according to a later report, "financial embarrassment" early in its history because of investments it had made.[20] (It recovered to become one of the leading societies in Yorkshire.) So co-operators, and in particular co-operative society committee members, took an increasing interest in the idea of housing development, not necessarily because like the Rochdale Pioneers they saw this as one of their core objectives but rather as a convenient place to sink their excess capital.

One writer in 1894 suggested that 279 societies were engaged in some way in this activity,[21] but data on house-building within the co-operative movement were not systematically collected until the start of the twentieth century. The first significant attempt at a comprehensive survey was undertaken for the Co-operative Congress in 1900. In headline terms this suggested that 224 societies had between them expended £5.1m in capital in relation to over 24,000 houses. How accurate this survey was had been questioned at the time: out of nearly 1,600 societies in membership of the Co-operative Union, only about 300 had chosen to complete it.[22]

A further attempt was made for the Congress in 1903 at which time 589 societies responded, of whom 344 advised that they had undertaken housing activity. Four years later, another survey for the 1907 Congress elicited 748 replies, with 413 societies reporting that they undertook housing work.

However, this work around housing needs to be separated into three quite distinct areas of engagement. Much the largest activity was the lending of money on a secured mortgage basis to members, to enable them to buy their own houses as owner-occupiers. In this respect, co-ops were effectively providing almost exactly the same lending service as that offered by building societies.

The 1903 survey found that mortgages had been advanced in total on 23,940 houses, with £5.3m lent. By 1907, these figures had increased to 32,600 mortgages and £6.5m advanced.

A much smaller area of activity did involve co-operative societies actually undertaking the building of new houses. In some cases, these were then immediately sold on to members of their society, so that ownership passed from the co-op to the individual (generally on a mortgage basis). The 1903 survey found that there were a little over 5,000 houses in this category, the capital expended being around £1.1m.

Finally there were those houses which co-op societies built and then retained in their own ownership, renting them out to tenants. In 1903, the relevant figures were 8,247 houses and a little under £1.7m.[23]

The 1903 and 1907 data show that co-ops were doing much more to promote owner-occupation than they were to build quality homes for the rental market. This point was a live debate in the movement in the later years of the nineteenth and early twentieth centuries. Was this desirable? Was owner-occupation the best solution for working class housing? Should there be, in fact, a 'co-operative' form of housing, one which was more collective and less individualistic?

Opinions differed. We can take as an example a local co-operative conference held in Watford in January 1900, where one speaker maintained that "the best plan for the artisan was to possess his own house" while another talked of the "evils arising from individual house ownership".[24]

Or we can move forward a few years, to hear Aneurin Williams addressing the Co-operative Congress in 1907. Williams, who we will encounter later in this book in his role, among other things, as president of the company that developed Letchworth Garden City (in later life he was to be chairman of the International Cooperative Alliance executive), made his own position clear. The original aim of those who founded the co-operative movement was to build up co-operative communities, he said. By contrast, houses provided by societies for owner-occupation pass out of the movement. "The houses so acquired are, of course, scattered here, there and everywhere ... They are bought and sold, and may eventually pass into the hands of ordinary investors in house property or even of the slum owner," he said. By contrast, those co-op societies that built estates for renting were able to look after them, keeping up the "character and good condition" of the area. This was "a real piece of joint ownership and democratic regulation in the common interest," he maintained. Why should co-operative power which might create permanent co-op owned housing be "frittered away" in the merely individualistic acquisition of privately-owned houses?[25]

His namesake (although no relation) Bernard Williams, who will also feature later in this story, had put forward a similar argument a few years earlier. Very many societies had lent money to their members to enable them to purchase houses, he said, and this was good, "so far as it goes". But "this would be still better if the houses were co-operatively owned, so as to prevent them slipping back into private hands".[26]

But (as at that 1900 Watford conference) there was also a strong current of opinion that argued for support for owner-occupation. Mrs Bury, who was active in the Women's Co-operative Guild in Darwen (and was later to serve as the Guild's president) was one of these. "A house purchased by the thrift of a man or woman added to the dignity of that man or woman," she said. And anyway, she added, were co-op societies really best qualified to start building houses? She was not convinced that "a committee of weavers and spinners were capable of undertaking the building of houses". It was a fair point: co-operative society committees had been elected by their members primarily to run efficient and profitable stores.[27]

Another argument against holding houses for rent was the risk of the society losing income, if it was unable to find tenants. On the other hand, generally only the better-off members of a society were in a position to contemplate a mortgage. Co-operative societies which focused their housing activity around owner-occupation were effectively benefiting only part of the membership, and not those who perhaps needed most help – so was this fair?

Some societies followed a middle course. According to the 1900 survey Derby, for example, was reported as renting 65 houses, having sold 26. Leeds had sold 567 houses and was renting 178 (a further 674 had been funded through mortgage loans). Huddersfield had 180 houses rented out, but had sold 128 and had also arranged mortgages on 109. The large Manchester and Salford society was reported to have simply focused on providing mortgages, while Gateshead's activity was limited to renting out 125 houses.

There was also the particular spin given to the idea of co-operative engagement in house-building by the powerful south London society based in Woolwich, the Royal Arsenal Co-operative Society (RACS). In 1900 the society, which at the time was well supplied with surplus funds, had taken the decision to buy 120 acres of building land at Bostall near Abbey Wood to add to around fifty acres which it had purchased previously and had used in the interim as a market garden (as well as a place for members to go for Saturday afternoon teas in a country setting).[28] The plan was that all the land would be developed as a major new housing estate.

The society pondered its options: it could choose to erect the houses and rent them out but this course of action would have required excessive capital. Instead, Woolwich decided to erect the houses and sell them to its members – but to sell them on a leasehold basis on 99 year leases which at the end of the lease period would revert to the society. By retaining the freehold, the society aimed to maintain the integrity of its development, and to keep the houses in some sense within the co-operative movement.

Woolwich initially provided the 90% mortgages to members from its own funds, although these dried up fairly soon after the estate development had begun and members were at that point advised to approach building societies. The society also made provision for less well-off members who would have struggled to find the 10% deposit required by enabling them to rent initially and, if they wished, to staircase later to buying the property. The rent they paid in the interim (which was calculated as a fraction of the build cost, and was probably around eight shillings a week[29]) was used to bring down the eventual cost of the mortgage. According to Woolwich's secretary who described the scheme in 1902, it would typically take three years for the sum to be reduced by 10%, after which a lease and mortgage could be provided.[30]

The development at Bostall progressed steadily, with around 760 houses completed by 1907 and the thousand mark reached well before 1915, at which point 820 houses had been sold leasehold and 180 were tenanted.[31] In 1925, the society went on to purchase the Well Hall estate in Eltham, taking over around 1,300 houses built for munitions workers at the Arsenal works during the First World War. (In best co-operative tradition RACS renamed Well Hall as 'Progress Estate'.)[32]

Woolwich's particular solution at Bostall to the owner/tenant debate became well known in the co-operative movement. Not everyone was convinced, however. A CWS representative at a Surrey co-op conference, Henry Pumphrey, raised the scenario that, were the RACS to fail, the whole estate would fall into the hands of property companies, "the big people". If this happened "the evil would then become as bad as ever". Anyway what was wrong, Henry Pumphrey asked, with everyone owning their own houses outright?[33]

It has to be said that the RACS did not go under, or at least not until the mid-1980s when it encountered financial difficulties and had to be rescued – ironically – by the CWS. Nevertheless its potentially innovative 99 year lease arrangement did not last the course: RACS's scheme turned out in the end to be not so very different from the more conventional routes by which co-op societies were helping their members into owner-occupancy.

By the time that Bostall's fields were in the hands of the RACS, however, another experiment in co-operative housing had been under way for more than a decade. The Tenant Co-operators were operating to a different model, one which – by translating the idea of the co-op 'divi' into the area of housing rent – was trying to provide working-class housing in London in a definitely co-operative way to those unwilling or unable to become owner-occupiers. It is time to consider this venture.

CHAPTER 2

"THINKING OVER THE DWELLINGS QUESTION": BEN JONES AND THE TENANT CO-OPERATORS

It was a Tuesday, the first day of July 1884, and the members of the Royal Commission on the Housing of the Working Classes were settling down once again in a room just off Whitehall to hear from those they had summonsed to give evidence. It was their twenty-sixth day of hearings. Ahead of them would lie many more similar days before, finally in May 1885, the last of the interviews would be completed and the Commission's eventual report (or, more accurately, the three volumes of its reports) could begin to be prepared for publication.[34]

One of those that the Commissioners would be hearing from that Tuesday was a leading figure in the British co-operative movement. Benjamin Jones was in his late thirties at this point. He had been born in Salford in 1847 of working-class parents, both of whom worked in the weaving and dyeing trade. Ben himself had started work aged nine.

In 1866 in his late teens he had been taken on by the Manchester-based Co-operative Wholesale Society. This was just three years after the CWS had first been established by co-operative activists, as a self-help method of providing wholesale goods for the growing number of Northern co-operative retail societies. Thereafter had followed a series of promotions for Jones which enabled him to have a good overview of the CWS business: he had worked for a time as a book-keeper and he had also the experience of acting as an assistant buyer for the essential stock items of butter and cheese. By 1874, by which time the CWS was already turning over more than a million pounds in sales and had also started what was effectively a banking operation, the society was ready to establish its first London branch office. Ben Jones was chosen to head this operation.

Jones moved south from Manchester to London to establish the office. He was to remain there for almost thirty years, finally leaving the CWS in 1902. After a difficult start (London was recognised as something of a co-operative desert, in terms of active societies) Jones built up a strong foundation for the CWS in the south and the business quickly began to contribute a valuable additional significant share to the CWS's turnover.[35]

This was his day job and, as he told the Royal Commissioners, it kept him very fully occupied. However Jones found several other voluntary ways of contributing to the development of the co-operative movement. He was actively engaged in the Co-operative Union as both the secretary of the Union's Southern Section and as a Southern Section delegate to the Co-operative Union's Central Board. He took a leading role in his local independent co-operative society, in south London. A little later, in his forties, he was to research and write the major 800-page opus *Co-operative Production*, the detailed story of early worker-run co-operative businesses in Britain which was first published in 1894 and is still an invaluable resource for researchers today.

But in the years before the Royal Commission began its deliberations Jones had also turned his attention to the housing crisis in London and had begun to ponder how the experience of the co-operative movement could be brought to bear here. It was for this that the Royal Commissioners had invited him to appear before them.

The questioning was opened by a sympathetic Royal Commissioner, Henry Broadhurst, a radical MP who came to Westminster from a trade union background and who was at that point sitting in Parliament as the Lib-Lab member for Stoke-on-Trent. Broadhurst offered Jones a gentle way to get started: "You have been thinking over the dwellings question, and you have formed an opinion that the principle of co-operation might be applied to provide the working people with dwellings of their own?" he asked. Jones was able to reply simply: "Yes, I have that opinion".

Jones went on to précis some of the housing problems facing those of London's working classes who would have liked to have improved their position. "The cost of dwellings in London is so great that it is very difficult for a working man by any possible habits of providence or thrift to become the possessor of his own house," he said. Even if this were possible, for example by borrowing from a building society, there were significant risks. Income from work could be unpredictable, but London-based building societies penalised harshly those who fell into arrears. Almost certainly the reality of the housing market was such that the would-be owner-occupier would live in only a handful of rooms, sharing the rest of their house with rent-paying tenants: but of course taking in tenants constituted a further risk. In any case, workers also needed the ability to move away at short notice for their employment, and the difficulties of selling property quickly and the legal costs of conveyancing all meant that it could be extremely difficult to get back money spent on acquiring the house in the first place.

Jones's solution was instead to offer would-be owner-occupiers a share in a co-operative society which would own property jointly on their behalf. "Instead of a person possessing the freehold of a room, or suite of rooms, the sale of which would probably cause as much trouble and expense as the sale of a house, he is put in possession of stock in the company, which stock can be sold with scarcely any expense and with much greater ease," Jones claimed. And, in an analogous way to the way that retail co-operative societies paid dividends from profits to their members, so tenants of the housing society would be entitled to dividends from profits, according to the rent they paid. External investors would receive a fair, fixed, rate of interest (initially 5%, falling to 4% once the scheme was well established, Jones suggested) but after that the remaining surplus would be there to be enjoyed by the tenants. This 'dividend' would not be paid across as cash, however, but would be capitalised and retained in the co-operative.

"Each year the tenants could have stock certificates issued to them for the amount of this surplus, in proportion to the amount of rent they had paid," Jones explained. He offered a worked example of a co-operative undertaking a £100,000 property development, which suggested that the tenant-members could have paid off the initial capital borrowings and begun to own a large share of their society's property outright in little more than twenty years.[36]

Ben Jones had been working on this proposal. In fact, Henry Broadhurst was already well briefed before the Royal Commission hearing in July 1884: he and Jones knew each other and shared similar politics, and Jones had talked through his idea when the two of them had met previously. Broadhurst had recommended that Jones approach the London Trades Council to solicit their support, and indeed Jones had prepared a pamphlet which had been discussed by the Trades Council in late May 1884.[37]

According to one later account, Ben Jones had started pondering a co-operative way forward for housing the year before, in part because he had seen the problems caused by eviction of tenants from properties as a result of local authority efforts towards street improvements – ironically, a side effect of the half-hearted attempts by parliamentary legislation to improve the worst areas of slum housing in London and the industrial cities.[38] 1883 was, in any case, a year when housing issues rose towards the top of the political agenda, partly as the result of the publication of a short campaigning tract by the nonconformist minister Andrew Mearns.

It would be fair to say that Mearns' book *The Bitter Cry of Outcast London* had a similar effect for its time as the BBC TV play *Cathy Come Home* was to have when it was broadcast over eighty years later. *The Bitter Cry* was an overtly Christian call to arms to do something to tackle London's slum housing: that "great dark region of poverty, misery, squalor and immorality". Mearns told his readers that he felt obliged to self-censor his account, in case they failed to believe him. "So far from making the worst of our facts for the purpose of appealing to emotion, we have been compelled to tone down everything, and wholly to omit what most needs to be known, or the ears and eyes of our readers would have been insufferably outraged," he wrote at the start. But nevertheless, he was uncompromising in relating what he had seen at first hand on forays into some of London's worst slum streets and courts. "How can those places be called homes, compared with which the lair of a wild beast would be a comfortable and healthy spot?" he demanded.[39]

Following the publication of *The Bitter Cry*, housing continued to be at the forefront of political discourse. The autumn of 1883 saw a series of articles appearing in influential journals, the first being by Lord Salisbury in the *National Review* in November. Salisbury adopted the rather unexpected stance for the Tory leader of the time by suggesting that the problem of working class housing would have to be addressed by greater state intervention in the housing market. A second political heavyweight Joseph Chamberlain (at that stage a leading Cabinet minister in Gladstone's Liberal administration) entered the fray to respond in another widely-read journal the following month.[40]

Housing as an issue was not going away. Gladstone's administration had already in 1882 had one go at housing legislation, in the weak Artisans' Dwellings Act which offered only minor reforms. It was evident that more was required to address concerns. Following the time-honoured way that governments have of establishing enquiries to address complicated political issues, the Gladstone government set up the Royal Commission on the Housing of the Working Classes in March 1884. The Liberal politician Sir Charles Dilke was appointed as the chairman. Two MPs Sir Richard Cross and William Torrens, both of whom had as MPs shepherded earlier housing legislation through Parliament, were among those appointed as Commissioners, and others included the Prince of Wales (the future Edward VII), the Roman Catholic Archbishop of Westminster, the Anglican Bishop of Bedford and Lord Salisbury himself. Henry Broadhurst represented the working-class voice.

Ben Jones's proposal for a new type of co-operative solution for the housing crisis needs to be put in this broader context, therefore. However, it would probably be misleading to imagine that Jones was simply reacting to the upsurge of interest in housing in 1883-4. He would almost certainly have been aware of the coverage in the co-operative press a few years earlier of the development of Le Familistère in Guise, in northern France, the co-operative housing development undertaken by the utopian-minded industrialist Jean-Baptiste André Godin, which in some ways echoed Robert Owen's much earlier development at New Lanark.[41] He would also probably have read the suggestion from his fellow Southern Section Central Board member Edward Owen Greening writing in *Co-operative News* in early 1881, who had called for co-operative societies to build and own houses for their members on "real co-operative terms", so that members ended up not as home owners but as holders of shares in the co-op equal to the value of the house. "Thus all the members would own all the houses," Greening had concluded.[42]

There were admittedly some rough edges still to Jones's idea, which emerged in the questioning he received in his appearance before the Royal Commissioners. Would tenants have absolute rights of occupancy even if they turned out to be unruly, he was asked? What about someone who took rooms later on in a co-operative house: would they be expected to become a co-op member and how would they acquire shares, if all the shares were already issued and the co-op wasn't expanding? Could non-tenants be obliged to sell their shares? And what would happen to a tenancy in the event of a co-op member's death? – could the right to acquire the tenancy be bequeathed or simply the value of the shares?

Jones made a valiant effort in his responses, stressing again and again that a co-operative solution to housing need was very much preferable to the sort of patronage being practised by the philanthropic housing associations. We can suspect that it was the social reformer Octavia Hill, who combined her housing reform activism with a strong moralistic attitude towards her tenants, who was in Jones's sights when he railed against the "'goody goody' style of saying 'now you must do this and be very good' and all that sort of thing". But Jones was also clear that external capital from well-disposed investors would be needed to get his scheme off the ground. Surely there were people out there who would be prepared to help?

"A start is wanted. The effort is too much to be made by people without capital," Jones said. "A combination of wealthy men could start it and say 'Now, as you pay us out you shall have the management; when you have paid us all out you shall have the whole management to yourselves'. That is one way in which it could be done."[43]

Ben Jones's idea was indeed to come to fruition, and in a manner which was very close to the approach he suggested here. But it was to take several more years until the co-operative society known as Tenant Co-operators Ltd came to be established.

Nothing immediately came of Jones's appearance before the Royal Commissioners, and their final report makes no mention of his proposal. Nothing came either of his presentation a few weeks earlier at the London Trades Council. But by 1887, there was a sense of forward movement. Early that year, in a debate with the socialist journalist Henry Hyde Champion held at the Toynbee Hall settlement in Spitalfields, Jones had again spelled out the essence of his idea.[44]

Jones once more described his housing plan when he was invited before a select committee of MPs looking at leasehold reform issues in August 1887.[45] Finally, on November 17, came the inaugural committee meeting of the embryonic co-operative society. It was held in Jones's place of work, in the board room in the CWS's impressive new London headquarters in Leman Street, Whitechapel, which had only been opened a fortnight earlier.[46]

Jones had, it seems, mercilessly used his London contacts to pull together the initial interim committee. As Martin Spence has pointed out in his account of the Tenant Co-operators,[47] the early committee members came from three interlocking categories. Some were colleagues from the co-operative movement, some socially minded businessmen and some linked to nearby Toynbee Hall, opened in 1884 by Canon Samuel Barnett and his wife Henrietta as an East End centre committed to social reform.

From the co-operative movement Jones recruited, for example, H.J. Vansittart Neale, the son of the Co-operative Union's long-serving general secretary Edward Vansittart Neale, and J.J. Dent who led the workingmen's club federation the CIU and who was also on the Co-operative Union's Central Board. The barrister William Minet was another a supporter of co-operation, albeit a well-heeled one; he owned substantial land in Camberwell which he was later to develop sensitively (in the process donating a park and public library to the local community).

The Oxford don Arthur Acland (A.H.D. Acland) had strong co-operative credentials, too. Acland had co-authored the co-operative practical manual *Working Men Co-operators* with Ben Jones in 1884, and like Jones had been a Central Board member representing the Southern Section.

From the business community the most important recruit was the wool merchant Pascoe Fenwick, who having been impressed when he had come across a copy of *Working Men Co-operators* had sought out Ben Jones and told him he would make an initial £1,000 investment if the new housing co-operative society could be launched.[48]

The task now was to try to convert Ben Jones's vision into practice. A sub-committee worked with the Co-operative Union's J.C. Gray on suitable rules, and the new co-operative society was formally registered under the Industrial and Provident Societies Act on March 21 1888. The rules confirmed the principle that investors would receive no more than 4% and that the profits from the venture would be allocated to tenants in proportion to rent paid, a 'fundamental' rule which would require a special general meeting with at least half the members present and at least a 75% majority vote to overturn.

Prudently this distribution of profit was to take place after allowance for depreciation, the paying-off of preliminary expenses, the 4% dividend to share capital, a reserve fund contribution, Co-operative Union membership subs and contributions to an educational and social fund. The rules followed best co-operative practice of the time of pledging 2.5% of net profits for educational work.

In other respects too, the rules were progressive. The principle of 'one member one vote' was enshrined, regardless of the number of shares which individuals or organisations might hold. Finally, rule 71 made it a condition that anyone applying to become a tenant must be a member of the co-operative.[49]

At the same time as the rules were being drawn up the new co-operative society began the search for capital. Its first prospectus, launched in early 1888, appealed for capital of £10,000, in the form of share capital and loan stock, both of which would receive 4%. (Co-operative societies were at this stage unable to take more than £200 in shares from a single individual, so larger individual investments needed to be made in part through loan stock.) "Subscriptions to the share capital of the Society or to the loan stock is earnestly solicited from those friends of the working classes who believe that the best manner of showing friendship is to help the workers to help themselves," the society asserted, claiming that it already had £4,000 of the £10,000 in promises. One of those investing was presumably the wool merchant Fenwick. Ben Jones, we know, was another. He later revealed that he had had to borrow the £100 which he put in to Tenant Co-operators, paying 5% for the loan in order to receive back 4% from the co-operative. He didn't appear to consider it a hardship: "It has been an intense pleasure to me to see the development of Tenant Co-operation," he was to say.[50]

By the time of the first General Meeting of the co-operative, held on April 21 1888 again in the CWS London office, the talk could turn to the first development. According to the *Co-operative News* report,[51] there was debate about whether to opt for blocks of flats or individual houses. There was also discussion about where in London to site the properties, with both Chelsea and Tottenham apparently considered at an early stage. In the end, it was Upton Park, between West Ham and East Ham, which was selected and a conventional row of six new terraced houses (already constructed) which were bought in August that year. The houses were in the appropriately named Terrace Road.

Tenant Co-operators immediately started planning a much more ambitious project, the construction from scratch of houses in Penge, in south London. In March 1889 the society purchased land in what was to become Lucas Road. By this stage Tenant Co-operators had attracted share capital of £2,330 and loan stock of £2,438, although only just over £2,500 of this had actually been paid up. It had, however, been able to offer its Terrace Road tenants their first dividend from profits, from the first year profits of £9 3s 6d. The dividend was set at the rate of 1s 6d in the pound*, or 7.5%.[52]

---

* Before decimalisation there were 12 pence to the shilling and twenty shillings to the pound

The Penge development could be progressed only because the society had been able to receive further investment capital in the form of a £3,000 loan from the state, from the Public Works Loan Commissioners. The loan was at the relatively good interest rate of 3.25% and was repayable over thirty years.

Since, as will be seen, the Public Works Loan Board (PWLB) and its Commissioners will play a significant role in the financing of many of the other co-operative housing projects described in this book, this is perhaps the moment to introduce the agency. The origins of the PWLB can be traced back at least to an Act of 1817, but it was the Public Works Loans Act of 1875 which established the structure and objectives of the board which were in operation at this time. It was an independent statutory body which could lend money from the state to local authorities and other public bodies for public works. It also had other powers: significantly for our story it could provide loans to housing associations and societies and indeed to individuals for the provision of houses. The capital was in the form of secured loans, and was not grant-finance: it would take the First World War for the government finally to accept that grants would also be needed to finance the building of affordable houses.

In an example of the problems of new-build construction which may elicit wry smiles of recognition from some in today's community-led housing organisations, Tenant Co-operators were initially held back in the Penge build because of a rise in the cost of building materials. Nevertheless, the build contract was awarded in May 1889, nine of the houses roofed in by July, and the whole 24-house development completed by very early 1890.[53]

The contract was itself undertaken by a co-operative, the Brixton-based Co-operative Builders. This was a co-operative society which, although only formally registered in December 1889, had grown out of a building firm used by William Minet to construct his Public Library in Camberwell. The original contractor had gone under, and Minet had taken the opportunity to restructure the firm on co-operative lines, paying a dividend from profits to its employees.[54]

The accounts for Co-operative Builders for 1889 show a healthy profit of £1,582 on turnover of around £23,000, with a dividend on wages paid of 7.5%. The co-operative at this point had 195 shareholders, including 22 bricklayers, 49 carpenters and joiners, 80 labourers, 14 painters and polishers, and a smaller number of clerks, foremen, masons, plumbers and plasterers. The dividend on wages was continued for 1890, at the slightly lower rate of 6.25%, but had to be suspended in 1891 mainly for cash-flow reasons. By this stage, as well as the Tenant Co-operators contract, the co-op had undertaken work for the RACS (Woolwich co-operative society), had built the new central shop for the Sheerness Co-operative, and had also done some further private work for William Minet.

The 1890s saw a number of co-operative societies established in the building industry, a sector at that stage undergoing enormous growth. Their story, while a separate one to that being recounted in this book, is one where nevertheless the links could be close. By the turn of the century, there were building co-operatives established in, among other places, Kettering, Oxford, Cambridge, Lincoln and Leicester.[55] As we shall see in the next chapter, there was also another London venture: General Builders co-operative, based in west London, was to have a role in the development of the next wave of co-operative tenants' societies in the very early 1900s.

In 1891, the Tenant Co-operators purchased the land on the opposite (north) side of Lucas Road and once more contracted with Co-operative Builders, this time to erect a further 24 houses. These were deliberately designed as smaller 'double tenement' houses (effectively a type of maisonette), to meet requests the co-operative had received for cheaper rents.

Who moved in to the Lucas Road homes? Martin Spence's study draws on Census and other local records of the time and his conclusion is that "Most of the road's inhabitants sat firmly within the skilled working class and lower middle class: technical workers such as engineers or printers; traditional craftsmen such as carpenters or tailors; clerical workers such as clerks; and retail and distribution workers such as shop assistants and warehousemen. The female occupations recorded include teacher, housekeeper and charwoman."

Spence also points out that the tenants would have been recruited from within the co-operative movement. The surprisingly high numbers of tenants shown as employed in the printing industry, Spence suggests, might well be directly connected to the fact that the London branch of the Co-operative Printing Society had Ben Jones as its chairman.[56]

Minet himself offered land for the next stage in the co-op's growth, and twelve tenement flats were completed in late 1892 in Brief Street, Camberwell. Minet was described at the time by Beatrice Potter

(Beatrice Webb after her marriage) as "a barrister nominally, a man of large means actually who has devoted money and energy to bettering the conditions of the working class".[57] Potter, working closely with Ben Jones at this point on her book on co-operation, had been a very early additional recruit to the Tenant Co-operators committee; Minet by this point had stepped down from the committee in order to become the society's internal auditor. He had also taken on the role of chairman of Co-operative Builders.

From south London the committee turned their focus back to the East End and in 1895 acquired land at Plashet, East Ham, on which they agreed a build contract for 32 tenements. The co-operative was not finding its remit altogether easy: "It becomes somewhat difficult to erect houses of a sound, sanitary, and commodious character at rentals common to many of the localities around London," it told *Co-operative News*. There was also a shortage of capital, even with loan finance coming in from the Public Works Loan Commissioners. The committee would be "glad to receive subscriptions to the shares or loan stock of the society," the *Co-operative News*'s readers were told.[58]

The Plashet development went ahead but turned out to be, as a later account of the society was to admit, "the worst investment made by the Committee".[59] The full story was honestly set out by Howard Hodgkin in 1901 (Hodgkin had been the co-operative's secretary until 1896 when work pressures had obliged him to resign) and is worth quoting: "In their desire to provide for the poorer classes of the community, the Committee seem in this instance to have made a mistake; whether it be because no higher rented houses are mixed with them as at Penge, or because the houses are not well planned, and are too far from a railway station, or from the character of the neighbourhood – great difficulty has been found in securing suitable tenants."

In order to avoid the flats remaining empty, one of the key principles behind the co-operative had to be sacrificed: henceforth tenants would be taken on who did not contribute their £1 share and were therefore not members of the society. "The result is that, as regards the tenants, they do not gain the legitimate advantages of the Society, and that, as regards the Society, it does not gain the security of the pound share, so that when the tenants take to 'flitting', as often happens, there is usually some loss of rent from arrears," Hodgkin wrote. Being a volunteer-led landlord organisation, even a co-operative one, was not always a straightforward affair.[60]

Eventually, the Tenant Co-operators' committee had to decide to undertake major external and internal works to the flats to turn them into more lettable propositions.

There was to be one final property development, and this in the perhaps unlikely location of the market town of Epsom, Surrey.[61] This development of 26 properties (originally known as Neale Terrace, in memory of Edward Vansittart Neale; the houses are now 239-289 Hook Road) was set in motion in 1900 and completed in 1901 at a total cost of just over £8,750.

Ben Jones's original vision was of a network of fifty separate estates around London, so that tenant-members of the society who needed to move for their work could easily find another Tenant Co-operators property to move to. This was always an idealistic prospect and the society ended with five estates located, rather randomly, at East Ham, Penge, Camberwell, Plashet and Epsom. This in itself diminished the co-operative nature of the undertaking: each estate was too small to create much sense of community, and certainly tenants in one estate had little chance of socialising with those in another many miles away. "It cannot therefore be claimed that the spirit of Co-operation is very strongly developed in the majority of tenants," was the assessment of John Yerbury.

We have two contemporaneous accounts of the Tenant Co-operators written by insiders, Howard Hodgkin's article in 1901 which was written for a Quaker journal and Yerbury's longer account from 1913 at a time when he was chairman of the committee. Both Hodgkin and Yerbury are frank in acknowledging that Tenant Co-operators had failed in many ways to lived up to Jones's original vision. "We failed in much," Yerbury says at one point. Hodgkin calls it a success "... but not a brilliant success".[62]

Their frankness has perhaps tended to encourage later historians to play down the co-operative's significance. Any assessment today, looking back more than a century, has to begin by acknowledging that this was a co-operative venture which was financially very competently run. It remained profitable, producing over its first 25 year period the revenue to service its loan stock and share capital and the Public Works Loan Commissioners borrowings. It also found the funds to pay the profit dividend to tenants, which over these 25 years averaged out at a very respectable figure of 6%.

Nevertheless, the problems of achieving tenant engagement affected this aspect, too: in 1913, only 51 of the 344 shareholders were tenants.

Given that there were 122 properties in total, slightly more than half of the co-operative's tenants were not at this point holding shares.[63]

Yerbury stresses several times in his account the voluntary nature of the venture. The committee had always consisted of busy volunteers, he says: "the Tenant Co-operators was founded to help the working classes and was started by men willing to give their unpaid services for the benefit of those poorer than themselves".

This was, in 1913, an important point to stress because by this point a very significant new wave of co-operative housing had taken off. In Ealing, in Sevenoaks, in Letchworth, in Hampstead, and outside London in places such as Manchester, Birmingham, Liverpool, Stoke-on-Trent and Leicester new 'co-partnership tenant societies' were developing. These followed a rather different model to that of the Tenant Co-operators, a model which – certainly by the time Yerbury was writing – had found it necessary to become increasingly hard-nosed in the way that business was done.

CHAPTER 3

CO-PARTNERSHIP IN HOUSING: ENTER HENRY VIVIAN

It is conventional to begin any account of the 'co-partnership' housing movement in the west London settlement of Ealing, and more precisely at a meeting held at the Haven Arms in Ealing on February 16 1901. It was here that the idea of what would shortly become Ealing Tenants Ltd had its first proper discussion.

The plan before that meeting seems to have been that a small group of local men, almost all involved in the building trade in some way, would acquire land and build their own homes. The plan as it emerged afterwards was to undertake the building as a collective venture, so that the land and the buildings would be jointly owned by a new 'co-partnership society'. Instead of being owner-occupiers, the men involved would be both members and tenants of the new society.

The impetus for the change of plan, we can be sure, came from a man called Henry Vivian. Vivian was at this stage aged thirty-two. Born in a village on the edge of Dartmoor, Vivian's father had been an estate carpenter and Vivian himself was apprenticed in Plymouth to his father's trade. However he was clearly a young man destined to go places: "a Devonian, with something of the spirit of adventure" according to a later writer.[64] He moved to London probably while still in his teens and there he became an active trade unionist in the Amalgamated Society of Carpenters and Joiners. He became the elected president of the union's Pimlico branch.[65]

In London, he became acquainted with Edward Owen Greening. Greening, it will be remembered, was the author of the 1881 article in *Co-operative News* which had called for 'real' co-operative forms of housing. Greening was by this stage a leading figure in the co-operative movement, if not an entirely uncontroversial one. Originally from

Lancashire, he had moved south to London twenty years earlier and at this stage was running the Agricultural and Horticultural Association (the 'One and All'), structured as a co-operative society although one in which Greening was very much the dominant figure. Although representing a somewhat different part of the movement, Greening was, like Ben Jones, for many years an elected member of the Co-operative Union's Central Board as one of the representatives of the South of England. From 1888 he undertook the organising of the National Co-operative Festivals at Crystal Palace, a major annual event which comprised performances from co-operative and temperance choirs, flower shows and other kinds of entertainment, and which at its peak attracted tens of thousands of participants. The Crystal Palace events, which ran until 1910, were for most of that time organised under Greening's direct oversight and quite independently of the Co-operative Union.[66]

Significantly for our story, Greening was also an active member of a spin-off from the mainstream co-operative movement known as the Labour Association. This had been set up at a fringe meeting at the Co-operative Congress in Derby in 1884 and was enthusiastically backed among others by George Jacob Holyoake and by Edward Vansittart Neale, the Co-operative Union's general secretary. In 1890 at the age of twenty-two, almost certainly through his friendship with Greening, Vivian was appointed as the secretary of the Labour Association.

The later years of the nineteenth century were a time when the co-operative movement experienced a period of considerable internal acrimony over what I have described elsewhere as almost a doctrinal dispute.[67] Disagreements, even on occasions vituperate attacks on fellow co-operators, could be a feature of Congress proceedings. The disputes were a feature from the 1870s right through to the start of the twentieth century, despite periodic attempts (as at the 1895 so-called 'Conciliation Congress') to work towards unity.

The issue which proved so divisive could be seen, at one level, to reflect simply the rather different interests of 'distributive co-operation' (the retail co-operative movement and the Co-operative Wholesale Society and Scottish CWS which serviced them) and 'productive co-operation' – what we would now call workers' co-operatives. Then as now, this latter sector was by far the smaller part of the overall British movement. In the early days the point of contention was focused on the so-called bonus to labour, or in other words whether or not employees in a co-operative concern should receive a share of the society's profits on top of their wages, as a reward for their participation. Productive co-operatives generally were committed to this (after all, their primary role as they saw it was to provide decent employment for their employee-members). A minority of retail societies also gave a profit dividend to their staff. The Co-operative Wholesale Society experimented in its early days with a bonus to labour but then became opposed to the concept.[68]

More broadly, the issue could be seen as a debate over how co-operative societies should treat their own employees. Should co-ops develop different employment practices from conventional capitalist concerns? Should their workers be encouraged to participate directly in the management of their businesses?

Standing up for the concept of profit-sharing, and later for the concept of workplace participation, were working class leaders of productive co-operatives such as Hebden Bridge's Joseph Greenwood (the father of Crossley Greenwood, the speaker at the inaugural Keswick meeting), who argued strongly that the workers at his co-operative textile mill should share in the fruits of their labour. Also supporting this argument were co-operative leaders such as Holyoake and Greening and E.V. Neale.

On the other side of the debate were equally heavyweight figures from within the movement, such as the CWS's J.T.W. Mitchell. The CWS was an autonomous second-level co-operative society, owned by all those separate societies who chose to become its members. Its argument (or one of the several arguments it advanced) was that it shared its profits collectively with all these societies and not with a handful of lucky individuals who happened to work for the society. It claimed therefore to be promoting what it called the 'federalist' approach, as opposed to the 'individualist' approach which – the CWS said – wanted to reward the few.

There were, in fact, persuasive arguments which could be raised by both sides in the dispute,[69] and plenty of opportunities to make these arguments. The Labour Association was intended as a propagandist vehicle to support the profit-sharing side of the debate, as its original cumbersome title of the 'Labour Association for Promoting Co-operative Production Based on the Co-partnership of the Workers' makes clear. It complemented the more practically-orientated Co-operative Productive Federation which had been established two years earlier to help develop the productive co-operative sector. The CPF's secretary at this time, Thomas Blandford, was another acquaintance of Vivian's after he had first moved from Devon to London.

Vivian, through his work with the Labour Association, was demonstrating that he was firmly in the 'co-partnership' camp – or as he explained to the Royal Commission on Labour when he gave evidence before it in 1893 "that party in the co-operative movement which seeks to establish workshops in which the workers share in profits and participate in management" as opposed to those co-operatives merely employing "wage-paid labour".[70]

Vivian's background as a joiner, his trade union experience and his work for the Labour Association fused in his plans for what eventually became General Builders, a co-operative society which he saw as providing work for those in the building trade. Vivian was to assert that General Builders had been set up as far back as 1891 although there was clearly a long period of what was later called "preparatory work",[71] and financial returns from the co-operative only appeared for the first time in the data prepared for the Co-operative Congress in 1898; at this stage, the co-op was recording that it had 693 members, a turnover of £5,609 and a profit of £56. (By comparison, Co-operative Builders that year had sixty members and a turnover of £11,419.)

Clearly few of General Builders' reported 693 members could have been actively expecting to earn their living at this time from work undertaken for the co-op, but this was probably never how Vivian envisaged that the society would work. "The machinery for the management of our Society is in many ways the same as that for the management of our Trade Union," he said in an early speech introducing the idea to union colleagues.[72] It is evident that from the start Vivian was planning for a mass membership body. There would, he told his audience, be branches of General Builders established wherever at least twenty members signed up, with each branch electing at least one Council delegate (further delegates would represent each further 100 members). So visualise 30 branches, Vivian went on, each with 300 members: together they would elect a Council of ninety delegates who in turn would instruct the co-op's executive.

It was a highly ambitious concept, very different from the small worker-run productive co-operatives with whom the Labour Association was primarily working at this time. And it would need strong leadership: "When the Society is in thorough working order it should appoint a man to superintend its affairs who would create confidence in the Society both of its workers and the public. A man whose experience and character is good, and one whose good business knowledge is not rendered next to useless to us by his lack of Co-operative spirit and enthusiasm," Vivian added. It is perhaps not too difficult to decode here who Vivian felt might be suitable for this role.

Ambitious or not, General Builders did recruit members in the building trades, and it was the president of the Ealing branch, a plasterer called Hubert Brampton, who was instrumental in setting up the meeting with Vivian on the evening in February 1901 in the Haven Arms which led to Ealing Tenants becoming the first 'co-partnership' tenants' society. According to Aileen Reid, who has written the definitive history of Ealing tenants, an initial group of local men had been meeting regularly over the winter of 1900-1901 to discuss a building venture of some kind. Brampton himself was politically active as a Liberal member of the local Urban District Council, as well as being secretary of a locally-based sickness club which offered its members help in times of illness and access to beds in a convalescent home.[73]

Vivian would undoubtedly have been delighted to have the chance to act as a kind of godparent to a new co-partnership. He was able to introduce Brampton and his colleagues to the model already in use by Tenant Co-operators, which as we have seen brought together the idea of limited rewards for external investors with tenant dividends. Vivian later described Ealing Tenants as a society which is a partnership of capital, tenants and employees[74] and clearly he was hoping initially to refine the Tenant Co-operators model to include also some element of profit-sharing for those actually building the houses. However, "owing to various practical difficulties the idea of enabling the employees engaged in the production of the buildings to become interested in the profits on production was not adopted".[75]

Nevertheless, this new 'co-partnership' tenants' model which Vivian and the Ealing workers were bringing about could be presented in a very positive light. According to Vivian, writing here in 1905, tenants potentially benefited in a number of ways:

"He gets a house at a rental which, if accommodation and other things are compared, is not higher and is probably less than he would have to pay elsewhere. He can invest in the society of which he is a tenant at 5 per cent any savings he finds it possible to make out of his earnings. Should values go up, the tenant gets the benefit either by way of a dividend on his rent or by paying a rental which is below the market value. He secures practically all surplus profit after the fixed charges have been met."

Vivian added that, over time, the tenants collectively could accumulate sufficient capital to dispense with the need for external investors altogether. And in the meantime the capital would be coming in at a lower than commercial rate, cheaper than "any other system that is commercially sound".[76]

By the time Vivian was writing this, Ealing had successfully acquired five plots of building land on which it had erected fifty houses with another twenty or so under way. It was about to engage in a rapid expansion which would lead it to purchase several additional very sizeable areas of building land so that finally more than six hundred houses would be built. The coverage in the Labour Association's *Co-partnership* magazine was uniformly upbeat about the success of the venture, as the 'pioneer' co-partnership suburb which had beaten the path for others to follow, and one national newspaper had even described the community there as the "Ealing Paradise".[77]

Nevertheless, reading between the lines, it is clear that the early years at Ealing were by no means plain-sailing. The challenge was to find the capital to fund the land purchase and, particularly, the build costs. Vivian used his Labour Association and co-operative contacts as much as he could. The first investment appears to have been that from John Herbert Greenhalgh, a retired barrister who was a member of the Labour Association and who provided the £441 needed to complete the purchase of the first building plots, in Woodfield Road; Greenhalgh was later to make further investments. Further early investors included other well-heeled supporters of co-partnership and the Labour Association.

Ealing Tenants Ltd was registered as a co-operative society in April 1901,[78] with the ceremony to mark the cutting of the first sod taking place the same month. Vivian took upon himself the role of chairman of the new society, a position he was to maintain until December 1911. No doubt with Vivian's encouragement, the initial building work was contracted out to General Builders. However the relationship between the builders and Ealing Tenants quickly broke down, with the Ealing society complaining that General Builders was prioritising work being undertaking elsewhere. By the end of 1901 General Builders had been dismissed as contractors and Ealing thereafter undertook the building work on a direct labour basis, appointing one of their members Harry

Perry, a bricklayer, to oversee the works.[79] Given that Vivian was also chairman of General Builders, this must have been an embarrassing turn of events. Almost certainly these were the "various practical difficulties" which Vivian mentioned euphemistically in his 1912 article quoted above.

There was another area of disagreement between Vivian and some of the Ealing society members, and this time Vivian's view triumphed. Again according to Vivian, there was a strong desire initially to limit the scope of the Ealing venture to houses for craftsmen, particularly for people in the building trade. Vivian pushed back: "Some of us opposed this idea strongly. Firstly I hold that the estate will be on a more sound basis commercially, educationally and socially if it includes tenants who earn their living in a variety of ways rather than only as craftsmen. Secondly I believe the tendency to separate those who earn their living into 'workmen' and others is anti-social ... We all lose something of life by making these divisions," he wrote.[80]

The idea of mixed communities – mixed in social and class terms – is in many ways a very attractive one, and it was a concept which would feature later in the co-partnership tenants' history, particularly in relation to developments at Hampstead Garden Suburb. However, Vivian certainly had no desire to see tenants at Ealing from less skilled parts of the working classes. The one substantive change he made to the Tenant Co-operators model was to increase to £50 the amount which tenants would be required to hold as shares in their society. Fifty pounds (in the form of five £10 shares) was a very significant amount of money for working men and was comparable to (if not more than) the 10%-20% deposit which a would-be home-owner would be required to provide as a deposit for a building society or co-operative society mortgage loan.

Admittedly tenants were not obliged to fully pay up the £50 when taking up tenancies, the requirement being for £5 up-front and the remainder in regular instalments. However any members wishing to stand for the society's committee had to have invested more than the £5 initial minimum, the argument advanced by Vivian being that this would ensure they took their management responsibilities more seriously.[81]

Given the problem that Tenant Co-operators had encountered at Plashet in attracting tenants able to invest even £1, the £50 requirement was a significant pointer to the approach Vivian wanted to take in the development of co-partnership societies. Even one of Vivian's close collaborators in the movement was later to admit that the rule was "somewhat stern" and some later tenant societies chose to water down the commitment. In this context, it is clearly relevant to note that as early as May 1906, according to Aileen Reid, only forty of Ealing's 67 tenants were shareholders.[82] Tenant participation, emblazoned as one of the cornerstones of the co-partnership housing movement, was already perhaps proving problematic.

CHAPTER 4

WITH THE GARDEN CITY MOVEMENT

The houses built by the Ealing Tenants in the years up to 1906 may have been brought about as a collective endeavour but they were in most respects very conventionally designed. Aileen Reid describes the houses as "in an unexceptional style, a late-Victorian metropolitan vernacular that owed little to the 'cutting edge' of architectural thinking and fashion".[83] They were built as terraced housing facing on to streets which had been put down on former agricultural land following the sort of orthodox grid framework being adopted at this time by speculative builders throughout English urban areas.

The development by the Ealing Tenants after 1906, however, was completely different. Even a casual stroll from the pre-1906 streets (Woodfield Road, Woodfield Crescent and Woodfield Avenue) through the latter area of the estate (streets such as Brentham Way, Holyoake Walk and Ludlow Road) makes this abundantly clear. The new houses, built on development land which the society was able to acquire freehold over the period from 1906 to 1909, have been designed to a very different planning paradigm, one which pays obvious tribute to the Arts and Crafts movement. The houses face on to gently curving roads, located to make the most of the topography of the site and to maximise the potential to create attractive views. This is the part of the Ealing Tenants' development where the 'cutting edge' of architectural and planning thinking was indeed allowed to take charge. And this is the reason why the estate merits the name by which the area is known today: Brentham Garden Suburb.

The co-partnership tenants' movement would have been unlikely to have developed in the way that it did had it not become inextricably enmeshed with the parallel movement promoting the idea of garden cities and, more particularly, of garden villages and garden suburbs. From around the middle of the first decade of the century, all the new co-partnerships were designed in line with garden suburb principles. Indeed it was this aspect of their development which was often the driving force behind new projects, persuading (among others) landowners wanting to turn their farm lands into property to look to the co-partnership concept to realise their ideas.

Ebenezer Howard's book, setting out his vision for a network of new 'garden cities', was first published in 1898 under the title *To-morrow: a Peaceful Path to Real Reform*. Its more widely-read second edition came out in 1902, with the new title *Garden Cities of To-morrow*. Today the book is seen as a classic, something that helped kick-start the town planning profession as well as providing inspiration for the network of new towns created across Britain after the Second World War.

Howard's story is well-known and has been widely covered. He earned his living as a stenographer, had relatively modest means and had initially struggled to get his book published. The time he spent in the United States, and especially in the 'garden city' of Chicago, undoubtedly influenced his thinking. So, too, were books he had read, including Edward Bellamy's utopian novel *Looking Backward* (1888), which posits a future harmonious society based on state ownership of business, and William Morris's delightful libertarian socialist riposte *News from Nowhere* (1890).

Howard's own vision was based on his recognition that both urban living and rural life had benefits and disadvantages, and that a way needed to be found to maximise the benefits and reduce the downsides of both. In a celebrated diagram entitled the 'three magnets' which he included in the book he suggested an approach whereby the 'town-country' could bring together all the benefits of city and countryside. The list of the advantages was a long one, including "beauty of nature, social opportunity, fields and parks of easy access, low rents, high wages, low rates, plenty to do ... pure air and water, good drainage, bright homes and gardens, no smoke, no slums." He ended his list with the two words "freedom, co-operation". Although not directly involved in the co-operative movement, Howard certainly identified with the political impulse behind co-operation. Shortly after returning to Britain from the US in 1876 he had joined the Zetetical Society, a debating society on political and philosophical issues, where he fraternised with, among others, the future Fabian Sidney Webb and with George Bernard Shaw, who was to remain a lifelong acquaintance.

Howard's book is focused much more on the economic foundation on which his garden cities could be developed rather than on planning and town design issues, which are mentioned as something of an afterthought. The key factor, as he pointed out, was that while development land in urban areas was extremely expensive agricultural land was cheap: "while in some parts of London the rent is equal to £30,000 an acre, £4 an acre is an extremely high rent for agricultural land," Howard wrote.[84] This was, after all, a time when there had been a long period of recession in agriculture and significant rural depopulation.

If land could be acquired cheaply in rural areas and then converted into Garden Cities, the vision of a better life in the 'town-country' could be realised, Howard argued. Not only that but the increase in land values which would result from a garden city's development could be captured and held collectively for those who moved in to the new settlement. "By buying the new land *before* a new value is given to it by migration, the migrating people obtain the site at an extremely low figure and secure the coming increment for themselves and those who come after them," Howard explained.[85]

In other words, the organisation responsible for acquiring the garden city land (a sort of quasi-municipality) would continue to hold the freehold for the good of all, with residents being given only leasehold ownership rights. Thereafter they would pay a combined ground rent and rates, to meet the interest on the capital borrowed for initial land purchase and infrastructure costs, to enable all borrowings to be repaid (hopefully within thirty years) and to cover the services which a local authority would conventionally provide – schools, libraries, museums and everything else necessary for strong community life. Howard offered a worked example of the likely level at which this 'rate-rent' would have to be set and declared that it would be "insignificant".[86]

Because of its focus on land value, Howard's book directly engaged in what at this time was a significant issue in Britain. Not surprisingly, given the way that rapid urbanisation of Britain's cities and towns had led to astonishingly high windfall returns for those individual landowners lucky enough to hold the land required, the 'land issue' was high on the political agenda. In November 1909 David Lloyd George would attempt to tackle it in his Budget when he would propose a series of taxes on land values (Lloyd George's budget, rejected by the House of Lords with its strong landowner representation, led directly to the subsequent constitutional crisis and eventually to the Parliament Act of 1911). However the 1909 Budget followed more than thirty years of lively debate, some of it inspired by the US writer Henry George's book *Progress and Poverty* (1879). One of the active pressure groups leading the propaganda on the issue was the Land Nationalisation Society (LNS), originally established in 1881. It was members of the LNS who, a few months after Howard's book had first appeared in 1898, were instrumental in helping Howard establish the Garden City Association (GCA); the embryonic GCA (today the Town and Country Planning Association) was given office space in the LNS's premises.

The Labour Association's magazine *Labour Co-partnership* reviewed Howard's *To-morrow: A Peaceful Path to Real Reform* early in 1899 and the GCA's first AGM was also reported in the magazine in December that year.[87] But it was an editorial in *Labour Co-partnership* in February 1901, with the title The Extension of Co-operation: Garden Cities, which seems to have been instrumental in bringing co-partnership and the fledgling garden city movement together.[88] The writer of this article was Ralph Neville, a barrister who had long been a member of the Labour Association and who had also served as a Liberal MP for Liverpool Exchange from 1887 to 1895.[89]

The opportunity to strengthen this new partnership came in the autumn of 1901 at a highly influential conference held south of Birmingham in the model village of Bournville, created by the Quaker businessman George Cadbury but now (following a transfer by Cadbury in 1900) in the hands of an independent trust. Ebenezer Howard was one of the speakers at this conference, as was Ralph Neville. Neville had by this point become the chairman of the Garden City Association.

The architect Raymond Unwin, then in his late thirties, was a third speaker at Bournville. It was the beginning of a relationship which would see Unwin emerge as a central figure in the developing story of co-partnership housing societies and as the key figure in the development in England of garden suburbs and garden villages. He was at this stage working with his brother-in-law Barry Parker in a practice which they had set up jointly in 1894, and which was initially based in Buxton. Their work was strongly influenced by the Arts and Crafts movement, but Unwin was inspired not just by the Arts and Crafts aesthetic but also by the radical politics which underlay it. He had been for a time the secretary of Manchester's branch of the Socialist League, the socialist organisation set up by William Morris and others following their split with the Social Democratic Federation in 1884. Unwin was also a frequent visitor in the 1880s to Edward Carpenter's 'simple life' community in Millthorpe south of Sheffield, where Carpenter lived openly with his young working-class partner George Merrill. Carpenter described Unwin in his autobiography *My Days and Dreams* as a "young man of cultured antecedents, of first-rate ability and good sense, healthy, democratic, vegetarian".[90]

With excellent timing, Unwin and Parker had published in 1901 a book of lectures called *The Art of Building a Home* which effectively acted as a manifesto for their ideas. In a chapter in the book entitled Co-operation in Building, Unwin describes ways that working-class housing could be developed on co-operative lines. "The houses could be grouped together and so arranged that each would obtain a sunny aspect," he wrote. "The success of the plan would depend largely on the clustering of the buildings, the avoidance of mere rows on the one hand and of detached villas on the other." Local materials should be used. Anything pretentious or showy should be excluded.[91]

Later Unwin was to restate the importance of the idea of co-operation in working-class housing: "I look to the principle of co-partnership to give us again, in a new form, a communal civic life which will once more infuse harmony and beauty into the homes and into the suburbs and villages," he wrote.[92]

This is an appropriate moment to report that it was Raymond Unwin who was the architect asked by the Ealing Tenants committee to prepare plans for the development of the new part of their estate, work which Unwin delivered to the society in the spring of 1907. Ealing Tenants, after its shaky start, was beginning to become a more secure venture. Unwin's ideas would directly inspire the later development of Brentham Garden Suburb.

Long before Unwin was asked to turn his attention to Ealing, however, other high-profile work had come the way of his practice. Almost immediately following the 1901 Bournville conference, he and Parker had received a commission from another Quaker chocolate-making family, the Rowntree brothers, to design and build the model village of New Earswick just outside York city centre. Unwin summarised his approach in a Fabian pamphlet *Cottage Plans and Common Sense* (1902). Then in 1903 Unwin's practice received a further, highly significant, commission: they were to be directly involved in the efforts to turn Ebenezer Howard's 1898 vision into practice, at the first actual Garden City.

The story of how agricultural land was successfully acquired close to the then village of Letchworth in Hertfordshire and how thereafter the new Garden City took shape has been well documented and need not be repeated here. In summary, the fact that Letchworth happened at all is an extraordinary achievement. It came at a cost, though: Letchworth today can disappoint those expecting to find a Howardian utopian planned community. The problem essentially was that First Garden City Ltd (the company established to develop the new community) was engaged in its early years of life in a desperate struggle to find the necessary capital to develop the land, and this meant that significant compromises were necessary. Considerable concessions had to be made to the proposed leasehold arrangements, for example, in order to persuade businesses and individuals to relocate. Perhaps inevitably, business realism and idealism clashed. Howard, who had initially assumed the role of managing director of the company, was politely but firmly told to step down by his board. Ralph Neville had by this stage assumed the chairmanship of the company.[93]

Another director of First Garden City in these early days was the significant figure of Aneurin Williams, already introduced (page 15). Williams had been born in Glamorganshire in 1859 and was seven when his family moved to Middlesbrough, where his father took over the management of an ironworks. Williams went to Cambridge University and later was called to the Bar, but he was strongly moved by Andrew Mearns' *The Bitter Cry of Outcast London* and became actively involved in the Toynbee Settlement in Spitalfields where he worked with Canon Samuel Barnett. His father's death took him back to Teesside to work in the management of the family ironworks before his wife's ill-health prompted a move south again in 1892, this time to Hindhead in Surrey. Once settled, he quickly became active in the Labour Association, becoming for a time the editor of *Labour Co-partnership* after the magazine was established in 1894.[94]

Aneurin Williams threw himself into the work of building Letchworth with the same enthusiasm he displayed for the Labour Association. Creating a new urban development from scratch had all sorts of challenges, one of which was to create the business base which would enable migrants arriving in Letchworth to find work. Aneurin Williams used his co-operative and co-partnership contacts here. Even before the Letchworth site had been identified and bought, he had had a quiet word with his namesake Bernard Williams, at that stage managing the successful productive co-operative Leicester Printers. As Aneurin Williams later recalled, he said to Bernard, "If an estate is purchased will you go there to establish a printing business on co-partnership lines?" Bernard Williams had reportedly replied, "Yes, with pleasure".[95]

Bernard Williams was as good as his word. He left his post at Leicester Printers and moved to Letchworth to establish another co-partnership productive co-operative, Garden City Press (in the process bringing some of his Leicester co-operators with him). Aneurin Williams accepted the post of president of the new co-operative, which was established at the start of 1904.

Garden City Press quickly built up a business, employing 22 people by the end of 1904 and 32 by 1906, despite the misfortune of losing its new purpose-built premises in 1905 to a fire.[96]

The success of Garden City Press posed another problem, however, and that was the shortage of working-class accommodation in the 'Garden City'. Bernard Williams himself was obliged to live initially outside Letchworth, in Hitchin. The solution was an obvious one: to establish a new co-partnership tenants' society. Garden City Tenants was planned in the autumn of 1904, with a prospectus issued at the year's end which appealed for share capital at 5% and loan stock investment at 4.5%. The prospectus reported that the Letchworth development company First Garden City was fully co-operating, offering sites "on most reasonable terms".[97] (Later commercial builders claimed that First Garden City had unfairly favoured the new co-partnership, an allegation which was firmly denied.)[98]

Garden City Tenants got off to a fast start. By May 1905, Bernard Williams was able to write in *Co-operative News* that the society had begun operations with the building of thirteen houses, each with half an acre of land attached: "The future tenants of these houses have each agreed to give up a small portion of their land for the creation of a common green of one-and-a-half acres, on which the houses will front in an irregular semi-circle. The effect is expecting to be delightfully reminiscent of an old English village."[99]

Bernard Williams himself was very quickly able to move from Hitchin to become a tenant of the new co-partnership. Three months later he was able to tell his co-operative readers in no uncertain terms of the pleasures of his new home: "Every breath is a joy; every glance an inspiration; every movement a growth. It does not seem possible to us (erstwhile town-dwellers) that landscapes could always have been so fair, grass so green, atmospheres so gloriously and translucently blue, nor breeze so caressingly soft," he wrote.[100] (Letchworth at this stage undoubtedly needed good propagandists.)

Garden City Tenants took over the Ealing model, and indeed as at Ealing Henry Vivian was asked to act as chairman. Bernard Williams would have known Vivian through the Labour Association, and an established 'name' could be valuable in attracting the capital needed. Indeed, by June 1905 a two-page advertisement in *Labour Co-partnership* was reporting that Ralph Neville, Aneurin Williams (by this stage the First Garden City chairman), George Cadbury's son Edward, and William Lever (of Lever Brothers, and the inspiration behind the Port Sunlight model village in the Wirral) were all applying for shares in Garden City Tenants. Later George Bernard Shaw was to join their number.[101]

It was no surprise that Raymond Unwin was asked to undertake the design of the Garden City Tenants developments. There were, in fact, several separate sites in Letchworth which First Garden City Ltd made available to the new co-partnership society. Two areas, Eastholm Green and Westholm Green, were small and Unwin chose to arrange the houses in each case around a central 'village green'. Bird's Hill and neighbouring Pixmore Hill were larger and required more detailed planning. Unwin himself was later to explain the reasoning he followed. Bird's Hill, "an irregularly shaped piece of land on the hillside, commanding considerable views to the south and west" included breaks in the lines of buildings in order to maintain views from the houses. "On the adjacent piece of land known as Pixmore Hill, also developed by the Garden City Tenants, the general shape of the plot being square, the development was carried out on more regular lines, and except that a few of the groups were set across the north-eastern corner to preserve the existing copse at that corner, nearly all the groups of cottages on this site were placed square with each other," Unwin added. Regularity of design was not necessarily unacceptable. However, "it is the mere aimless arrangement, such as one finds springing from an ill-considered reaction against formal design that offends against one's sense of order," he explained.[102]

Unwin was also anxious that the co-operative movement generally got the message he was trying to put into practice in places such as Ealing and Letchworth: "Many estates have, of course, been developed in the past by co-operative societies with a view to housing their members ... Too often, however, co-operation has ceased with the purchase of the estate, and the development has been carried out very much on the old lines without a full realisation of the opportunities which co-operation offers. It is the importance of these opportunities which I wish to emphasise."[103]

By the end of the decade the Garden City Tenants had built close to three hundred homes across Letchworth, and the society would finally complete about 320 houses. Pixmore Hill, much the largest of the sites developed by Garden City Tenants, was chosen to house a central meeting hall, the Institute. It was also provided with a bowling green, several open spaces and several allotment gardens. Allotments and gardens, which residents could use to grow the vegetables they needed, were seen by Unwin as a central requirement for well-planned working-class housing estates.

The workers at the Garden City Press had not been alone in thinking of combining co-operation in the workplace with co-operation in housing when in 1904 they set up Garden City Tenants. Two years earlier, in 1902, a similar idea had been actively discussed by workers in Bernard Williams' old home town of Leicester, at the Anchor Boot and Shoe Co-operative, a productive co-operative which specialised in producing children's footwear.

Leicester (where the Co-operative Productive Federation was based) was in many respects the heartland of the productive co-operative movement in Britain at this time. The Anchor co-operative was a spin-off in 1892-3 from the successful boot and shoe co-op in the city, the Equity, and by 1895 the Anchor had developed into a strong business in its own right. It had moved to new premises in 1895, had been able to reduce its member-worker hours of work from 54 to 49 in 1897, and had also introduced a week's paid holiday in 1898. By the turn of the century it was turning over around £25,000 a year.[104]

Leicester Anchor's leaders J.T. Taylor (for many years the co-op's manager) and Amos Mann (the co-op's president) were active both in politics and in the co-operative movement. Mann, a socialist in his politics although one who believed in trying to unite all progressive tendencies, was a town councillor for Leicester from 1897 to 1908 (nominally sitting as a Liberal member). Taylor was treasurer of the local Independent Labour Party and was also a town councillor for a short time (in his case standing for the ILP).[105] Leicester's footwear workers, it should be said, were known for their radicalism.[106]

Mann was also treasurer for many years of the Co-operative Productive Federation as well as being for a time on the committee of the local distributive co-op society. He was later to play an active role in the Labour Co-partnership Association (as the Labour Association had chosen to rename itself in 1901),[107] becoming their paid organiser in 1912.

It should be no surprise to learn therefore that Henry Vivian, on behalf of the Association, had been invited by Leicester Anchor to speak at a meeting on 'co-operators and the housing question' held in October 1902. Bernard Williams, still at that stage at Leicester Printers before his move to Letchworth, took the chair. Vivian was able to call his speech the "Advantages of Co-operative Tenancy on what has come to be known as the Ealing Tenant Society system".

Vivian's speech immediately had results: the Anchor workers decided that they would replicate Ealing Tenants by creating a co-partnership tenants' society in Leicester. By December 1902, *Labour Co-partnership* was able to give the news that plans were already under way to register Anchor Tenants Ltd. Amos Mann later reported that at this stage 45 of the Anchor co-op's workers were subscribing towards the venture: "The desire was that a real co-operative community should be established ... that life, as far as that was possible with our own independent ideas, should be lived in common," he wrote. This was after all, Mann pointed out, what the Rochdale Pioneers had wanted too, when they had drawn up their original aims. "Leading spirits in the movement let their imagination carry them forward to a time when they would be able to provide a house, with a garden of a fair size, and to create a sort of workmen's community, that would provide collectively some of the advantages that a rich man can obtain for himself".[108]

Admittedly, realising this vision was to prove initially challenging. Weekly subs from members managed to bring in £200 after the first year. Efforts continued, and after two years the sum was £339. Potential land had been identified, just outside the Leicester city boundary at Humberstone, but £339 was barely enough to build one house, let along an estate. It was becoming clear that there would need to be a radical change of direction before Anchor Tenants had sufficient capital to be able to offer anything to compare with the housing erected by Ealing Tenants or Garden City Tenants. (That change was to happen, although not until 1907.)[109]

Meanwhile, the idea of co-partnership tenants' societies was also taking root in a fourth location, in the small town of Sevenoaks in Kent. Sevenoaks Tenants Ltd was registered in 1903, this time with the local distributive co-operative society taking the lead. The Sevenoaks store (formed in 1896) was, according to *Labour Co-partnership*, "one of the most thriving in the south of England" in 1904, with over 850 members and an annual turnover of £19,000.[110] It was also one of the minority of co-operative stores to offer their shop workers as well as their customers a share of the profits through the 'divi'.

Sevenoaks' commitment to profit-sharing was perhaps not surprising, given that it had among its leading lights several members of the Labour (Co-partnership) Association, most notably the local Liberal councillor and businessman (an 'Africa merchant') Francis Swanzy and Laura Gilchrist Thompson, the wife of the local vicar Percy Thompson. Indeed, unlike the other three co-partnerships described so far, the Sevenoaks venture was very much a top-down affair. Mrs Thompson made available approaching two acres of land near Sevenoaks station in 1904 and (according to Aileen Reid) Swanzy was the most likely source of the society's founding capital of £700.[111]

The first 25 houses were completed and occupied by January 1906. Unwin's influence had yet to be felt and the houses constructed (in St Botolph's Avenue) were of conventional design, similar to the first streets constructed in Ealing. In fact, Sevenoaks Tenants arranged for Fred Watts, an Ealing Tenants' committee member, to act as their clerk of works.

Francis Swanzy was to provide Sevenoaks Tenants with its second plot of development land in 1905, a slightly challenging site where the street named Holyoake Terrace was to be constructed over the next two years. By this stage Sevenoaks had got the message about garden suburbs, and had asked Unwin to contribute his advice. Sevenoaks Tenants was later to extend its work to rural housing in neighbouring villages outside Sevenoaks, ultimately ending with 89 houses on six separate sites.[112]

By 1905, in fact, there was enough momentum to begin to formalise this new movement. Ealing, Letchworth, Leicester and Sevenoaks together made four co-partnership societies; add in the Tenant Co-operators and that made five. It was enough to start a new federation. The Co-partnership Tenants Housing Council held its inaugural meeting on February 27 1905.[113]

CHAPTER 5

SCALING UP: A NATIONAL INFRASTRUCTURE

From its founding in 1884, the Labour Association had focused its work on propaganda to promote the success of productive co-operatives. As the years had gone by, it had widened its reach to begin campaigning also on behalf of those conventional commercial businesses which were introducing some element of employee participation, of the kind which today we would associate with employee share-ownership plans and employee benefit trusts. Firms such as South Metropolitan Gas were featured as exemplars of what the Association referred to (perhaps optimistically) as the 'Transformation of Capitalism'.

In other words, the Association was keen to promote ways to reconcile the interests of capital with those of labour. This was what it meant by 'co-partnership'. It was an approach that could attract the liberal-minded, concerned perhaps at what this new and growing creed of 'socialism' might imply, and the Labour Association could count among its members not just pioneering worker-run productive co-operatives but also representatives of the aristocracy, politicians and leading churchmen.[114] Sidney and Beatrice Webb were later to critique the concept of co-partnership in forthright terms: "not the finding of a new organisation of industry, so that it may be governed in the interests of the community rather than those of individuals, but the discovery of a way to avoid conflicts between the capitalist employer and the wage-earners in his service".[115] Supporters saw it differently, of course, as a way of creating a harmonious society that benefited all.

Now, following Henry Vivian's involvement with the launch of Ealing Tenants, it became apparent that the Labour Association – the Labour Co-partnership Association from 1901 – potentially had a third string to its bow.

The model of 'co-partnership tenant' societies, as it developed, was based on the principle that both investors and tenants would benefit. It is worth looking at this model in more detail. Although tenants would not be owner-occupiers of their own houses they would instead, through their membership of the society, have a collective interest in their whole estate. The title of this book 'These houses are ours' is taken from a 1914 book by Birmingham housing reformer John Nettlefold, but the same language was used regularly by those promoting co-partnerships in the early years of the twentieth century. For example, an unsigned article in the GCA's magazine *Garden City* in 1906 stated "No individual may say of any particular dwelling 'This is my house'; but he may say, with his fellow-members 'These are our houses'".[116] The Garden City article may well have been written by Vivian, who regularly used this language.

As we have seen, Vivian had taken from the Tenant Co-operators the concept of the 'divi' to tenants, a distribution of the profits on the basis of the rent they had paid. This was to be a distribution from net profits, to be calculated after other deductions. Typically this meant after the repayment of any setting-up costs still outstanding, after payment of loan interest and share dividends to investors, after a depreciation allowance for writing down the value of fixed assets such as property, and after transferring whatever level of profits which the committee felt was appropriate into a reserve or contingency fund.

As at Tenant Co-operators, any dividend which became due to a tenant was paid in the form of shares in the society rather than in cash, until the time that a tenant had reached the minimum holding required of them under their society's rules. Leicester Anchor's rules in 1902 fixed this at the maximum permitted under co-operative legislation at the time, £200, but in a 1910 rule revision changed this so that tenants' bonuses would remain capitalised in the society (if need be as loan stock rather than shares) until they actually held the equivalent of the whole value of their house.[117]

As shareholders, tenants also benefited from shareholders' dividends, but of course the funds held in their name were not easily turned into liquid cash. Again taking Leicester Anchor as an example, tenants giving up their tenancy and moving out could request that their funds be returned. We can assume that this request was normally fulfilled, although the rules did give the committee discretion not to repay, in which case the tenant was allowed to try to find someone to buy their shares from them.

It is not clear from the records how often the tenants' dividend was actually paid in practice. Vivian in a book published in 1908 said that no tenant dividend had yet been payable in Ealing, the committee apparently waiting until they had more experience of the scheduling of building repairs;[118] by 1910, however, he was writing that "older societies" had been able to declare a dividend on rent of 1s (5%) – 1s 6d (7.5%).[119] Nevertheless it is clear that the tenants' dividend was by no means automatic.

Of course, societies also potentially had the scope to benefit their tenants by fixing rent levels below the market rent. However this does not seem to have been the general practice. Just as co-operative stores tended to adopt the policy of fixing their grocery prices at market prices, tenant housing societies appear to have pitched their rents at commercial levels.[120]

The standard arrangement in tenancy agreements was that tenants had responsibility for internal decorations and repairs, while the society took responsibility for external repairs (a system similar to that applying today for many social housing tenants). The society reserved the right when tenants left to use tenants' share capital to pay for any costs of redecoration or refurbishment, if it was felt that the condition of the property had not been left in an adequate state. This is certainly a reasonable policy in principle, but in fact disputes over internal decorations were to become a significant cause of controversy. Many tenants appeared to feel that this provision was unfair.

Anyone reading the preceding paragraphs might conclude that the benefits to tenants from the co-partnership model were not particularly generous. Nevertheless the communal facilities provided on many estates, and the opportunities for social and educational activities which these facilities offered, also need to be taken into account. Chapter 7 looks in much more detail at the social side of life in these co-partnership estates.

What about the benefits to investors? One of the arguments often advanced by Vivian and his associates was that investors were putting their money into estates which attracted a better class of tenant and therefore into estates which would be much less at risk of suffering from a decline in quality or reputation. The tenants' obligatory financial stake through their shareholdings meant greater commitment, it was said, and also gave access to funds which could be used if tenants fell into rent arrears or, as we have seen, left their property in a poor state.

Investors were strongly encouraged too to identify with the garden suburb ethos adopted by the co-partnership tenants' movement. It is fair to say that, after the early housing built at Ealing and Sevenoaks, Raymond Unwin's planning principles were adopted to a significant extent in every single subsequent development. Nevertheless, investors were taking some risks in placing their funds in co-partnership societies, an issue explored in the next chapter.

As an aside, Ewart Culpin, the long-serving secretary of the GCA and the Garden Cities and Town Planning Association (as the GCA became in 1909), thought there should be a very definite difference made between 'garden villages' (new self-contained communities, smaller versions of Garden Cities) and 'garden suburbs' (extensions to existing cities).[121] In practice, however, the co-partnership housing movement tended to use the two terms more or less interchangeably, and this book will follow that lead.

From the original Ealing meeting in the Haven Arms onwards, Henry Vivian seems to have been given very much free rein by his Labour Co-partnership Association employers to devote time to developing the co-partnership tenants and to undertake his role as chairman of both the Ealing and Garden City societies, as well of course of General Builders. The financial side of this arrangement is opaque; there would have been remuneration payable to Vivian for holding these positions, which it would appear he had agreed would be paid (at least in part) to the Association rather than to himself. The money was probably not actually paid until 1907, when Ealing was asked to pay the Association the significant amount of £236 0s 6d "in respect of Mr Vivian's services from the commencement of the Society" until the end of 1906. Garden City Tenants were similarly required to pay back-pay of £95 0s 0d.[122]

The idea for a federated body linking the first five societies, the Co-partnership Tenants Housing Council, took shape in 1904. Vivian had gained approval from his executive committee in December 1904 for the proposal, at that point called the 'Tenants' Societies Committee'. Again there was a certain financial vagueness involved: it would appear that Vivian had asked for £50 from the Association as seed-corn funding, although the spending decision had not been minuted and had to be rediscussed (and retrospectively agreed) late in 1905.[123]

The Co-partnership Tenants Housing Council had signed up an aristocrat, the co-partnership advocate Earl Grey, to be its initial president and there was a long list of vice-presidents (a position that represented a statement of endorsement, rather than of active participation). These included the veteran co-operator George Jacob Holyoake, the eminent Cambridge economist Professor Alfred Marshall, and the trade unionist and Liberal politician Fred Maddison (an MP from 1897-1900, and again from 1906). Two leading housing reformers active in local government, both of whom we will meet again later, were recruited too: Alderman William Thompson from Richmond (Surrey), the chairman of the National Housing Reform Council, and Cllr John Nettlefold, the chairman of Birmingham City's housing committee. Aneurin Williams was a further vice-president and there were others from within the co-partnership world.

More relevant to the development of the new Council was its executive committee, which was chaired, as might be expected, by Henry Vivian. Ealing Tenants were represented by William Hutchings, a retired civil servant who had moved into one of the Ealing houses in Woodfield Avenue, and by Harry Perry the bricklayer-turned-overseer. Bernard Williams represented Garden City Tenants. Anchor Tenants were represented by its secretary J.S. Wilford, a fellow activist of Amos Mann and J.T. Taylor. Francis Swanzy the local politician and businessman was one of two Sevenoaks representatives, and Tenant Co-operators despite their different background were also represented, by John Yerbury. Although the Council was presented as the tenant societies' own federation, there were also several others on the executive committee with no direct links to any of the five societies. It was predominantly a very comfortably middle-class committee.[124]

It was also, predictably, predominantly male. Nevertheless, among all these men there were two woman. Annette Churton, who was active particularly around rural housing issues, joined the executive committee as representative of an organisation called the Rural Housing and Sanitation Association; the part she played in building that association was a valuable one but it must be said that her engagement with the Housing Council was to be a modest one. The other woman, who agreed to take on the position of honorary secretary of the Council, was to play a much more significant role in the development of the movement. Her name was Sybella Gurney and at this point she was in her mid-thirties.

Gurney had been born in Paris in 1870, her father at that point being the chaplain to the British embassy. The family returned to Britain after the disturbances of the Paris Commune and settled in

Oxford, and later Sybella was able to study to degree level at the pioneering women's college the Royal Holloway. She developed close links with the co-operative movement and, particularly, with the Labour Association. For a period she undertook the editorship of *Labour Co-partnership*.[125]

One of the central roles of the new Council was to propagandise for the idea of co-partnership tenant societies, and Gurney quickly got things started. In a paper given at a conference in Derby that April, for example, she called for an alternative to the mean streets put up by speculators and the "dreariness of modern life" which they represented.[126] A little later she was to elaborate these ideas in an article in the sympathetic journal *Charity Organisation Review*: "Under the ordinary plan we find all new building areas are developed in the interests of the building speculator and the land speculator. The object is to get the greatest return out of capital ... It is found cheapest to reproduce the same type of house indefinitely, and so we get the dreary monotony of the modern suburb."

There were benefits to the co-partnership way of providing working-class housing also for investors, Gurney added in her article: those with capital had responsibilities in how they used their money, she argued.[127] She was as good as her word: Gurney had inherited wealth and was shortly to make a number of significant investments in the co-partnership tenants' societies. Indeed it would appear that it was Gurney who provided the £300 finance needed for one of the very first actions taken by the new Housing Council.[128] This was to arrange for a pair of houses to be erected in the Cheap Cottages Exhibition which was being organised by *County Gentleman* magazine and which was staged in Letchworth in the summer of 1905.

The exhibition, which attracted tens of thousands of visitors, was designed to see if adequate working-class houses could be constructed for no more than £150 each, and the Co-partnership Tenants Housing Council exhibited a pair of completed 'cottages', together costing £300, which it said could be replicated and constructed within two months. The houses may not have been lavish but they were not ungenerous in terms of space: each had a living room (16ft by 7ft 9 in) with a range and a scullery, while upstairs were three relatively decent-sized bedrooms. The houses also came equipped with a WC. After the exhibition the houses were passed on to the Garden City Tenants and one of the two became Bernard Williams' own home.[129]

The momentum which had led to the establishment of the Council continued in the months thereafter. *Labour Co-partnership* magazine quickly reported possible new tenant societies being discussed in, among other places, Eccles near Maidstone, Bromley, Hindhead and Brockenhurst. By the autumn there was interest recorded from Manchester, Liverpool and Sheffield and by the middle of 1906 from Brighton, Birmingham, Berkhamsted, Cardiff, Oxford, Winchester, Ruabon, Oldham and Hampstead.[130] Clearly Sybella Gurney was struggling to handle the administration on a voluntary basis. "The work of the Housing Council in correspondence and in advice to new societies had increased so much by the autumn [of 1905] that the appointment of an organising secretary had become essential," *Labour Co-partnership* reported in January 1906. The person appointed was Frederick Litchfield, previously general secretary of the National Deposit Friendly Society.[131]

Several of these would-be tenant societies were being willed forward by active Labour Co-partnership Association members. Hindhead was, as mentioned, the home town of Aneurin Williams (he and his wife lived in a large Arts and Crafts style villa called Wheelside, still extant but now split into several flats; Williams had already been responsible for establishing the Haslemere Builders co-operative, which at this point was doing good business, turning over more than either of the two London-based co-ops, Co-operative Builders and General Builders).[132] The Brockenhurst proposal was undoubtedly the initiative of Sybella Gurney, who lived nearby. The Brighton proposal, which was eventually to be registered legally as the Brighton and Sussex Tenants but which did not progress beyond that, was particularly associated with the suffragist and humanist Emilie Holyoake-Marsh, the daughter of George Jacob Holyoake; she lived in Brighton, as did her father before his death in 1906. Oxford's strong co-operative and co-partnership links were also utilised; meetings were held in the city several times from 1905 with a twenty-five acre site near the river being at one stage actively considered, but the venture ultimately did not proceed.[133]

In fact, most of the towns optimistically mentioned in *Labour Co-partnership* at this time did not see tenant co-partnerships come to fruition. But some did. By the end of 1906 three new societies were legally registered and actively beginning the work of planning their new estates – all three, of course, adopting garden suburb principles. The first of these was Bournville Tenants, where George Cadbury provided twenty acres of land to the south-west of his existing model village on a 99 year leasehold basis, eighteen acres to be developed for low-density housing and two to be left as open space; Cadbury also contributed investment capital towards the overall costs. Cadbury had kept in touch with the co-partnership movement following the 1901 conference and as early as 1902 had been talking with Fred Maddison about the possibility of a co-partnership tenant society.[134] Bournville Tenants got under way following a June 1906 meeting in the city addressed by Sybella Gurney and Henry Vivian and was fully autonomous of the Bournville Village Trust, the charity with responsibility for Cadbury's model village housing.[135]

Oldham Garden Suburb Tenants was also registered in 1906, although it would be two years before building work commenced. Here the equivalent role to that played by Cadbury was undertaken by the philanthropist Sarah Lees, in her sixties and widowed and living in a mansion in Werneth Park, Oldham, with her daughter Marjory. Sarah Lees (later Dame Sarah Lees) was to become, in 1907, the first female councillor in Lancashire and, in 1910, the Mayor of the town, only the second female Mayor in the country. A committed Liberal, she had been one of those involved some years earlier in establishing the 'Beautiful Oldham' society, influenced by the City Beautiful movement in the US; she also helped bank-roll the new tenant society through a sizeable donation.[136]

Almost all the new co-partnership housing societies which were to be established after the formation of the Housing Council were, as in Bournville and Oldham, 'top-down' initiatives created by those with money concerned to do something for working-class housing in their areas. The one exception, at least in its early days, was Manchester Tenants Ltd, the idea for which came from discussions among employees at the Co-operative Wholesale Society at its head office in central Manchester. Sybella Gurney addressed a meeting at the CWS in June 1906 and returned again to the city in the Autumn with Frederick Litchfield.[137] Manchester Tenants was to be a great success: the society was to go on to build a garden village in Burnage in south Manchester, complete with bowling green, tennis courts and meeting hall, and it remains one of the most attractive areas of Manchester to this day. Nevertheless, as we shall see in the next chapter, the initial search for capital was not at all easy.

Henry Vivian understood that there was a pressing need to develop a more effective and methodical way to tap into the capital potentially available for new co-partnership tenant societies. By 1906, he and his colleagues at the Housing Council were well advanced with plans for a second nationally-based federated body for the growing movement, which would be launched in 1907 as Co-partnership Tenants Ltd (CTL). Thereafter the Housing Council's role was limited to propaganda and educational work. CTL was the agency which was designed to actually work closely with new tenant societies, providing the professional expertise needed to enable them to come to fruition.

CTL was based, it should be said at the outset, on a very good concept. Frederick Litchfield, who moved across from the Housing Council to become CTL's organising secretary (his role at the Council being taken by Crossley Greenwood), was later to describe CTL's role as "a kind of Clearing House for the movement, raising financial assistance where it is satisfied of the solid foundation of the societies, doing educational work in acquainting people of the real ideals of the co-partnership plan, advising with regard to the purchase and planning of estates, and generally supplying the financial, technical, and expert knowledge that is frequently lacking among the pioneers".[138]

Indeed, CTL quickly developed these areas of operation into separate departments. There was a finance department which took on the task of raising investment capital, both for CTL member societies and for CTL itself. There was an accountancy department, whose role was to help societies with their book-keeping and financial management – and implicitly to ensure that CTL did not suffer any reputational risk from any of its associated societies running into financial difficulties. There was a buying department, designed to help societies save money by pooling orders for building materials. CTL also had a preferred building contractor, in the shape of Henry Vivian's original co-partnership General Builders.

There was a further section of CTL described as the "surveying, planning and building supervision department". Raymond Unwin was signed up as CTL's architectural and planning consultant.[139] Later, in 1910, an in-house architect's department would be created, with Hebden Bridge-born George Lister Sutcliffe as CTL's own architect.

The presence of CTL certainly offered a new, and potentially faster, route for new tenant societies to get going. It was pro-active in its approach: "The option of a suitable site at a suitable price is first secured, and after a certain number of persons have undertaken to join the proposed tenants' society, the land is planned out with due regard to health, economy, and artistic appearance; capital is subscribed in shares of not more than £10 each, payable by monthly instalments, and 4 per cent loan stock is raised," explained one writer, writing in 1908.[140]

CTL was very much Henry Vivian's creation, and he was the society's chairman right through until his death in 1930. CTL was established under co-operative legislation as a society in its own right and it had from the start a strong business orientation, looking to ensure that it made the profits necessary to employ its staff, service its borrowings and also remunerate its directors. Its prospectus described it as a "business centre or federation for the movement"[141] but it was much less obviously structured as a federation than the Housing Council. Societies could choose to become members of CTL and were then required to use CTL's services in their development and building work (it seems that sometimes there was a small amount of discretion allowed in the imposition of this rule). Member societies were also obliged to acquire shares in CTL (one £10 share for each £1,000 of its assets, with a minimum of two shares). However voting in the new society was skewed towards those who had invested the most: votes were on the basis of one vote per share held, and a further vote for each £50 of loan stock invested. Members of the board of directors (the term used for the co-operative's management committee) were also required to be shareholders themselves.[142]

Inevitably, therefore, the CTL board was primarily made up of those who were investors rather than tenant-delegates. At its launch it consisted of Sir John Brunner MP, who was also its president, John Greenhalgh (who, as we have seen, had financed Ealing Tenants), William Hutchings (the retired civil servant now living in Ealing), Francis Swanzy (the Sevenoaks businessman) and Henry Vivian himself, as well as Garden City Press's Bernard Williams.[143]

Ealing, Sevenoaks, Garden City Tenants, Leicester Anchor, Oldham and Manchester Tenants quickly signed up as CTL members. Not every tenant housing society wanted to accept the CTL embrace, however. Bournville Tenants (although a member of the Housing Council) never chose to affiliate to CTL and neither did Tenant Co-operators.

To appreciate Henry Vivian's thinking when CTL was launched in 1907 we have to understand the event in early 1906 which had dramatically changed his position in life. The General Election held early that year saw a massive landslide for the Liberals, who gained a 124 seat majority over all the other parties combined. One of the 397 Liberal

MPs returned was Vivian, who had stood as the Liberal candidate for the Birkenhead constituency.[144]

Vivian had no obvious links to Birkenhead before the election but was probably helped in his selection there by William Lever of Lever Brothers, who was the Liberal MP for next door Wirral. Vivian had stood on a Lib-Lab ticket, one of the group of so-called 'trade unionist' Lib-Lab MPs which included Fred Maddison, now once again returned as an MP and a close political ally of Vivian's. Vivian had no political links with the 29 Labour MPs who had been returned under their leader Keir Hardie, the first time that there had been a significant Labour presence in Parliament. While the Labour MPs occupied part of the opposition benches across the floor, Vivian was a backbencher on the government side of the Commons.

In fact, Vivian showed a degree of hostility towards the Labour MPs. One of his most notable interventions in a Commons debate was during the 1907 debate on the King's Speech when he critiqued directly both Hardie and the idea of socialism: "The Hon. Member had suggested that in order to solve the problem, we should reconstruct our industrial system from top to bottom. For himself, he was in favour of a gradual change."[145]

Vivian was indeed politically very much in the free trade Liberal tradition. His commitment to the attributes of self-help, self-reliance and freedom from state intervention – a commitment which of course had underlain his work for the Labour Association – meant that among other things he opposed measures being discussed in Parliament for the state to help the unemployed find work. Together with Fred Maddison he was to be censured by the TUC in 1907 for failing to endorse the Labour candidate Pete Curran, an active trade unionist and one of the founders of the ILP, at a bye-election in Jarrow held that year (their lack of support turned out to be immaterial: Curran was elected regardless).[146]

Vivian's election gave him a significant platform to advance his co-partnership views but it also brought new obligations, and what it didn't bring him was any new money. MPs were unpaid until the passing of the Parliament Act of 1911, when finally the demand of the Chartist movement for MPs to be remunerated would be fulfilled. So he remained reliant on his paid work at the Labour Co-partnership Association and whatever further income he received from the co-partnership societies he chaired. The exact arrangement for his salary at the Labour Co-partnership Association was discussed by the Association's committee shortly after Vivian's election when it was agreed that he would be paid £250 a year plus £50 expenses. It was also agreed that Vivian would pass income up to £150 he received from the tenant societies to the Association; anything from the societies above £150 a year would be his to keep.

A year later, in April 1908, Vivian's salary was discussed again, and was fixed this time at £150 a year. In exchange, the Association agreed to forego all the income it had received from tenant societies, "Mr Vivian being left to receive from them direct any payment for his services to them," as the minutes put it. This would refer primarily to income from Ealing, Garden City, General Builders and particularly from CTL.[147]

Although not regularly contributing to Commons debates, Vivian was able to work behind the scenes to advance his housing agenda and he quickly found himself with a valuable platform when in the spring of 1906 he was asked to serve on the Select Committee looking at a proposed Amendment Bill to the Housing of the Working Classes Act of 1890. From May to October the Select Committee called witnesses to give evidence, and Vivian found himself in the intriguing position of being able to question some of those in the housing reform movement with whom he had previously collaborated. These included the Richmond Alderman William Thompson, who was called back before the committee no less than three times, and Cllr John Nettlefold from Birmingham. Vivian had changed his position in life since that time in 1893 when he had himself given evidence to the Royal Commission on Labour and when asked his trade had replied 'joiner'.[148]

John Nettlefold's evidence before the Select Committee is perhaps the most relevant for our purpose. Nettlefold was born in 1866 into a Unitarian non-conformist family whose family business was Nettlefolds Ltd, later to merge into Guest Keen and Nettlefold, now the aviation and motor components multinational GKN. He became a Liberal councillor in 1898 for Edgbaston-Harborne in Birmingham and from 1901 chaired the City Council's newly established Housing Committee, effectively establishing the council's strategic approach to housing. He was related through marriage to Birmingham's powerful Chamberlain clan (his wife was Joseph Chamberlain's niece and Neville Chamberlain's cousin), although he later fell out politically with the Chamberlains over free trade and tariff reform.[149]

Nettlefold's approach to housing was to eschew the powers available to the council under the 1890 Act for slum clearance and municipal rebuilding but instead to put pressure on private landlords to improve housing in poor condition themselves. "In Birmingham we never demolish houses if we can possibly help it, we always try to persuade the owners to repair them, because we do not want to create a sudden shortage," he told the Select Committee.

As regards new development, Nettlefold said that he was against councils erecting their own housing (the approach being adopted by London County Council as well as cities such as Liverpool). Instead he called for councils to have much stronger compulsory purchase powers to acquire building land, which could then be let to others to develop. His position here was partly pragmatic, in that council funds could go much further in land acquisition than in actual house construction: "a pound spent in municipal land purchase goes at least seven times as far towards solving the Housing Problem as a pound spent in municipal house building," he claimed.

The chairman of the Select Committee suggested to him that he was advocating "what you might call localisation instead of nationalisation" of the land. Nettlefold agreed, although he added that the land would be paid for: "It is not confiscating it".

Land ownership would facilitate town planning, an issue whose importance he stressed, going as far as to hand in to the Committee a draft town planning bill he had had drafted for their consideration. Nettlefold was worried that, without proper controls and open spaces, suburban developments would simply create the slums of the future. Later in 1906 he was to chair a Birmingham meeting to promote what he called 'intelligent town planning' and he was also to show himself to be a strong advocate of children's playgrounds in housing developments.

Nettlefold was influenced in his approach to town planning by Unwin and the garden suburb movement, but particularly by the approach being adopted for urban growth through town planning in Germany. The German experience, which relied on active engagement by municipal authorities, had been communicated to British housing reform circles through a 1904 book from Thomas Horsfall, a Manchester community activist and philanthropist. Nettlefold had led a Birmingham delegation to a number of German cities and towns in 1905 to see for himself what was being done. He mentioned to the Select Committee the role in Germany of state-endorsed 'public utility societies', the agencies who undertook some of the actual housing work, and at this point Vivian took the opportunity to point out these were effectively exactly the same thing as those housing societies in Britain registered under co-operative legislation – or in other words the tenant housing societies. The term 'public utility society' would shortly become widely used in Britain too.

It is not surprising that Bournville featured in Nettlefold's evidence. Nettlefold revealed that he had accepted a recent offer to join the committee of Bournville Tenants, partly he admitted with an ulterior motive: "I want to follow out all the details and know the inner working absolutely, hoping some day or other to be able to introduce a similar idea in Birmingham, and there is nothing like practical experience if you want to carry out new ideas". He went on, "My hope is that some day or other we shall have twelve Bournvilles all round Birmingham, on the lines of municipal land purchase and land leasing". Land away from the city centre should be sought at no more than £200 an acre, and then a tramway developed. "We nowadays put our tramway down first, force up the value of the land and then try to buy it. Let us buy the land first and force up our own land instead of other people's."[150]

The proposal that public authorities should acquire land and then let it on lease to 'public utility societies' duly made it into the Select Committee's final report, along with a recommendation that these societies should be able to borrow more from the Public Works Loan Commissioners. The report was delivered in December 1906, but then followed a hiatus which meant that its recommendations were somewhat pushed to one side. It was not until 1909 that new Parliamentary legislation, the Housing, Town Planning &c Act, would finally reach the statute books. The Act was to be a step forward, if a rather more modest one than many housing reformers and town planning advocates had been hoping for. Nettlefold himself was disappointed with the Act, which he argued had been designed to be unworkable.

But long before the 1909 Act had worked its way through Parliament, Co-partnership Tenants Ltd had grown its membership. One of the new societies was Harborne Tenants, in Nettlefold's own ward in Birmingham. It was Nettlefold himself who brought it into being: he had indeed been able to put into effect the practical lessons he had acquired at Bournville. Another new co-partnership, Fallings Park Tenants, was under way near Wolverhampton, a development promoted by the landowner there, Sir Richard Paget. And, thanks to CTL assistance in finding capital, Anchor Tenants were finally moving forward.

But even with external assistance, finding the resources to create affordable homes was not necessarily straightforward. Manchester Tenants, as we shall see, teetered on the brink of financial failure before eventually bringing their project to fruition.

CHAPTER 6

FINDING THE MONEY

A special meeting of the Manchester Tenants committee was held on May 1 1907. The society was facing a difficult financial situation.[151]

As reported above, the idea for a tenant society in Manchester had originally come from staff working for the Co-operative Wholesale Society, whose head office was just across from Victoria station at the northern end of the city centre. Manchester was the centre of the co-operative movement: the Co-operative Union, led at this stage by its general secretary J.C. Gray, was also based in Manchester.

The idea had clearly been mulled over for some time, perhaps since an early lecture Ebenezer Howard had given in the city and certainly since 1904. Sybella Gurney's attendance at the June 1906 meeting in the CWS committee room started things moving again and the following September saw a follow-up meeting held in Manchester Town Hall, with the theme, *A Garden City for Wholesale [CWS] Employees. Is it possible?*[152]

The answer seems to have been 'yes'. The decision to formally register Manchester Tenants Ltd as a new society was taken at this time, and a preliminary committee appointed which tracked down suitable land just off Burnage Lane in south Manchester. Ten and a half acres of land were on offer, together with four existing houses, for about £7,250. The arrangement was that £4,000 of this money could be left unpaid as a mortgage loan, but the remainder needed to be found.

The preliminary committee handed over at the start of 1907 to a permanent committee, and at their first meeting in the New Year (again held in CWS premises) they took stock of the capital they had available. Eighteen members had applied for shares totalling £470, along with £550 of loan stock; a further £400 of loan stock had been promised. It wasn't enough even to complete the land purchase.[153]

The committee had appointed a man called J.W. Greenwood as their organising secretary, a post which was paid for on a commission basis,

Greenwood retaining 1% of any investments he brought in. (This was common practice at the time, and was the basis of Litchfield's initial employment at the Housing Council; Litchfield's first efforts were directed towards helping Ealing Tenants find capital.) Greenwood, together with an assistant James Rowbottom, reported regularly on the efforts they had taken, including a trip to Westminster where they had tried to persuade local MPs to become investors. Greenwood was resolutely upbeat when he attended committee meetings but his success, in terms of the capital he actually raised, was modest.

Meanwhile Vivian had been to Manchester to speak at a public meeting in late January and Frederick Litchfield (a speaker with Gurney at the September 1906 meeting) had also been back in touch. Faced at the May committee meeting with the need to find further capital, the committee agreed to ask Litchfield to undertake national fundraising on their behalf. His commission was to be 2%. Greenwood and Rowbottom's commission was also increased to 2%.[154]

Litchfield attended several committee meetings in June and July, taking the opportunity in early July to strongly promote the concept behind the CTL, just at that stage being launched. He must have also praised Raymond Unwin's work, for Manchester Tenants immediately asked him to arrange for Unwin to consult with them on design matters, at a fee of "not more than ten guineas". The society had by this stage already appointed the architect it planned to work with, but was clearly having second thoughts (the architect was later paid off).

As the Summer of 1907 progressed the committee became more and more convinced that they needed to belong to CTL. A minute for the September 6 meeting recorded, "That this Committee feeling that the advice of the Co-partnership Tenants Limited is of the utmost importance to the welfare of this Society place themselves in their hands entirely" and the society's seal was affixed to a legal agreement with CTL in October. The financial aspect of the deal was that CTL would charge 2.5% commission on share and loan capital it acquired, and 0.5% on bank mortgages and any borrowings arranged with the Public Works Loan Board.[155] The land having been by this stage acquired, an opening ceremony with among others the Lord Mayor of Manchester and Henry Vivian was held on November 2.

By now (probably at Litchfield's prompting) the composition of the committee had been partly changed, mainly to bring in 'names' who could attract broader support for the fledgling society. Manchester

Tenants made an inspired choice for their new chairman: it was the housing and social reformer Thomas R. Marr.

Marr had moved to Manchester about five years earlier from Edinburgh, where he had been an associate of the pioneering biologist and sociologist Patrick Geddes. He took up the post of joint warden at the University Settlement in Ancoats, and also became involved in the local ILP. He worked closely with Thomas Horsfall (the housing reformer who had brought Germany's town planning ventures to Nettlefold's attention) in the Citizens' Association for the Improvement of the Unwholesome Dwellings and Surroundings of the People, a Manchester/Salford organisation on which Marr served as secretary. In 1904 Marr published the report *Housing Conditions in Manchester and Salford* which included a detailed coloured map of the cities' streets, showing the housing stock in each area and identifying slums and back-to-backs.[156]

Marr threw himself wholeheartedly into his work as Manchester Tenants' chairman. There was no shortage of issues for him to try to resolve. The society had cast its lot in with CTL, but by the Spring of 1908 stresses were developing in this relationship, particularly over investment money. The committee, it appeared, had been led to anticipate that Litchfield and the CTL would be able to contribute £10,000 of the capital needed. But Litchfield, at a meeting in mid-March, rejected this assumption. "We were asking too much of CTL when we ask them to raise the sum of £10,000," the society's minutes reported. Litchfield criticised the society for not having adequate architects' plans available. "After five months he was sorely disappointed ... There was apparently some misunderstanding ..."[157]

The financial situation hardly improved during the summer of 1908, by which point the building work on the land was in full flow. Marr reported to his committee in July that £1,000 was immediately due, and invoices and bills would require them to find altogether £2,950 by early September. A very short-term loan from CTL of £1,500 also was due for repayment. On the revenue side, a bank overdraft of £1,000 (with personal guarantees from the committee) was necessary and the first tranche of a loan from the Public Works Loan Board was also impatiently awaited. Further borrowings from CTL would also be necessary, however, even though relations with Vivian's organisation were clearly becoming very tense. The minutes of that July meeting report that "exception was taken to many statements" being made to

CTL's board about Manchester Tenants. The minute added "It was agreed that probably no good would ensue by combating the same at this time". There were to be further tussles with CTL in the months ahead.[158]

Today's community-led housing groups would probably understand the challenges facing Manchester Tenants as they sought the funding package and tried to manage the cash-flow during the build process for their estate. An assessment of the committee minute book suggests that the society only narrowly escaped insolvency at this time. The minutes also make clear just how hard Marr worked behind the scenes to resolve matters. At the members' half-yearly meeting in September he was honest about the difficulties being faced, although he added that he was "confident of the ultimate success of the undertaking".[159]

At this time the society was anticipating that the total estate would cost £46,000[160] (the eventual costs appear to have come in at around £55,000, according to a much later report[161]). So where did the capital come from?

A significant part came from the government via the Public Works Loan Board, an agency already introduced (page 26). During this period the PWLB was authorised to lend (on a secured basis) up to 50% of the costs of building working-class housing to those societies which limited their dividend payments to 5%. Manchester Tenants had initially included provision for dividends to be higher than this for early shareholders but amended its rules in April 1908 and in July 1908 the PWLB confirmed that it would lend £23,205 at 3.5% interest, repayment to be over a thirty year term.[162] (PWLB interest rates changed over the years, and were also set higher for longer repayment terms). The loan was to be paid across in instalments, as the building work was completed. It was the first part of the PWLB loan that Marr and his colleagues were eagerly anticipating when assessing their financial situation that July.

The loan with the PWLB was negotiated on Manchester Tenants' behalf by CTL, as it was to do for other co-partnerships in CTL membership. Although individual societies could have dealt direct with the Board, there were advantages to this approach in that CTL could develop an ongoing relationship with PWLB staff and could handle the necessary administration. Nevertheless Vivian and the co-partnership tenants' movement seem to have been somewhat slow to take advantage of what was clearly a key funding source. As late as March 1906, only the (non-CTL) Tenant Co-operators among co-operative societies had taken advantage of this borrowing facility, having been lent originally £9,075 and having repaid by this stage about a third of the principal.[163] It was a tiny percentage of PWLB's total lending: at this point it had about £900,000 outstanding in loans made for working-class housing, to local authorities, to philanthropic housing bodies, to other types of housing society and to individuals. Co-partnerships were at risk of missing a trick.

The first CTL-affiliated society to receive PWLB funding was the Garden City Tenants, who were lent £9,000 for the Bird's Hill development during the 1906-7 financial year. Thereafter, the pace quickened very considerably. In addition to Manchester, the societies at Ealing, Harborne (Nettlefold's project in Birmingham) and Sevenoaks all received loan capital during the next few years, as did two other newly established co-partnerships, those in Wavertree (Liverpool) and Penkhull near Stoke-on-Trent. Both these latter societies chose to join CTL.[164]

There was also another co-partnership which took PWLB finance during this time, one we have met already: Leicester's Anchor Tenants. At long last this society was making progress. The breakthrough came in 1907 and the key decision taken by the society was to affiliate to CTL. Thereafter finance became considerably easier to find. The first houses were erected in 1908 and building work continued steadily from then on.

Because of the PWLB's importance as a provider of capital, there were demands on the government during this time to widen its lending criteria. Henry Vivian and his colleagues in the 1906 Select Committee called for the interest charged to be reduced considerably and for the loan limit to societies to be increased from 50% to 75%.[165] In the end, the 1909 Housing and Town Planning Act did increase the lending threshold, although only to two-thirds; the call for lower interest rates went unanswered. Local authorities were given more generous terms. (Later still, as we shall see, the government's lending rules were to change again, in the 1919 Housing Act, when for the first time a grant subsidy was to be introduced).

Despite their slowness in turning to the PWLB, there is no doubt that the co-operative and co-partnership housing societies of this period could not have developed in the way they did without the Board's funding. However, commercial borrowing from banks on a standard mortgage basis (as well as overdrafts) was also a familiar part of societies' funding packages. The CTL appears to have developed at an early stage a relationship with the Surrey-based London and South Western Bank (later taken over by Barclays).[166] Manchester Tenants banked with Lloyds, who were persuaded in the Autumn of 1908 to increase the overdraft to £4,000. By contrast, the co-operative movement's own banking operation, run by the CWS, appears to have shown no interest in financing this new area of co-operative activity. The CWS turned down a membership request from the fledgling Manchester Tenants in January 1907.[167]

If the PWLB was essential as a source of capital for societies, so too were the investments made by private individuals. The concept of 'community shares' has been mentioned in the Introduction in relation to activities in Keswick (page 3), with the point made that this form of direct 'buy-in' by private investors is being widely used today to fund a host of community ventures, including village shops and community pubs as well as community-led housing projects. There can be a sense within today's community shares movement that this form of ethical investment is a new creation. In reality, although the community shares name is modern, the idea is not. Almost from the start of the modern British co-operative movement, motivated investors such as Edward Vansittart Neale were helping to bank-roll new co-operatives. Productive co-operatives in particular used this mechanism: Neale was one of a number of external investors to help Crossley Greenwood's father Joseph start his textile productive co-operative in Hebden Bridge in 1870, for example. Later, after the creation of the Co-operative Productive Federation in 1882, the CPF itself attempted to raise capital for its member societies by borrowing at 4% and lending at 5%. The sums were relatively small: by 1897 the CPF had £4,000 out on loan.[168]

Bernard Williams after his move from Leicester to Letchworth also sought capital from private investors to help provide the finance to launch the Garden City Press. *Are your investments right?* read the headline of an advertisement for the society in one of the Garden City publications. "Capital spells responsibility. It depends on HOW it is invested whether it produces Wealth or Ill-th," the advert continued.[169]

Wealth or 'ill-th' – this may have been an advertisement run by the Garden City Press rather than by Garden City Tenants, but it was also the message which, in different ways, was used to encourage investors to put their money into co-partnership housing societies. As we have seen, the PWLB restricted dividends to shareholders to a maximum of 5%, but in fact there was a long tradition of so-called 'Five per cent Philanthropy' in relation to the nineteenth century philanthropic housing societies such as Peabody. When Octavia Hill persuaded John Ruskin to lend her the money to begin her own engagement in philanthropic housing in London (the purchase of the inappropriately named Paradise Place in Marylebone), the bargain was that Ruskin would receive 5% interest each year.[170]

So co-partnership tenant societies were picking up on this older tradition when the share dividend was set at 5%. However there was a legal difficulty in relation to share capital: as we have seen, co-operative legislation restricted individual holdings in societies to £200. Investors were therefore also strongly encouraged to top up their shareholdings with additional loan capital. Loan stock received 4%, or sometimes 4.5%.

Technically, loan stock was safer than share capital, in that its holders had a prior claim on the society's assets in case of insolvency. In practice, almost all the societies, and especially those under Vivian's control through CTL, made sure that share dividends were paid annually. Effectively these were treated not so much as a distribution of profit but as a necessary fixed cost.

Prospectuses for investment capital were issued by each society (sometimes in several different iterations) and from 1907 regular advertisements were run in *Co-partnership* magazine (as *Labour Co-partnership* had been renamed in January 1907), initially under the auspices of Ealing Tenants and Garden City Tenants and then from October in the name of the CTL. The names of investors and the size of their investments were frequently given, presumably as encouragement to others. By the end of the year, for example, CTL was reporting a total investment of £6,000 from Sybella Gurney and of £4,500 from John Nettlefold. Others mentioned included Ralph Neville (£2,500), John Brunner (£2,200), Leopold de Rothschild (£1,000) and Mrs Thompson from Sevenoaks (£1,000).[171]

The most familiar name on this list, however, is George Bernard Shaw, who had invested the considerable sum of £5,400. Shaw did not have inherited wealth and it was only around the 1906-1907 period that, thanks to the success of his plays, he found himself beginning to be very comfortably off. He was to be one of the most significant investors in the garden suburb and co-partnership tenants' movements.

Writing later, in 1921, Shaw explained some of his motivation: "You know what the ordinary man does: he goes to his stockbroker who recommends something and he invests in rubber, minerals, 'Shell', or some other stock. Now, in doing that he gives up all control of his money, for he is in the most part buying shares in a Company which is already formed ... If I have any money to invest, I really do like to think that something has been done with it."[172]

Later still, in the early years of the Second World War, Shaw sent a letter to the author and Garden City advocate Frederic Osborn which again revealed his approach to investment: "I am one of those investors who like to see something for their money instead of merely changing transfers with some old shareholder and adding nothing to the country's fixed capital. I found the new garden cities just what I wanted. I saw waste places changed into pleasant and well planned dwellings and handsome markets by my spare cash. The investments never gave me a moment's anxiety or trouble: they were and are entirely satisfactory, both morally and economically."[173]

Shaw's interest in housing issues went back to his very first play *Widowers' Houses*, first produced in 1892, which had explored the moral dilemmas of wealth generated from slum landlordism. As we have seen, he had first met Ebenezer Howard through the Zetetical Society, and they remained friends. Shaw had also been at the influential Bournville conference in 1901 (page 42).[174] Nevertheless the size of the investments he was prepared to make is remarkable. He invested initially in Ealing Tenants (£2,500) in the Spring of 1907, and shortly after also invested in Garden City Tenants. Later he was to put money into one of the co-partnership societies becoming established in Hampstead Garden Suburb, as well as in CTL itself. In addition he made sizeable investments in the Letchworth development company First Garden City Ltd, in the second Garden City Welwyn after it was established by Howard after the First World War and also in a Letchworth-based housing association, the Howard Cottage Society (run on conventional rather than co-operative lines).[175]

The co-partnership housing movement proved remarkably successful in attracting share and loan capital, in a very short period of time. The Labour Co-partnership Association network was clearly valuable in this respect, and we know that Vivian was prepared to use his own contacts to solicit investments. From 1909, regular advertisements from the CTL in *Co-partnership* magazine (together with data published elsewhere) allow us to build up a picture of the growth of the capital invested (Table 1).

	Shares (£)	Loan stock (£)
Jan 1909	13,730	32,750
Apr 1909	n.a.	n.a.
July 1909	16,760	42,270
Oct 1909	24,340	63,871
Jan 1910	28,980	72,720
Apr 1910	31,460	81,389
July 1910	34,530	83,174
Oct 1910	35,550	89,653
Jan 1911	42,610	102,252
Apr 1911	49,220	109,045
July 1911	56,150	113,753
Oct 1912	68,190	190,174
June 1914	81,860	241,260

Table 1: Share and loan investments reported by CTL[176]

It is not clear how CTL compiled these data but it is likely that this table conflates investments made to CTL-affiliated societies (such as Ealing Tenants and Garden City Tenants) with investments made to the CTL itself for onward investment to individual societies. Nevertheless, the growth in the sums raised is impressive.

Henry Vivian and CTL were not alone in trying to harness the potential of this form of ethical investment. In south Wales, Stanley Jevons resigned his post as professor of economics at University College Cardiff in 1911 to lead a new venture dedicated to creating a string of garden suburbs in and around Cardiff. The Housing Reform Company was registered early in 1912 and quickly identified land to the north of Cardiff, at Rhiwbina,[177] as suitable for the first development. In keeping with contemporary progressive thought, the prospectus appealing for investors did so in reformed spelling, offering "4,000 shairz ov £1 eech and £4,000 loen stoc". The prospectus explained that "the Sosiety haz puchast 10 aicers ov the Pentwyn Estate ... The cost ov the land is £200 per aicer, and the Sosiety haz the opshun for 18 munths ov acwiering a further area ov 20 aicers at £220 per aicer".[178]

The plan, as envisaged by the Housing Reform Company, was to adopt the usual co-operative and co-partnership principles: "the tenants of the houses are also shareholders; in other words, everyone is in part his own landlord," wrote Jevons in early 1912 in the organisation's own publication *Housing Reformer*. He described his plans for a very ambitious new co-operative society, partly based on the CTL model, which he saw as attracting shares and loans from the public to invest onwards in garden suburb societies. After all, "Why is it, we must ask, that if a South American Railway wants £1,000,000 it can have it in London for the asking? Why do Englishmen find £100,000,000 for Canadian Railways and Tramways in a few years?"[179]

Jevons foresaw his 'Co-operative Garden Villages Societies' Federation' as offering a home-based investment alternative. It would very soon, he said, have attracted hundreds of thousands or "perhaps millions" of pounds in shares and loan stock.

The first houses in Rhiwbina, which were to be owned and occupied by members of the newly created Cardiff Workers' Co-operative Garden Village Society, were completed in 1913 when another prospectus was issued (this time in standard orthography).[180] The Housing Reform Company rapidly went on to take up other development land opportunities, including in Caerphilly where it established the Caerphilly Co-operative Garden Village Society, and at Peterston-super-Ely north of Cardiff.[181]

But alas Jevons and his colleagues had overreached themselves. The magazine *Housing Reformer* didn't outlast 1912 and in 1914 the Housing Reform Company itself crashed into insolvency. It was an exceptionally bitter blow for Jevons and for the other pioneer investors. The liquidator's reports have survived and make difficult reading. The share capital was lost. Jevons had himself taken up the majority of shares in the venture, at least 1,200 in all, but as these were not fully paid up Jevons was required to pay the amounts outstanding on his shares to the liquidator. He paid in instalments. When the company was finally wound up in 1920, the loanstock holders and other creditors received precisely 7¼ pence in the pound – or in other words only about 3%. Raymond Unwin, for example, who was a creditor to the tune of about £39 (presumably for his professional advice) ended up with just over £1 4s.[182] Jevons himself had by this stage left the country, taking up a post at the university in Allahabad in India in 1914.[183]

There was a rather happier outcome if not for the investors at least for the Rhiwbina development, which was taken over by a new organisation the Welsh Town Planning and Housing Trust, funded by the much deeper pockets of David Davies MP, Liberal member for Montgomeryshire and a noted philanthropist.

Nevertheless, the Housing Reform Company's fate demonstrated that there could be problems for investors keen to have returns which were, using Shaw's words, morally as well as economically advantageous. The issues became more apparent as the years went by, and particularly when investors wanted to realise their assets. Lack of liquidity was a significant concern. Generally if investments could be sold on it would be at a loss. One holder of loan stock in the Hereford co-operative tenants' society accepted an offer of £35 for his £50 holding in early 1918[184], and perhaps he was fortunate. Writing in 1916 Thomas Marr reported that many investors were "sadly disillusioned" when they found they could get back only "half or less" of their capital.[185]

Another investor, this time the MP Sir Richard Winfrey speaking in the Commons in 1914, appeared to accept that his money would never receive any interest. He had invested in a small rural housing society (probably Wayford) in his constituency in Norfolk: "We were able to borrow only two-thirds of the money from the Public Works Loan Commissioners, and they lent it for only forty years; so that there is a considerable sinking fund, and, so far as I can see, those of us who found the other one-third of the money will not get any interest or any return whatsoever". Had the PWLB loan been over sixty years, he went on, the revenue put aside for the sinking fund would have been less and a dividend to private investors might have been possible – albeit probably only 3% or 3½%.[186]

Among some of the leaders of the co-partnership movement there was recognition that there needed to be a much more effective structure imposed on the co-operative share and loan market, to better reassure investors and to enable them to access their money when they needed it. Sybella Gurney, for example, saw this as the main cause of hesitation by would-be investors. "There is a large and growing class of investors to whom the social effect of their investment is, or could become, of great importance. They are contented with a moderate and safe return, but they must have the power of withdrawal," she wrote in 1915.[187] Gurney posited the idea that share and loan investments could be underwritten by some third party, perhaps she added (highly optimistically) by the trade union movement.

Thomas Marr went a step further, by calling for the development of a formal market for investments in what, following the 1909 Housing Act, were now increasingly being referred to as public utility societies. "More than once I have had to be content with an investment of £100, whereas if I could have assured the investor that his capital could be repaid or that he could easily find a purchaser for his stock, the amount would have been £1,000 or more," he wrote a year after Gurney. "We need a 'market' in which public utility society securities can be bought and sold. Some people will think this suggestion opens the door to all kinds of speculation, but that is not the case. Bargains are even now made, but partly because our societies are so little known, partly because their registration under the Industrial and Provident Societies Act puts them outside the lists of the lawyers, brokers and others, there is no regular market."[188]

What is interesting is that, a century on, this issue has not gone away. The latest surge in 'community shares' follows a debate within the co-operative movement early in the twenty-first century about how to harness ethical investment funds for co-operative ventures. The debate was rehearsed in the book *Co-operative Capital* published in 2004, which among things called for the creation of an 'ethical exchange' to facilitate the growth of the market.[189] A number of charitable foundations subsequently helped finance the not-for-profit Ethex exchange, which began operations in 2013 but which is focused primarily on new issues rather than the secondary market. The interest today in community shares and the good they can achieve is extremely positive, but investors still need to be aware that their money is not backed by any savings guarantee scheme and may not be easy to convert back into liquid funds.

CHAPTER 7

'FULL OF COMRADESHIP': LIFE AS IT WAS LIVED IN THE ESTATES

According to Sybella Gurney, there were four principles behind the co-partnership tenants' housing developments. Firstly, the estates were the result of better town planning. Secondly, the houses themselves were better. Thirdly, the societies practised a form of common ownership, rather than individual ownership. And fourthly, there were opportunities for a good social life.[190]

As Thomas Marr and his colleagues at Manchester knew, and as the committee at Anchor Tenants knew too, the task of erecting the estates could be a challenging one. But once the buildings were completed and the houses tenanted, here, finally, was the chance for the residents, together, to build their own community. Here, as Anchor's Amos Mann had put it, was the opportunity for working people to have, collectively, some of the advantages that the rich could automatically enjoy. Away from the grime and squalor of city life, residents (to quote this time a member of Liverpool Garden Suburb Tenants) could be "full of the comradeship that arises on a Garden Suburb where people seek to make the most of life".[191]

An historical account of the early co-operative and co-partnership societies such as this one needs to explore the financing arrangements, the internal governance of the societies, the issues, the problems and the difficulties. But a focus just on these areas would be misleading. In the period before the First World War many of the co-partnership estates developed a vibrant social life. To ignore this side of the picture would risk the account being an unbalanced one.

Liverpool Garden Suburb Tenants Ltd was established in 1910 on land at Wavertree, almost due east of Liverpool city centre which was owned by the Marquess of Salisbury. Salisbury was prepared to pass as much as 150 acres to the new society on a 999 year leasehold arrangement and was also prepared to make an initial investment of £10,000 in the venture. CTL immediately offered to match Salisbury's sum and to increase this to £20,000 when an additional £10,000 had been subscribed locally. The committee behind the co-partnership included some familiar names, including Vivian who was the chairman, William Hutchings, and Sir John Brunner (CTL's first president). Viscount Howick, the son of the long-time advocate of co-partnership Earl Grey, was also on the committee. The Wavertree society was self-evidently a 'top-down' venture, incubated very much within the CTL networks.[192]

Things moved quickly. The first houses were completed and lived in by December 1910, and six months later 34 were completed and a further 38 were under construction. It was time to set up a Tenants' Committee and a constitution was approved. As *Co-partnership* reported: "That 'votes for women' has been granted goes without saying. Every adult resident who cares to register his or her name will be entitled to vote and eligible for a seat on the Tenants' Council."[193]

One early initiative from the Tenants' Council was a letter hand-delivered to new arrivals, extending a "hearty welcome" to them. "As you are doubtless aware, one of the chief aims of a Co-partnership Suburb is the promotion amongst its members of mutual co-operation and friendly intercourse," the letter continued.[194]

Perhaps not everyone was immediately ready for the proffered friendly intercourse. "At first the newcomers felt surprised at this collective welcome and invitation from their neighbours; it was a new experience and unexpected, an undeveloped imagination characterised it as rudeness, but this objection soon vanished when a friendly call followed the little note and explained the new Constitution, the new ideals, the new hopes that exist in the bosom of the citizens of this Garden Village."[195]

There were certainly plenty of new arrivals in Wavertree. By March 1912 a hundred houses were occupied, and the population was about 500-strong, including about 150 children. The estate was equipped with a meeting hall (converted from two existing cottages and comprising a billiard room and reading area), a bowling green, a children's playground and two tennis courts. Residents had organised themselves into a choral society, a magazine club, a ladies' guild, a horticultural society and a savings club.[196]

Bryce Leicester, the Liverpool society's secretary and also an employee of CTL, summed up the differences between garden suburb life, as experienced at Wavertree, and ordinary town life for readers of *Co-partnership* magazine in 1913:

> *Gardens v Backyards*
> *Playgrounds v the Street*
> *Bowling Greens v Nothing*
> *Hedges for Brick Walls*
> *Grass Margins v Slippery Pavements*
> *Healthy Living v Tired Feeling*
> *Neighbourliness v Isolation*
> *Billiards and games in the evening*
> *Open spaces all day long*[197]

Leicester, of course, had a vested interest in focusing on the positives, but nevertheless his list is a fair one. Thanks to Raymond Unwin's vision for garden suburbs, the density of the houses erected was far less than it would have been in a conventional urban development. Typically, garden suburbs were laid out with between 10 and 12 houses per acre, compared to perhaps 50 to 55 houses in streets which were commercially built. Unwin was insistent too that adequate open space for recreation and playgrounds was included. Leicester's mention of hedges rather than brick walls rings true, as well: privet hedges in particular were a familiar feature, and indeed are an enduring feature to this day in some garden suburbs dating back to this period.

Mutual CTL affiliation linked the Wavertree society with the society in Manchester and in the Autumn of 1911 Wavertree's residents challenged the residents at Manchester Tenants to bowls and tennis matches, an invitation that was later to be reciprocated.[198] After all the efforts of Thomas Marr and his committee, it is pleasing to report that the estate at Burnage was by this stage successfully developed. By January 1909, 26 houses were being lived in and in March that year the fledgling community celebrated a new arrival, a "wee baby girl", the first child born on the estate. Building work had continued actively during 1909 and into 1910, and by the summer of 1910 Marr was reporting that the last fourteen houses were being progressed. The development included a bowling green, two tennis courts and a meeting hall.[199]

Manchester Tenants' estate at Burnage remains today much as it was in 1910. It primarily comprises a set of four roads (South Avenue,

West Avenue, North Avenue and East Avenue, plus a short cul-de-sac) which are reached from Burnage Lane via Main Avenue, the whole estate being essentially square-shaped. The hall, bowling green and tennis courts (only one now, the second having been turned into a multi-user games area) occupy the heart of the estate, with footpath entrances from the avenues. Of all the co-partnership developments, this is perhaps the one which is most obviously immediately attractive.

As at Wavertree, the Burnage residents organised a tenant committee which took in hand the arrangement of social activities. The meeting hall (opened in 1911, to replace a previous ad-hoc conversion of two houses into a meeting space) was equipped with billiards and a library and was also the venue for "a long round of social functions". An amateur dramatic society, later a mainstay of the estate, had its first production in 1912. "We 'villagers' boasted that we made our own pleasures and amusements," recalled one of the residents at the time when the Burnage Garden Village Amateur Players celebrated their 21ˢᵗ anniversary. "The bowling green, tennis courts, annual sports, rambling clubs etc were our recognised social activities, and supplied the simple needs of our neighbours. We were mostly young married couples, enjoying the novel experiment of a co-operative garden suburb."[200]

After the birth of the first 'wee baby girl' in 1910, the numbers of children on the estate rapidly increased. The experience of living in a co-partnership society obviously rubbed off on them: *Co-partnership* reported in 1911 that the children "have elected a committee of their own. This little committee does not believe in hiding its light under a bushel, and has already sent several urgent demands up to the Village Council!"[201]

In Leicester, Anchor Tenants were progressing at almost the same rate as Manchester Tenants. There had been, according to an early account of the history, "four years of patient plodding ... a testing time, eliminating the waverers, leaving a smaller band, more determined than ever to persevere". The society had taken the decision to widen membership beyond simply those working in the Leicester Anchor shoe co-operative, and in hindsight 1907 was seen as the key year when progress was finally made. Sybella Gurney supported them at this time, offering encouragement and also offering to be an early investor.[202] The first sod of the 48 acres acquired at Humberstone was cut in October 1907 (John Nettlefold having been persuaded to come from Birmingham to undertake the ceremony) and the first pair of cottages were completed a year later. By the Autumn of 1909 21 houses were finished and by October 1910 the estate was sufficiently established to have its own monthly newspaper the *A.T. Forerunner*, complete with a quote from John Ruskin on its masthead: "Not greater wealth, but simpler pleasures".[203]

Anchor Tenants, as Wavertree, established an estate committee elected by votes from all on the estate over sixteen, women and men.[204] Although – predictably – it is the men behind the venture, including the leaders Amos Mann and J.T. Taylor, whose version of Anchor Tenants' history predominates, there are tantalising glimpses of a community where women were also playing an active part. Certainly women attended estate meetings, for in December 1910 we hear that they were complaining about the atmosphere caused by the men smoking. The women also had their own Ladies Cricket Team, which on at least one occasion during the summer of 1911 took on the men's team. The women cricketers, *Co-partnership* reported, lost by 40 runs but in the evening "had their revenge, by handsomely beating the gents at skittles".[205]

Anchor Tenants, although CTL-affiliated, seems to have been successful in keeping something of its original emphasis on collective self-help and to have avoided relying too heavily on external investors. In 1908, of the society's eighty members, sixty were prospective residents already choosing plots for their houses and only twenty were outsiders.[206] The society's PWLB loan clearly helped provide the necessary capital for the development.

Anchor Tenants was an estate where the leadership was strongly non-conformist, with Mann and Taylor among those who were members of the small Congregationalist denomination known as the Church of Christ, a highly democratic but also fundamentalist sect. Gardening, for example, was definitely banned on Sundays, and one resident who disregarded this rule was required to leave.[207] An early initiative by the society was to construct a Church of Christ chapel on the estate which was opened in October 1910.

Although the formal links with Leicester Anchor co-operative were severed, the society's leaders remained active in the wider co-operative movement and support in the form of investment capital came from, among others, the boot and shoe productive co-operative in Kettering and, reportedly, from the main Leicester retail co-operative. CTL were matching each £100 of local investment with a further £100. "By

co-operation our estate has been founded," reported an early issue of
A.T. Forerunner.[208]

In terms of social life Liverpool, Manchester and Leicester Anchor
Tenants were all following in the footsteps of Ealing Tenants, who
by dint of being the first co-partnership society established under
Henry Vivian's leadership increasingly was referred to as "the Pioneer
Co-partnership Suburb".[209] (Ever since Rochdale, co-operators have
liked to talk of 'pioneers'.) Ealing had been encouraged by Vivian as
early as mid-1903 to "make the social life of the estate all that the
idealists hoped for".[210] Aileen Reid in her history of Ealing Tenants
recounts what this meant in practice. A social committee, established by
1904, helped organise among other things estate tennis teams (Ealing
had four tennis courts in 1906 and as many as twelve by 1913), a choir,
and regular debates and lectures. There were summer sports events
including intra-street tug-of-war, and from 1905 – in something of the
spirit of the English folk revival – the celebration of May Day. May
Pole dancing arrived for the 1906 celebration and remained an annual
celebration in Brentham right through to the present century.

As elsewhere, somewhere to meet was important for Ealing Tenants.
A temporary meeting space was created in 1905 by leaving a newly
built house as an empty shell inside, without even a staircase. However
Ealing Tenants was eventually to get its own purpose-built Brentham
Institute, opened with pomp and ceremony in May 1911 by Queen
Victoria's youngest son Prince Arthur, the Duke of Connaught.

Not everyone who took up residency in one of the co-partnership
estates would necessarily have bought in to the full set of principles which
encouraged participation in the social, educational and sporting activities
being organised, and we need to be conscious that accounts of estates'
active social life (as reported particularly in *Co-partnership*) represented
good propaganda for the cause. Nevertheless, life in these estates was
undoubtedly considerably different from that which many residents
would have previously experienced in their former homes. There was a
sense too in the years up to 1914 that some at least of the original vision
when the estates had first been discussed had been brought to fruition.

So who found their way to a new home in a co-partnership estate?
The Public Works Loan Board had a legal remit to lend only for
working-class housing, but this was never defined very precisely and
gave wriggle-room for societies wanting to stretch the boundaries.
In general, the co-partnership societies provided homes for the most

skilled sections of the working class and for white-collar workers from the lower ranks of the middle classes. Certainly these were not homes for the unskilled working classes or the very poor. As one writer put it in *Co-partnership* in 1909, housing for this latter group would have to be left "for municipal action or philanthropic zeal".[211]

Michael Harrison undertook detailed research into the occupations of Manchester Tenants' first residents which he reported in a journal article in 1976. He found that the houses were being lived in, among others, by clerks (24), by salesmen and travelling representatives (11), by engineers (6), by engravers (3) and by teachers (4). As Harrison pointed out these occupations represented 'Labour aristocrats' and the lower middle classes. Burnage was not a place for casual labourers or the "pound-a-week man".[212]

Similar research, published in 1997, was undertaken by Antony Taylor for the Penkhull co-partnership established near Stoke-on-Trent and his findings mirror Harrison's. At Penkhull, skilled craftsmen from artisan trades were the lowest status group represented on the estate and remaining tenants were from salaried occupations. Eleven of the 65 tenants at Penkhull in 1912 were local authority workers. Also represented were sales reps (7), teachers (6), clerks (4), agents (4) and even clergymen (3). Taylor argued that, since there was a waiting list for would-be tenants, the society's committee could choose salaried middle-class applicants when vacancies arose.[213]

The rents which were charged on the estates would have excluded those on low or irregular incomes in any case. A comprehensive list of rent levels on the CTL-affiliated estates which was published in 1912 gives the weekly rent at Ealing as ranging from 6s 6d to 21s. Anchor Tenants' rents were from 6s to 10s 9d, Manchester from 5s 3d to 11s 6d, Garden City from 4s 6d to 10s, Liverpool (Wavertree) from 5s 7d to around 12s, and Sevenoaks from 4s 9d to 12s 6d, but these data by themselves do not tell us much. Rates to the local authority were also payable by tenants and could be substantial. In some cases (for example Anchor Tenants, Garden City and Sevenoaks) rates were included in the rent charged, but other societies (Ealing, Liverpool and Manchester, of those mentioned) separated rent from the rates payable. There was an argument that, if rates were paid separately, tenants would take more of an interest in the democratic workings of their local council.[214]

There is an opportunity, if only a very limited one, to compare co-partnership rent levels with those being charged on the commercial market at this time by using the 1908 report from the Board of Trade into working-class rents and housing prices. Board of Trade data suggested, for example, that houses in Ealing at this time were being rented from 6s to 8s per week where there were four rooms (upstairs and downstairs) and 6s 9d to 9s for five rooms. 'Modern' properties with four rooms would be charged between 7s 6d to 9s 6d.

The data for Manchester from the Board of Trade suggested rent levels between 4s 6d and 5s 6d for three rooms, 5s to 6s for four rooms and 6s to 7s for five rooms. In Liverpool in 'more modern' terraces, rents were 4s 6d to 5s 6d for three-roomed houses, rising to 5s to 6s for four rooms and 6s to 7s for five rooms (ie houses with three bedrooms).[215]

These data reinforce the conclusion that tenants in the estates were those who had achieved some social status and security in class terms (some, if not all of them, might have been able had they wished to become owner-occupiers rather than tenants). But this should come as no surprise, for the mainstream co-operative movement was also skewed very much towards the upper working classes and lower middle classes. A valuable analysis of the share ledger for one West Yorkshire co-operative society undertaken by John Butler found 223 of the 377 shareholder members represented 'skilled labour' and a further 60 comprised a lower professional, small shopkeepers and farmers category, and although Butler was examining records no later than 1876 there is no reason to imagine that the situation changed markedly thereafter or that the class composition in the society he examined (Mytholmroyd) was not typical of many other co-op societies.[216] Indeed a short-lived experiment in the Coronation Street slum area of Sunderland, launched very early in the twentieth century mainly as a Women's Co-operative Guild initiative, implicitly acknowledged that co-operation was not a movement reaching the very poor.

But within the overall demographic, did the nature of the co-partnership estates attract tenants with a certain attitude or political affiliation? A distinction probably needs to be drawn between those predominantly 'bottom-up' ventures, such as the ones at Burnage (Manchester), Garden City and Leicester which emerged indirectly from within the co-operative movement, and garden suburb co-partnerships launched by well-meaning landowners or philanthropists, in which category we can include for example Sevenoaks, Wavertree (Liverpool), Penkhull (Stoke) and Oldham, as well as the Hampstead Garden Suburb societies (to be introduced in the next chapter). Bournville probably also belongs in this category. Ealing Tenants is more difficult to categorise but despite its start in life as a venture by individual General Builders co-operators its trajectory was firmly in this direction too.

Let us consider the question then specifically about the communities at Burnage, Letchworth and Leicester. In their early days Burnage residents were apparently known to some in the outside world as the 'inmates' and regarded as rather cranky.[217] The design of the estate, with just a small road connecting it with the rest of south Manchester, perhaps encouraged the view that the garden village was a place apart. Letchworth Garden City certainly had to put up with the reputation for being a little unusual and cranky, and according to Ebenezer Howard there were sixty vegetarian families in Letchworth in 1908 as well as "men who prefer knickerbockers to trousers" and wore sandals (Howard was, however, referring to the whole town here, rather than specifically to Garden City Tenants).[218]

Unwin's early engagement with socialism and his friendship with Edward Carpenter in Millthorpe undoubtedly influenced his planning and design of the garden estates, and there was perhaps something pre-figurative about the nature of these new communities which attracted those active in local community and political campaigns – a sense that they could experience in the here-and-now something of what they were striving to obtain in society as a whole in the future. Certainly, as well as the somewhat strident non-conformist Christianity, there was a political radicalism in the early days at Anchor Tenants, where early in 1911 a new "Socialist League" society was established, to encourage "the study and propagation of collectivist principles".[219] Amos Mann and J.T. Taylor, given their involvement in local political life, must have had a hand in promoting the society. (Henry Vivian's views on this initiative are not recorded but can be imagined.)

It is the estate at Manchester Tenants, however, which seems to have attracted the greatest number of political activists. The Manchester-based historian Alison Ronan has undertaken detailed research work in this area and regularly leads radical heritage walks around the estate.[220] She reports that 5 East Avenue, for example, was the home of Edgar Whiteley, the manager of the Labour Press who printed the ILP's *Labour Leader* newspaper – and who as a consequence was arrested in 1915 when the newspaper ran an anti-war article. At 21 East Avenue lived Richard Wallhead, an ILP activist and opponent of the war who was detained in 1917 and eventually became a Labour

MP. His daughter Muriel was also an anti-war activist who married a conscientious objector and later stood as a Labour candidate for Parliament, and his son was also a CO, imprisoned in Wakefield prison. At 31 South Avenue Maud Dean was a socialist and active suffragist, a member of the Women's Freedom League (WFL) while next to her at 33 South Avenue was Annie Brickhill, secretary of the south Manchester WFL which held meetings in her house. Clara Doughty, another WFL suffragist, lived at 26 North Avenue. Harold Wild, another CO in the First World War, lived at 21 North Avenue. And so the list continues.

Ronan quotes a resident in the 1960s who looking back suggested that the estate started as a "socialist ideal", a "community of everyone loving you and being kind". That may represent overly rose-tinted childhood nostalgia, but nevertheless it is definitely appropriate to be able to give the name of one other community activist who was able to make his home in the Manchester Tenants estate at Burnage, and that is Thomas Marr himself. After all his efforts, Marr was eventually able to reap some reward for his labours. He lived at 31 East Avenue.[221]

Ealing Tenants – Ludlow Road c. 1910
(Brentham Heritage Society archive)

A house on Hampstead Way (Hampstead Tenants), 1910
(Hampstead Garden Suburb Archives Trust held at London Metropolitan Archives)

The Triangle, Bournville Tenants estate, an early photograph
(Bournville Tenants Ltd)

Stoke-on-Trent Tenants, c. 1914
(The Potteries Museum & Art Gallery, Stoke-on-Trent)

Henry Vivian addresses Ealing Tenants, c. 1903
(Brentham Heritage Society archive)

Building workers on pay-day, Ealing Tenants c. 1909-1910
(Brentham Heritage Society archive)

Architect's drawing of design for Liverpool Tenants quadrangle at Wavertree

(From Garden Suburbs, Villages and Homes Vol. 2)

Plans prepared by G Lister Sutcliffe (CTL) for Ealing Tenants, 1911, showing garden suburb principles

(Brentham Heritage Society archive)

The children's playground, Stoke-on-Trent Tenants
(From Garden Suburbs, Villages and Homes Vol. 2)

The tennis courts at Anchor Tenants, Leicester
(Co-partnership magazine)

Sybella Gurney
(Labour Co-partnership magazine)

CTL advertisement for
investment, 1910
(Brentham Heritage Society archive)

Opening of first cottages, Stoke-on-Trent Tenants, 1910; John Nettlefold is the speaker
(The Potteries Museum & Art Gallery, Stoke-on-Trent)

Two views of Fairfield Tenants houses today
(Author's photographs)

The Green, Knebworth Tenants today

**A recent view of the bowling green, tennis court and meeting hall at Burnage
(Manchester Tenants)**
(Author's photographs)

CHAPTER 8

THE MOVEMENT IN 1911

Much had been achieved in the first decade of the twentieth century. Ten years on from 1901, the year of that first meeting in the Haven Arms in Ealing and of the Bournville conference, an active tenant housing society movement had been established. A central federation had been formed, in the shape of the Co-partnership Tenants Housing Council, and a central business advisory agency established, the CTL. The garden suburb model, as proposed by Unwin, had been widely embraced. Around £150,000 had been raised in share and loan capital (these are CTL's figures for the end of 1910), and considerable funds borrowed from the Public Works Loan Board. And from Sevenoaks to Keswick, tenants had moved in to their new homes, and were creating new communities.

1911 seems a good opportunity to pause, therefore, and to offer a brief summary of how the various tenant societies were progressing.

At the start of 1911, there were around twenty independently registered housing societies which could be seen as co-operative. Of these CTL had twelve established societies in membership and a further two which were fledgling ventures. CTL's societies – partly because their progress was regularly reported in *Co-partnership* magazine – tended to attract the most attention at the time and have also tended subsequently to be more closely researched by historians. But the co-operative housing movement was larger than the CTL. So before taking stock of the CTL co-partnerships it will be appropriate to look first at other housing society initiatives which had got under way.

Three of these societies, Tenant Co-operators, Bournville Tenants and Oldham Tenants, have already been introduced. Tenant Co-operators had chosen not to develop any further sites after its activity at Epsom some ten years earlier, but was continuing as a well-managed venture under John Yerbury's leadership. Bournville Tenants had almost completed their estate of 146 houses. Oldham Garden Suburb Tenants, Sarah Lees' initiative, had had to overcome difficulties at the development stage but had made progress; housing was now built, with rents starting at the relatively modest figure of 5s 11d a week.

Another society, mentioned so far only in passing, was Hereford Co-operative Housing. The model adopted in Hereford was innovative, in that it offered a way for local authorities to engage in the provision of affordable rental housing without providing directly-owned municipal housing or taking on landlord responsibilities. Hereford's story is closely tied to that of Edward Frederick (Fred) Bulmer, the older brother of Percy Bulmer who established the family's cider-making business in 1887. Their father was a Herefordshire clergyman, although earlier the family had been wine merchants. Fred returned to Hereford from King's College, Cambridge after graduating in order to work with his brother in the new business. From very small beginnings the company expanded, adopting techniques from French cider-makers to help improve the quality of their products.[222]

Fred Bulmer was a man with a strong social conscience who showed concern both for the conditions of his own employees and more generally for the poor of the city of Hereford as a whole. Among other things, he instituted a pension scheme for his workers in 1898. He called for a minimum wage, for better medical care and for improved educational provision and he was also concerned to do something to alleviate poor housing conditions.[223] John Nettlefold, in a private letter to Henry Vivian, described him as a "shrewd business man with unlimited public spirit".[224]

Fred Bulmer engaged in local politics, becoming a councillor and then an alderman and, in 1908, serving for a year as the Mayor of Hereford. It was the ideal platform to launch a new housing initiative. Bulmer was in close touch with Nettlefold who came down from Birmingham to Hereford in November 1908 and then showed a small delegation from Hereford round his own venture, Harborne Tenants, a few days later.[225] By this stage, it was already clear how Bulmer's housing project would be established: it would be done with the aid of Hereford City Corporation's funds. Indeed the Corporation had already acquired, for £1,500, about nine acres of land on the far side of the Hereford railway station from the city centre. The arrangement was that the council would put in the necessary roads and infrastructure but then immediately pass the land to a tenant housing society.

It meant that the land was safely protected from the interest of speculators and it also gave the society time to get established. (In fact, Hereford Co-operative Housing Ltd was registered only a short time later, in February 1909.)[226] The deal agreed between the council and the society was that the society would commit to ensuring that the land was developed within two years (at least thirty houses, and no more than 100, was the arrangement). The society also undertook to pay in ground rent over eighty years the actual cost the council was incurring in servicing the cost of its borrowings for the land purchase and infrastructure work. This worked out as £133 a year until 1932 and £62 a year thereafter. At the end of the eighty years the council agreed to pass its interest in the land to the society, at no further cost.[227]

"This is an ideal little scheme from every point of view," John Nettlefold informed Henry Vivian in his letter.[228] Interestingly, the model being adopted at Hereford was essentially the same as Nettlefold himself had been proposing in his evidence before the Commons Select Committee in 1906 – or in other words the idea that local authorities should take responsibility for acquiring land for affordable housing but then leave the development to others. It was an argument that Sybella Gurney had also put forward, in her 1906 article in the Charity Organisation Review when she had railed against the results of speculative working-class housing. The alternative to this in most people's minds, she went on, was municipal building. "But why should it be the only alternative? ... To me, it appears most desirable on the contrary that the municipalities should acquire and retain as much land as possible, but that they should let it for building to societies of [the co-partnership] type," she had written.[229] Hereford was to be the only significant venture to use this model at this time, but as we shall see the idea was to return in the debates on post-First World War housing policy.

Following its legal registration, the Hereford Co-operative Housing Society moved quickly, and the first house was built and ready for its occupants in October 1909. Mrs Bulmer as Mayoress of Hereford was the guest of honour for the opening ceremony. By the end of the year, a total of 43 houses had been completed, and all except one of these let. By this stage the society had raised £2,680 in paid-up shares and £4,680 in loan stock from about 46 individual investors and had negotiated a £4,800 thirty-year loan from the PWLB. A second PWLB loan was about to be sought for the next 23 houses.[230]

One has the strong sense of Fred Bulmer using all his local friends and contacts to raise the share and loan stock capital. The 1909 loan stock register, which has survived, gives the names and addresses of these first investors and with just one or two exceptions all were Hereford based. Bulmer, as might be imagined, was an investor himself and is shown as holding £300 loan stock. Details of the first shareholders are unfortunately not so easy to analyse, but Bulmer would certainly have been a shareholder too.[231]

Tenants were required to be members of the society and at the end of 1909 about half of the 85 shareholders were tenants.[232] In contrast to the 'Ealing' model there was no obligation to build up to £50 in shares: tenants in the smaller houses were asked to hold two £1 shares, with those in larger houses required to hold three shares. The funds for the shares could be paid in instalments, with only 5s required initially. But tenants had other obligations, of course, as set out in the tenancy agreement. One was to ensure that chimneys were regularly swept. Another was not to damage floors by chopping wood inside the house. A third was to look after their gardens properly and not to allow weeds to run to seed.[233] Rents (which included rates) were from 4s 9d to 7s 9d.[234]

There had also been activity in the time before 1911 in other cities and towns. Sarah Lees' commitment to a garden suburb in Oldham had been linked, as we saw (page 57), to her engagement in the Beautiful Oldham society and, across in Warrington, a similar interest was motivating Canon Morley Stevenson, who was principal of the Warrington teacher training college. Stevenson was chairman of the Beautiful Warrington society and was also the organiser in 1907 of a two-day British 'City Beautiful' conference, a movement which was arriving in Britain having become particularly influential in North America.[235]

In July 1909, a new company Warrington Garden Suburbs Ltd was established, with the ultimate aim of creating a string of garden suburbs round the town. The model was to some extent Letchworth, with the new company taking on the equivalent role to First Garden City Ltd. It quickly bought two sites, both of around twenty acres, at Great Sankey and Grappenhall and in each case established co-partnership societies to develop the housing. Warrington Tenants was registered in 1908 and Grappenhall Tenants in 1911, but both made slow progress. By 1913, 24 houses were erected at Great Sankey and 27 completed or close to completion at Grappenhall.[236]

In West Byfleet, Surrey, a development under the auspices of the Birchwood Tenants Society was completed and formally opened at a ceremony held in May 1911. The estate comprised around seventy houses in the cul-de-sac of Birchwood Road with a small number of additional houses on the adjoining Station Road. Parker and Unwin were the architects, and the estate is now a designated conservation area.

The society, according to local historian Iain Wakeford, was the initiative of a local Woking businessman F.C. Stoop. John Burns MP, the President of the Local Government Board, reported in the Commons in March 1912 that he had recently gone down to Byfleet and "found a generous band of a few men had got £32,000 together and had put up near a golf course a co-operative village as cheap as it is beautiful".[237]

The Hereford, Warrington and West Byfleet ventures were 'top-down' initiatives, undertaken by those who wanted to improve housing conditions but were certainly not intending to be tenants of the houses once they were built. The story of Stirling Homesteads is quite the opposite: here was a group of politically-committed local activists looking to build a small community where they could live a more communal life and enjoy a degree of self-sufficiency. A comparison with both today's co-housing movement and the various recent community agriculture ventures springs to mind.

The Stirling Homesteads story has become better known from valuable work by Scottish historians, primarily the 1984 local history from Peter Aitken, Cameron Cunningham and Bob McCutcheon and more recently through work by James Smyth and Douglas Robertson.[238] It was centred on forty to fifty acres on the outskirts of Stirling, relatively close to Stirling Castle. Much of this land was destined to be run as a dairy farm with one of the tenant members employed as the farm manager. A smaller area, about five acres, was to be a market garden (with the produce co-operatively marketed) and a still smaller area used for housing. The venture got under way in 1910 and ten houses were erected by the end of that year for the community's members.

The Stirling branch of the Independent Labour Party, set up in 1906, was very closely linked to the venture. As Smyth and Robertson point out, the ILP was taking a lead at this time in campaigning around housing issues: "The interest of the membership was both general, calling for large-scale municipal house building, and personal, keen to explore co-operative ways of living and working; three members of the original branch committee plus at least one more party member became original residents of the Homesteads," they report.[239] There was also a strong Arts and Crafts influence in the Homesteads, mainly through the involvement of ILP member Robert Maclaurin who was active in the Scottish Guild of Handicrafts, and work by Guild members was a feature of the furniture and fittings in the houses. The initiative was also influenced by the Garden City and garden suburb movement. Maclaurin was active in the West of Scotland branch of the Garden Cities and Town Planning Association, and Ebenezer Howard had lectured in Scotland in 1908, including in Stirling in November that year. As we shall see, the West of Scotland GCTPA branch would later help bring about a Glasgow co-partnership garden village to the north-west of the city.

The Homesteaders' motivation has been described by Smyth and Robertson as "socialist and based on what might be termed 'collective self-help'", although it did not constitute a back-to-the-land attempt to retreat from ordinary life: Stirling ILP continued to push for a major municipal house-building programme in the town, so that many others could escape poor housing conditions.[240] The dairy farm reportedly struggled and was closed in 1925 but the market gardening business was successful and the society itself continued into the 1970s.[241]

The Stirling Homesteads project was an outlier, both geographically and in the way it was structured. Returning to England, it is now time to report on the position in 1911 of those societies which had chosen to affiliate to Henry Vivian's Co-partnership Tenants Ltd. They included the tenant co-partnerships whose story we have been following: Ealing, Sevenoaks, Garden City, Anchor, Manchester (Burnage), and Liverpool (Wavertree). There were also eight other societies which by now were signed up: Harborne (Birmingham), Fallings Park (Wolverhampton), Penkhull (Stoke), Keswick, Sealand (Flintshire) and three societies in Hampstead Garden Suburb.

By the time of the opening of Ealing Tenants' Institute in 1911 the Ealing society was very well advanced in the development of the houses on the newer, garden suburb, part of their Brentham estate, on land they had acquired in stages between 1906 and 1909. Eighty-four houses were put up during 1911 itself and only some hundred houses would remain to be built thereafter in the years up to 1914 when the estate would comprise 600 houses.[242]

Sevenoaks Tenants had completed their first two estates, of 69 houses, by the end of 1907. The society was engaged in 1910-11 in two

smaller developments, the first being four houses on the so-called
Sevenoaks Farm site and the second comprising eleven more in
Sevenoaks Weald, a village south of Sevenoaks itself. Later, further
developments were to take place in the nearby villages of Kemsing
and Shoreham (Kent).[243]

Garden City Tenants in Letchworth had had their new Institute,
in Pixmore Hill, opened in 1909 by Sybella Gurney and were close to
completing the development work, a total of 322 houses on 39 acres. By
this stage, there may have been some shift in their orientation. It would
seem that the society was felt by some not to be fully meeting the need
for working-class housing in the town. In August 1911, First Garden City
Ltd helped bring about a new venture, the Howard Cottage Society,
aiming to provide homes for the less well-paid. As mentioned above
(page 72) this was a more conventional housing organisation without
co-partnership elements.[244]

Anchor Tenants' estate was developing steadily, although not
particularly quickly. Twenty houses were built in 1910, and there were
ten more under construction in the Spring of 1911 at which point the
society had raised capital of about £24,000. This included a forty-year
loan from the PWLB. Development was continued at a similar sort of
pace over the following four years, until eventually the estate comprised
93 houses (far fewer than the 400-500 originally envisaged).

There was debate in the estate newspaper *A.T. Forerunner* in 1911 as
to possible names for the estate, and we can perhaps be grateful that
'Hopedale', 'Gladburne', 'Edenville' and various other similar suggestions
were not pursued: Humberstone Garden Suburb it was to be. Some
further building was to take place in the 1930s but undeveloped land
originally held by Anchor Tenants was later acquired by the council
and developed less sympathetically. Regrettably, the houses today have
lost much of their original garden suburb feel.[245]

Liverpool Garden Suburb Tenants was moving quicker than Anchor
Tenants although in 1911 the site was still unfinished. 360 houses would
be completed before the war stopped further work; this was a long
way short of the original ambitious target, which had been for 1,800
houses.[246]

By contrast, Manchester Tenants had effectively completed the estate
by 1911. A grand opening ceremony was held in September 1910, where
the Lord Mayor of Manchester was presented with a symbolic golden
key to the estate and sportingly then played a game of bowls with the

chairman of the Village Association. The estate totalled 144 houses in all.[247]

Harborne Tenants in Birmingham (page 63) had been John Nettlefold's venture, launched in 1907. It acquired 54 acres of land on which it was to successfully erect just under five hundred houses. 455 of these were finished by mid-1911 and around 1,600 people were at that stage living on the estate.[248]

Harborne was Nettlefold's great achievement, built according to best garden suburb principles with an average density of fewer than ten houses on each acre. It can be seen as a demonstration by him of a practical alternative to the direct development of housing estates by local authorities which, as we have seen from his Select Committee evidence, Nettlefold was arguing against.

His role on Birmingham City Council clearly helped negotiate the planning process, in that Harborne Tenants were excused from many of the bye-law requirements which would normally have applied to the development. Unwin, Nettlefold and many others in the wider garden suburb movement were strongly critical at this time of the implications of the standard bye-laws in force in most cities. Ironically these had been introduced specifically to raise housing standards, initially via a series of early Public Health Acts and then in 1877 in a government-issued set of model bye-laws. But the bye-laws generally required wide tarmacked streets, granite kerbs and paved footpaths which tended, according to Unwin, to lead to standard urban street design, or what he called 'bye-law architecture'. Bye-laws imposed rigidity of design, something he was determined to avoid, and they also added considerably to the cost of infrastructure for new developments, so that as a consequence the number of houses developers tried to squeeze on to their land was pushed up.[249] Bye-laws could also have perverse consequences: Nettlefold complained at one point that mature trees were being cut down in new housing developments just to make sure that roads met the width requirements.[250]

Harborne Tenants negotiated an agreement with Birmingham City Council to construct roads on the estate only sixteen feet wide, with tree-planted turf margins, footpaths eight feet wide and front gardens to the houses fifteen feet wide. It meant that the width between houses facing each other worked out at 72 feet instead of the fifty feet required by bye-laws, but it also meant more green space for residents. "It is no small advantage that every window on the estate will look out upon some green and living thing," said one of the committee members in 1908. There were also savings on the usual groundwork costs – although Harborne Tenants still felt aggrieved that the council made them make up the main Ravenhurst Rd to bye-law standards and pay for a large sewer which later Harborne developments would use.[251]

There were innovative attempts to maintain the natural beauty of the site: the little Moor Pool in the site was left as open water and advice on tree-planting was sought from the curator of the city's Botanical Gardens.[252] And, as elsewhere, at the heart of the estate were constructed a bowling green, tennis courts and the Institute, Moor Pool Hall. The estate worked financially too: Nettlefold was proud to have been able to keep rents low on at least some of the houses, a little over fifty of them having rents (in 1914) of between 4s 6d and 6s. "The erection of 4s houses on Harborne Tenants' estate, where there is an average of only ten houses per acre and not more than twenty houses on any one acre, shows what could be done under the [1909] Housing & Town Planning Act," he was to write.[253]

As in other tenant societies, a loan from PWLB (this time, over thirty years) helped to complete the Harborne funding package.

Fallings Park in Wolverhampton has been briefly mentioned above (page 63) as a development promoted by the landowner Sir Richard Paget and his son Arthur. Sir Richard Paget, a Conservative MP from 1865 to 1895, lived in Somerset but owned four hundred acres on the outskirts of Wolverhampton which he wanted to develop on garden suburb lines. A small part of the site was earmarked for the co-partnership society Fallings Park Garden Suburb Tenants. It was established in 1907 to provide houses "for workmen who have not a sufficiently large amount of savings to utilize the ordinary building society, or who by reason of the mobility of labour find it difficult to purchase freehold houses under the ordinary system".[254] The tenant society's first houses were completed in January 1908 and by 1911 seventy-five houses were either completed or under construction.[255]

The initial design of the whole Fallings Park site was given to Thomas Adams, who had strong garden city and garden suburb credentials: he had been the first paid secretary of the Garden City Association in 1901 and had also had management responsibility for the early development of Letchworth as the secretary of First Garden City Ltd. He resigned from his Letchworth work in 1906 and was shortly afterwards appointed by Paget to Fallings Park. (Later Adams was to move on to other garden suburb projects, including Derwentwater Tenants at Keswick.)[256] It was perhaps Adams' experience of the Cheap Cottages exhibition in Letchworth in 1905 which provided the spur for a similar 'Model Housing Exhibition' held at Fallings Park in the summer of 1908 where around sixty houses (all full-size, it should be said) were on show. This was organised as a competition for prizes, which included a category for sizeable detached and semi-detached houses but also had a category for houses built for under £200. Several of these latter houses were destined for the Fallings Park Tenants society.[257]

Fallings Park seemed initially to be following the same trajectory as Harborne and there are reports of early social life of the tenants. (There was a debate held in spring 1909 on the theme "A non-Flesh diet, the Diet of the Future" where in the face of "much opposition" the speaker "very courageously held his opinions".[258]) But the whole Fallings Park venture hit a hiatus: Sir Richard Paget died early in 1908 and although his son Arthur inherited the land and remained actively involved, the momentum behind the tenants' society seems to have become lost.

The idea for the Stoke-on-Trent Tenants society at Penkhull near Stoke (page 69), another CTL affiliate, had first been discussed at a public meeting in 1908 although it was not until 1910 that the venture got under way when 38 acres of land were acquired. Penkhull was not the first development land considered and earlier a site at Trentham had been looked at. By 1911 eighty houses had been constructed, and over the next two years the total would reach ninety-five. Later some of the undeveloped land would be acquired by the council for a school.

Penkhull's early and later history has been the subject of a valuable essay by the historian Antony Taylor. His assessment is that this was very much a top-down venture. There was, he says, little that was democratic about the tenants' society, with the estate "supervised by a self-perpetuating elite, in no way answerable to the tenants".[259]

The further from London the less direct influence CTL seems to have exercised over its affiliates and certainly it is apparent that the Derwentwater Tenants at Keswick, introduced at the start of this book, did not have very close dealings with Henry Vivian and his colleagues. Share and loan books from that period[260] suggest that CTL's commitment to the financing of the project was limited to five £10 shares, so perhaps Derwentwater Tenants chose to affiliate to CTL more out of a sense of solidarity. Then as now, the residents of Greta Hamlet have tended to go their own way.

Derwentwater's little estate of twenty-five houses (there were planned to be 27, but two remained unbuilt) was occupied and virtually completed by early 1911. The opportunity was taken of the Whitsun holiday that year to celebrate, with tea and cakes for the children on the central Green followed by games and races. Meanwhile the adults could enjoy the "magnificent prospect of mountain, lake and woodland". Tenants' rents at this early stage in its history were set at between 4s 1d and 5s 3d.[261]

Building work had also been going on in the village of Sealand close to Shotton in Flintshire, a very short distance from the Welsh/English border. Sealand Tenants Ltd had been registered in 1910, at the behest of the iron and steel manufacturing firm John Summers and Sons which had expanded some years earlier from their original base in Stalybridge to a new site beside the river Dee, previously marshland. 1909-10 had seen a major year-long strike at the Flintshire plant with strike-breakers brought in from Liverpool, and this may have been a factor behind the company's plans for a new housing estate. Raymond Unwin was called in to plan the development, and by 1912 over a hundred houses had been built and occupied.[262] When completed, Sealand Garden Village was to comprise 283 houses and three shops.[263]

We have arrived at the last three societies in affiliation of CTL in 1911, and therefore at Hampstead Garden Suburb. The story of Henrietta Barnett's determination and persistence in bringing about this now highly-desirable area of north London has been recounted many times, and a summary will suffice here. Henrietta and her husband Samuel, it will be remembered (page 23), worked among some of the poorest communities in east London at the Toynbee Hall settlement in Spitalfields. They had a weekend retreat away from East End grime, however, in the form of a cottage in Hampstead. When plans to extend the Northern Line through to Hampstead were promoted in 1900, Henrietta began a long campaign to prevent the new tube line from leading to speculative building. With seven suitable worthies chosen from the great and good (including the Co-partnership Association's active supporter Earl Grey) she established the Garden Suburb Trust[264] which successfully negotiated to buy 323 acres of land from Eton College. Some of this land was to remain open space for recreation as the Hampstead Heath Extension, and this was immediately passed into the ownership of London County Council. On the remainder of the land, Henrietta Barnett conceived her plans for the garden suburb, a place where "the good and the gain [could] be shared by all classes of society", as she wrote in a 1905 article. "The classes will not be estranged and the estate will have the great advantage of being planned, not in piecemeal as plots are taken by different builders, but as a whole."[265] Unwin and his partner Barry Parker were given the responsibility of planning the new development, and Unwin moved from Letchworth to live in Hampstead and to oversee the work in 1906.

Henrietta Barnett's vision would have immediately faced the hard realities of the standard building bye-laws, but here Henry Vivian was able to assist. He shepherded through Parliament an uncontested Private Member's Bill which became the Hampstead Garden Suburb Act of 1906. The Act, as well as laying down that the housing density was to be no more than eight houses to the acre, made provision for access roads to be potentially exempt from the normal width requirements.

Given the direct involvement of both Vivian and Earl Grey, it was inevitable that the responsibility of building affordable housing in the garden suburb would be given to the co-partnership movement. Hampstead Tenants Ltd was established in 1907 and immediately began raising capital. At the end of 1907 it had raised £3,417 in shares and £6,668 in loan stock; eighteen months later these had increased to £19,950 and £24,150.[266] The usual 'Ealing' rules applied, in that tenants were obliged to hold £50 in shares, with £5 immediately due and the rest payable in instalments. As at Ealing, Vivian was chairman.

The Hampstead Tenants society's houses had been completed by 1910, the estate comprising 271 houses, a block of shops and also a block of flats designed primarily for widows and old people. The rents in the houses started at around 7s a week, although there were also houses let at considerably higher rents.[267] It wasn't just workers who were taking tenancies. *Co-partnership* reported in 1909 that large numbers were taken by "tenants of other classes such as artists, teachers, clerks, secretaries, chemists and architects".[268]

Another tenant society, Second Hampstead Tenants Ltd, was launched in 1909, primarily to take responsibility for buildings near the proposed central square of the Garden Suburb where the architect Edwin Lutyens had been commissioned to create a suitable civic heart to the settlement. The original plan was for around 300 standard houses and also for 110 more expensive homes.[269] Building work got under way in 1910, and – looking ahead to 1913 for a moment – the Second Hampstead society by then had 377 houses, another block of shops and two blocks of flats. Henry Vivian also assumed the chairmanship of this society when it was established.

Hampstead Garden Suburb was to have a very significant role in the later development of CTL, influencing the way that the organisation evolved. An embryonic further society, Third Hampstead Tenants, perhaps needs to be mentioned at this stage since it was also being claimed as a CTL affiliate in 1911, but this society's progress beyond 1911 seems to have stalled. We will return to the later Hampstead Garden Suburb history in a subsequent chapter.

As should be clear, the CTL affiliates were by no means uniform. There was certainly a distinction between those societies Vivian himself chaired (Ealing, Garden City, Hampstead, Second Hampstead, Liverpool), where the committees tended to comprise close colleagues or friends of Vivian's and those where there were other leading lights (Manchester, Sevenoaks, Harborne, Anchor, Fallings Park, Stoke and Keswick). Nevertheless all societies choosing to affiliate to CTL had to accept CTL's way of doing business, a requirement with implications which will be explored in the next chapter.

CHAPTER 9

THE TROUBLE WITH TENANTS?

Henry Vivian was returned as a Lib-Lab MP for Birkenhead in the General Election of January 1910, held in the middle of the constitutional crisis caused by the Commons and Lords dispute over Lloyd George's 1908 Budget, but with his majority slashed to just 144. The election resulted in a hung Parliament, and a new General Election was called for December 1910. This time, Vivian was less fortunate: his Conservative opponent took the seat, by a majority of over 1,000 votes.

From the start of 1911, therefore, Vivian no longer had the status of an MP. He immediately tried to return to Parliament. He contested a bye-election in November 1911 for the Liberal-held seat of South Somerset (its MP Edward Strachey had been made a Liberal peer), but unexpectedly Vivian was defeated by the Conservative, this time by about 150 votes.[270]

The loss of his seat at Westminster seems to have been a defining moment for Vivian, and because of this also for CTL and the CTL's co-partnership societies. He stepped down from his long-term role as secretary of the Labour Co-partnership Association early in 1911, instead taking on the unpaid position of honorary secretary.[271] (It is not clear precisely anyway how much time Vivian had been able to devote to his work for the Association in the preceding few years; in the Autumn of 1910 for example he was in Canada for three months at the invitation of Earl Grey, who by then had become Governor-General of Canada. One has the suspicion that the Association's committee members had the attitude that Vivian's continuing salary was a way of helping fund a useful MP.) Vivian also resigned his chairmanship of Ealing Tenants at the start of 1912, his staunch ally William Hutchings taking his place.[272]

Vivian remained very much the chairman of CTL, however, and now had the opportunity to steer his organisation much more directly.[273] Around this time he seems to have tried to put his various interests on a much more business-like footing. In an intriguing move, he set up a new company incorporated under the Companies Act, also with the name Co-partnership Tenants Ltd. Although this did not trade and was wound up in 1922, the initiative suggests Vivian was at this time contemplating moving CTL away from its incorporated status as a co-operative society.[274]

Something was happening too to General Builders, which in 1912 was absorbed into a new company called Woodworkers Ltd. This seems to have been a much more conventional business in terms of its governance: "though it shares profits with its workers, [it] cannot be included in [a] list of working men's societies," said *Co-partnership* magazine at one point.[275] Vivian was almost certainly chairman and was definitely a director of Woodworkers Ltd (as were his long-time collaborators William Hutchings and Frederick Litchfield). Vivian was also director of two other building industry companies, Garden Suburb Builders Ltd (based in Letchworth), and Brick and Tile Workers Ltd (based in Madeley, near Stoke-on-Trent). CTL had entered into agreements that these would be firms used by CTL to deliver its building contracts, although given the interlocking directorships involved the relationship was in practice much closer to that of parent and subsidiaries. Neither of these concerns filed returns to the Co-operative Union and clearly did not consider themselves to be co-operatives.

It was in Hampstead Garden Suburb that Vivian and CTL were to take their most ambitious step when, in 1912, CTL bought on a leasehold basis about three hundred further acres of land, to the east of the Hampstead Heath Extension. This was done independently of Henrietta Barnett's Hampstead Garden Suburb Trust, with CTL paying the Trust an 'acknowledgement fee' to be able to describe the new land as being within the Garden Suburb but with the Trust given no say in how the land was developed. Indeed tensions between CTL and the Trust began to grow in the subsequent years. Two new co-partnership societies, Hampstead Heath Extension Tenants and Oakwood Tenants were established, respectively in 1912 and 1913, to focus on developing this new land but by now the original co-partnership model was being interpreted rather differently from how it had been in 1901. Many of the houses on this land were built for sale.[276]

John Yerbury, who had been working away in the background on a voluntary basis as secretary for Tenant Co-operators could offer CTL only reserved praise in his 1913 book. It was, he wrote, "a business concern with paid officials ... catering for the well-to-do classes equally, if not more, than for the poorest of the workers".[277]

This is quite a criticism. To what extent was CTL's later trajectory set when it was first established in 1907 to be a central business federation for the growing movement? Is it even possible to argue that Vivian's organisation, far from helping the movement, effectively distorted it?

The answer is complicated. The services which CTL provided were undoubtedly services which were needed by new housing societies. Having a national business agency able to negotiate land purchase, raise capital, offer advice on planning, purchase business materials at wholesale prices, and then deliver the actual construction work was very valuable. Some would-be co-partnership societies would not have made it through to fruition without CTL on hand to assist.

But not every new society chose to have CTL involved. Fred Bulmer at Hereford Co-operative Housing Society, for example, definitely turned down the option of CTL affiliation. Although only one side of the correspondence appears to have survived, a letter by John Nettlefold to Bulmer written on December 7 1907 certainly suggests that Bulmer had not been impressed by CTL's terms (the background is the question of how the capital to build the estate could be found): "I quite understand your difficulty re building the houses, and am inclined to think you will find it best to operate in Hereford independently of London, but cannot of course take the slightest responsibility in deciding a question concerning the pros and cons of which you are far more familiar with than I am. On the other hand I do strongly advise you not to quarrel with London unless you can help it, as they may come in useful in various odd ways," Nettlefold wrote. He ended his letter with a postscript: "By-the-by, don't allow yourself to be angry with London. They have difficulties on their side to consider at least as great as the knotty problem you have to solve in Hereford ...".[278]

Nettlefold and his Harborne committee colleagues presumably had to assess the same pros and cons themselves, before deciding in their case that Harborne Tenants *would* affiliate to 'London'. It was, however, a decision taken "after very careful consideration", according to one of those involved.[279] There was also to be at least one case (that of Sealand in 1912) of a CTL-affiliated society reportedly later choosing to disaffiliate.[280]

So what was the downside? There was, as Thomas Marr and his Manchester Tenants' committee encountered, the potential for CTL to override local committees when it came to the practicalities of the building process. In July 1908, at the height of the Burnage building work, CTL was insisting that their works manager George Ramsbotham had authority over the Manchester Tenants' locally appointed manager Mr Sutton. The minute book for July 21 1908, when CTL's Frederick Litchfield was attending something of a crunch meeting, records, "Mr Marr asked that the committee of Manchester Tenants Ltd should be taken into entire confidence of CTL, final consent must rest with MTL committee. Mr Litchfield replied that CTL must have a free hand – meaning Mr Ramsbotham as manager to buy materials and to control Mr Sutton submanager."[281]

However the much more substantive issue encountered by Manchester Tenants was over CTL's requirement that their own model rules be adopted by the affiliate. This issue came to public attention in the news columns of the *Manchester Guardian* in September 1908. Some of the shareholder members of the society, the paper reported, were "much concerned" at a proposed amendment to the rulebook, due to be discussed at a forthcoming members' meeting. The members were arguing that the changes if adopted would "destroy the democratic basis on which the scheme was established".

The voting procedures in CTL, under which those who had invested the most were given the most votes, have already been described (page 59). However CTL also required its affiliates to adopt a similar principle in their own rules. The implications of this were spelled out later in the *Manchester Guardian* article: "At present the rules give to every individual member present at the meeting who is credited in the books of the society with a sum equal to one £10 share one vote, and no proxies are admitted. Societies and companies which have at least ten shares are also entitled through their representative to one vote ... The alteration proposed is to give one vote for every fully paid-up share and to admit voting by proxy. The fear of the shareholders, who have formed a committee to fight the proposals, is that if they are carried out the control of the estate will pass into the hands of the holders of large blocks of shares."[282]

CTL had been pressurising the Manchester Tenants committee in the summer of 1908 to make this change and it fell to Marr as chairman to try to persuade his members at the half-yearly meeting on September 14. It was obviously not an easy meeting. Several members spoke in particular against the proxy voting proposal, which, as the *Manchester Guardian* had implied, would have the effect that external investors would not have to attend meetings in person to be able to wield their voting power. With proxy voting written into the rules, the opportunity for tenants to challenge their committee would effectively disappear.

In the end the necessary two-thirds majority for the rule change at the September 14 meeting was not obtained and a reconvened meeting was held two weeks later where the rule change did go through. Resistance remained, however: Edgar Whiteley, the Labour Press manager, put the case against. He "strongly opposed the alteration on the ground that members should have only one vote and that on the ground of membership of the Society and not by reason of any amount of Capital invested in the Society".[283]

Some months earlier, in December 1907, a very similar rule change had been put to the Ealing Tenants members with a very similar response. Vivian and Hutchings had proposed the change, which was to introduce proxy voting and give multiple votes for each complete set of ten £10 shares held. As at Manchester, the two-thirds majority was not immediately achieved and a second General Meeting had to be called in January 1908 when the change went through. Aileen Reid, in her history of Ealing Tenants, reports that there was a larger turnout of shareholders in January, and that many of those who supported the change at the January meeting were not residents of the estate. At the subsequent AGM in February one tenant-member, R.P. Garrard, challenged Vivian's leadership by standing for the chairmanship. It was a gesture doomed to failure: under the new voting system Garrard lost by a large majority.[284] It can be added that after this Ealing Tenants' committee meetings were frequently held not on the Brentham estate but in central London, at the CTL office.

One by one the CTL-affiliated societies fell into line. Harborne's rules, for example, gave one vote for each share held. At Leicester, Anchor Tenants went further, giving not only shareholders one vote per share held but also a vote for loan stock holders for each £50 held.[285]

'One member, one vote' today is held to be such a fundamental principle of the co-operative movement that CTL's imposition of these rule changes strikes a very discordant note. So what could be the explanation for this?

Firstly, it should be said that 'one member, one vote' was at the time not quite such a cast-iron principle as some co-operators nowadays might imagine, or at least not in relation to secondary co-operatives (co-operatives owned by other co-op societies). For example in Britain the Co-operative Wholesale Society at this time gave larger member societies more votes than smaller societies. Even today, the International Cooperative Alliance's co-operative principles implicitly accept this sort of arrangement: "In primary cooperatives members have equal voting rights (one member, one vote) and cooperatives at other levels are also organised in a democratic manner".[286]

But CTL was going much further than, say, the CWS in its allocation of voting power to individual investors, moving indeed very close to the way that shareholder companies organised their governance. One reason for this could be that such a step was simply a necessity if CTL was to attract the investment into the co-partnership tenants' movement that it so badly wanted. Perhaps this was simply a pragmatic step and a regrettable necessity.

However, this is not borne out by evidence. The impression is much more that Vivian, by now in his role as Member of Parliament for Birkenhead, was happier having gentlemen investors on the management committees of CTL and its societies rather than potentially disruptive tenants.

In this context, we know that the Labour Co-partnership Association had debated this very issue at a meeting held in January 1907. The minutes report that "a discussion arose as to the best way of securing that the Government of our societies should be in the hands of men of experience. It was suggested that a large number of years' membership should be required before becoming eligible for the Committee." Vivian was at this meeting as the Association's secretary, and among those present were Sybella Gurney, Amos Mann and Bernard Williams. Aneurin Williams was the chairman.[287]

The issue of whether full-blooded member democracy could really be relied on in co-operatives or whether 'men of experience' were needed was something that Aneurin Williams had himself pondered in a Labour Association pamphlet called Government by the Fit, published in or around 1898. Williams wondered aloud if co-operative societies would be better run if they were in the hands of "true co-operators", committed to the co-operative spirit. At this stage, Williams rejected criteria based on investment: "It has been suggested that only those should be admitted to membership who are willing to take up a large sum in share capital; or, at least, that they only should be eligible for the committee. This is the fallacy of the property qualification all over again," he wrote, saying that this would risk co-operation degenerating to a "knot of little masters". But nevertheless, Williams remained ambivalent: perhaps co-operatives should only admit members who took up say five pounds in shares, he concluded.[288]

Others active in the co-partnership movement seem also to have convinced themselves of the value of what John Nettlefold called 'strong men'. Writing in 1914 he argued that "In any community of 100 or more persons there are sure to be a few who will endeavour to get more than they have a right to at the expense of their neighbours. It is, therefore, essential to success to have strong men in command of the society's affairs until the tenants have acquired a responsible stake in the concern and have had time to study and understand the working of the system that has been inaugurated for their benefit."[289] There is a strong whiff here of we-know-best patronage going on.

However the most extensive exposition of this argument comes from Henry Vivian himself, in an extraordinarily revealing article he wrote for *Garden Cities and Town Planning* magazine in 1914, explaining that CTL was introducing a new principle into its governance. "Unrestricted admission to complete partnership of tenants who have only a weekly tenant's interest, coupled with a small contribution of capital, which, as it is paid out on the tenant leaving, only in effect amounts to a deposit, is not the most satisfactory way of securing the co-operation of tenants in promoting the permanent welfare of the Society," he wrote. "Under this plan we admit to partnership those with the minimum of experience, sense of responsibility and capital at stake."

CTL would therefore change its way of operating. Tenants could if they wished acquire shares or loan stock, which would be refunded at par when they left. However, this would not give them a say in the society's governance.

"The right to become a full shareholding member under the rules will, broadly speaking, be subject (a) to a certain time of residence, perhaps three years, on the estate (b) to the holding of the minimum amount of share capital provided for in the rules or an amount proportionate to the issued Loan Stock (c) to there being no moral or legal right on the part of the shareholder to have his investment paid out on leaving the estate," Vivian went on.

It is hard not to see this article as Vivian's final renunciation of any residual co-operative element to the CTL co-partnership model. Just in case his message was not being understood by his readers, he concluded the article by pre-empting any would-be critics: "The idealist whose views are not disciplined by practical experience in administration or by actual contact with the realities of life's struggle is often the greatest enemy to the realization of ideals".[290]

Given this approach, it was perhaps not surprising if tenants sometimes seemed ungrateful. Ealing's tenant-members, or at least some of them, had formed an Ealing Tenants Committee in the summer of 1911 complaining that tenant-members were being frozen out of the society's affairs. New tenants after 1907, it was claimed, had been encouraged to buy loan stock (which carried no voting entitlement) rather than shares. William Hutchings, by now the Ealing Tenants' chairman, certainly was not inclined to parlay with the rebels and at one stage a solicitor's letter was sent by the management committee to the Tenant Committee's officers. A further tenants' attempt, via a specially-called Special General Meeting in 1912 to have external members' rights removed, was unsurprisingly unsuccessful and simply resulted in the rules being changed so that the power to call SGMs was removed from members and given to those holding share capital.[291]

Very similar moves were afoot in Hampstead, where an Association of Hampstead Tenants had also been established "to advocate the return to those principles of true co-partnership in housing, the wilful or careless neglect of which has been the fruitful cause of much discontent among the Hampstead Tenant Shareholders, and others". Control at Hampstead, the Tenants Association claimed, was "ultimately in the hands of an outside body of capitalists".[292]

Ealing and Hampstead tenants were in close contact with each other at this time and in 1912 they arranged for a friendly MP, John Roberts, to ask a Parliamentary Question of the Secretary of the Treasury on their behalf. The question was whether he was aware of their allegations that CTL was violating the requirements of the Industrial and Provident Societies Act in refusing to allow members to inspect the books of the Ealing and Hampstead Tenants' societies. The PQ started a flurry of internal memos between the Treasury civil servants and the Registrar of Friendly Societies (the responsible agency for co-operative registration). The Registrar made it clear that he was not minded to get involved. If the committee were refusing to allow access to members to the books, any legal redress was up to the members themselves, he wrote. He went on, "It would seem that the CTL have acquired a controlling interest in the other two societies. If this is so, it is the fault of the members of those societies who have permitted them to do so, and I do not see how the Registrar or anyone else can intervene."[293]

The mix of investor members and tenant members in the CTL version of co-partnership housing societies could indeed lead to tension and instability.[294] There were other potential flashpoints too where differing attitudes could rub up against each other. Top-down philanthropy could encounter bottom-up co-operative democracy. A desire for security of investment could clash with the practical challenges of actually building houses. Middle-class and working-class values could collide. And not all the factors that were motivating those involved in co-partnership were necessarily always apparent. Vivian and the Labour Co-partnership Association, as we have seen, looked to build a more harmonious society based on self-help rather than state-help, but there were hopes that decent working-class housing could achieve other, wider, goals for society. As the risk of European war grew, a slight whiff of eugenics entered the picture. Vivian at a ceremony being staged by Anchor Tenants in 1911 made the point that "Garden suburbs had a striking effect on the physique of the people, and were therefore important from the point of view of providing soldiers for the battlefield and men for the workshops". He was reiterating a point he had made a year earlier, in a speech at the Penkhull opening event, when he said that good housing was essential for the proper physical development of men, necessary if the country was going to need soldiers.[295]

So issues between tenants and their committees at Ealing and Hampstead could have been predicted. There were tensions in other co-partnerships as well, although an implicit consensus seems to have developed that societies' management committees would look after the business and financial side of things while a tenants' committee (separate and subordinate to the management committee) would concern itself with the social and educational side of estate life.

Even so, not everything was plain-sailing. At Manchester Tenants Thomas Marr had demonstrated immediately after the controversial rule revision of 1908 that he was himself uncomfortable with aspects of the CTL's requirements when he arranged for three tenant-members to join the committee; they were brought on to the committee in November 1908 and thereafter played an active role in committee deliberations. But even here at Burnage there were to be future problems. There was "a general feeling of hostility on the part of the residents towards the committee," reported a local newspaper in 1913, describing a meeting held at Burnage. One tenant had apparently started a rent strike. A speaker at the meeting was quoted by the paper as saying that "the committee are out for victory every time ... There is no co-partnership at the present time".[296]

It may have felt that way to some of the tenants at Burnage but to the outside world the co-partnership housing movement appeared in 1913 and 1914 never to have been stronger. New and prospective co-partnership garden village developments were springing up around the country. Vivian could tell his members at the 1914 AGM, held in March, that CTL's services were being deployed to help new societies in Hertfordshire, Cheshire, North Wales, Somerset and Middlesex.[297] This was a movement that still seemed able and willing to make a major difference to Britain's housing problems. This was a movement still with plenty of wind in its sails.

CHAPTER 10

'HOUSING IS A WOMEN'S ISSUE'

If housing is important for men it is even more important for women, said Huddersfield-based co-operative activist Catherine Mayo at the Annual Meeting of the Women's Co-operative Guild in 1898. "It is the woman who has the most time to spend in the house. Her home is the place where she does her daily work, and when there is anything wrong or unsanitary about it it is usually the mother and children who suffer first," she said.

As co-operators, she went on, we must aim at getting the right sort of houses built in the right places. "A woman would make many practical suggestions that would not occur to the men."[298]

Sybella Gurney was to make a similar point at the 1906 Co-operative Congress, where housing was the subject of a major debate. The housing question, she said, was pre-eminently a woman's question.[299]

Nevertheless, women only rarely had the opportunity to contribute their views on how housing could better meet their needs. The Welsh Housing and Development Association (a body which linked the Welsh Garden City movement with trades councils and unions) was unusual in choosing to canvass the opinions of 2,000 women for a survey it undertook during the First World War. The message from the survey came back loud and clear: "There seems to be a fairly general opinion amongst women that in the planning of the dwellings too little regard has been paid to the convenience of women who have to live and work in houses".[300]

The co-operative movement generally was not particularly advanced when it came to giving women positions of influence or responsibility. Out of the more than nine hundred co-operative societies in membership of the Co-operative Union in 1890,[301] not a single one appears to have had a woman on their management committee. By 1895 there were nine women elected and by 1900 the number had crept up to twenty-one – still a very tiny minority among the several thousand male committee members.[302] In this respect, therefore, the dominance of men on the management committees of the co-partnership housing societies was nothing out of the ordinary. It did mean, however, that women's ideas as to how housing could be improved were unlikely to get much of an airing.

In fact, the home was for many women in Victorian and early twentieth century times a place of sheer drudgery, particularly for working-class women living in poor conditions but also for many middle-class women unable to afford a team of domestic servants but nevertheless expected to maintain the home as a place of cleanliness and social refinement. Fires needed making and cleaning, meals needed cooking, children needed caring for and husbands needed attention – even if they did not consider it their role to lend a hand in domestic duties.

"The co-operative movement aims at improving the world, at making it a brighter and better place both for ourselves and for those who shall come after us," Catherine Mayo told her Women's Guild audience. So what *could* co-operative housing initiatives do to make things better? Could more co-operative ways of living be developed which removed at least some of the household drudgery?

According to Ebenezer Howard writing in the *Garden City* magazine in 1906, one answer could be what he called 'co-operative housekeeping'. "I believe the time has come when [co-operation] can be successfully tried as one of the central ideas of domestic life," he wrote. He had arranged for the architect H. Clapham Lander to draw up plans for a square of houses, very much in the style of an Oxford quadrangle. "In the centre of one of the sides of the square is the common kitchen ... and a common dining room, garage for bicycles, store rooms for boxes, telephone etc. Around the inside of the quadrangle a cloister would run, by means of which tenants could pass under shelter from their own houses to the common rooms." Meals would be prepared in the central kitchen by a qualified cook, and delivered to tenants in their own homes or, alternatively, "at their option, in the common dining-room".[303]

A vast amount of women's abilities and energy was wasted with the current way of running households, Howard was later to assert. Co-operative housekeeping, he argued, was a solution to this problem.[304]

Howard was certainly not the first to discuss co-operative housekeeping – that is, an arrangement so that several households share the costs and effort involved in necessary household tasks such as cooking and washing while at the same time maintaining their own home space and privacy (today we would use the term co-housing). The Women's Co-operative Guild had put the idea on the agenda at their Annual Meeting in 1893, when the co-operative author and activist Catherine Webb presented a paper she had written. She particularly stressed the value of co-operative washhouses and laundries ("About the discomforts of washing day in a working-class house I need not say one word," she told her audience). She also raised the possibility of co-operative kitchens, "another suggestion that we hope you will discuss with much vigour".[305] Later the Women's Co-operative Guild was to suggest co-operative housekeeping as a possible topic for branches to discuss, with a WCG Popular Paper on the subject available from the national office.[306]

Earlier, senior figures in the co-operative movement, including Edward Vansittart Neale, had debated the possibilities through the columns of *Co-operative News* and its predecessor *The Co-operator*.[307] Lynn Pearson, who has written the comprehensive history of the evolving story of co-operative housekeeping, in fact traces the idea within the co-operative movement back to the early short-lived Owenite communities such as Orbiston and Queenwood (Harmony Hall) although the term itself seems first to have been used in the late 1860s in relation to the ideas being promoted in the United States by Melusina Fay Peirce. Peirce was an early advocate of the benefits which women – particularly middle-class women – could realise by having to spend less time on the tedium of household management. As Pearson recounts, the idea attracted the attention of women in Britain too, and in particular Elizabeth Moss King, a member of the British Association for the Advancement of Science who raised the idea at a meeting of the Association in 1873. Later in the century there were to be mansion blocks put up in areas of central London by companies such as the Ladies' Dwellings Company and the Ladies' Residential Chambers Ltd, offering flats for professional women with services such as catering provided centrally.[308]

Ebenezer Howard in his 1906 article on co-operative housekeeping was certainly not breaking new ground, therefore. Raymond Unwin was also attracted to the idea. In the 'Co-operation in Buildings' chapter for the 1901 book he co-authored with Barry Parker (page 43) he allowed himself to imagine just what might be possible, not just for the middle-class residents who had hitherto been the main target group for co-operative housekeeping ventures but for working-class women and men too.

Unwin, who it must be said was never much in favour of the idea of the working-class parlour kept only for best, suggested the parlour be sacrificed and replaced with communal facilities. "Some of the space so often wasted in a useless front parlour in each cottage could be used to form instead a Common Room, in which a fire might always be burning in an evening, where comfort for social intercourse, for reading, or writing, could always be found," he argued. "To this Common Room could be added a laundry and drying-room fitted with a few modern appliances which would not only reduce by half the labour and time occupied in the weekly wash, but would take the bulky copper and mangle out of each cottage, and relieve them all of the unpleasantness of the steam and the encumbrance of the drying clothes."

From there it would only be a matter of time before there would be demand also for a central bakehouse and a central kitchen: "The advantage of it is obvious. Instead of thirty or forty housewives preparing thirty or forty little scrap dinners, heating a like number of ovens, boiling thrice the number of pans & cleaning them all up again, two or three of them retained as cooks by the little settlement would do the whole, and could give better and cheaper meals into the bargain."[309]

With the Garden City vision which Howard had presented in his 1898 book actually being transformed into reality in the agricultural fields of Letchworth, there appeared to be space opening up at the start of the twentieth century to explore new ways of living, and it was to be in Letchworth that Howard's proposal for a co-operative housekeeping venture would be realised. Letchworth Co-operative Homes was set up in 1907 to take on the task of developing Clapham Lander's design for the cloistered quadrangle of houses. The development was given the name Homesgarth. Lander amended his original plans slightly to offer three types of property, ranging from one-bedroomed flats to three-bedroomed houses. Heating was provided for the whole development from a central boiler and, although tenants had use of the main dining room and a smaller tea-room, each individual property also came equipped with a small gas stove. "At Homesgarth an attempt is being made to combine the privacy of the home with the advantages of a common kitchen and dining rooms," said Clapham Lander writing in 1911. Nevertheless, sociability was not obligatory: "Homesgarth offers just as much or as little society as the tenant may feel disposed to seek".[310]

Originally thirty-two houses were planned (to include a further option of bed-sitting room flats) and of these the first eight were built and occupied by the end of 1910 and another eight were ready in Spring 1912. There, unfortunately, the development stalled and despite Howard's best efforts (including writing an article about the benefits of co-operative housekeeping in the *Daily Mail*),[311] Homesgarth remained as just the original sixteen units. It meant that the quadrangle was never more than half-completed. Homesgarth can still be seen today, now renamed Sollershott Hall.[312]

Homesgarth, which was open to both women and men, was definitely pitched at middle-class residents and was promoted to an extent as helping middle-class women find an alternative to the difficulties they could face when trying to recruit domestic servants (Homesgarth provided accommodation for live-in staff servicing the tenants' needs). Rent and charges in 1913 ranged from £40 to £64 a year and – on the perhaps spurious grounds that Homesgarth was intended as an experiment – there was also a strict 'no children' policy. Ebenezer Howard himself moved into Homesgarth in 1911.[313]

Could the Homesgarth model be replicated for working-class residents? Clapham Lander in his 1911 article said that this was certainly a desired outcome, but there was a caveat: first of all, Homesgarth had to demonstrate that it was successful. It was to prove a significant caveat.

Later, in 1914, the Howard Cottage Society was to undertake a similar development to Homesgarth in Letchworth known as Meadow Way Green, a community of seven individual cottages which included a common dining room and kitchen. The scheme, extended in the early 1920s, was pushed for and financed by two young women, a teacher Ruth Pym and her life companion Miss S.E. Dewe, who moved in to one of the cottages when it was completed. Meadow Way Green was restricted to women, and the early tenants included a librarian, a governess, a secretary and a missionary.[314]

In Hampstead Garden Suburb, Hampstead Heath Extension Tenants (one of the two societies set up to develop CTL's later land acquisition) successfully built Meadway Court, a set of 55 flats designed by CTL's in-house architect G.L. Sutcliffe who again utilised the quadrangle principle. Meadway's tenants had access to a common dining room, a private dining room, a billiard room and a reading room, as well as use of four tennis courts. The communal facilities appear to have been run by a separate tenants' Club, and *Co-partnership* magazine reported in 1917 that the Club had "proved a very interesting and effective experiment in communal service".[315] Earlier another CTL affiliate, Hampstead Tenants, had built a block of 57 basic flats called The Orchard designed by Parker and Unwin and intended for older couples or widows. The Orchard had shared baths and washhouses but no communal dining arrangements. To complete the picture, Hampstead Garden Suburb's early developments also included a quadrangle of houses for women with central dining facilities and centralised heating known as Waterlow Court. This was erected not by one of the co-partnership societies, however, but by the long-established philanthropic housing organisation the Improved Industrial Dwellings Company, originally set up by the businessman and Liberal politician Sydney Waterlow in 1863.[316]

Separately, the garden city supporter and activist Alice Melvin was also promoting the concept of co-operative housekeeping, and from 1909-10 onwards she helped shepherd into existence a major development in Finchley, the Brent Garden Village (Finchley) Society. After the usual struggles in finding the capital, the venture was able to progress (albeit in a somewhat changed form) and by 1914 comprised a series of houses and a block of flats, Cedar Court. In late 1911 Melvin moved on from Brent Garden Village to launch a new organisation, the Society for the Promotion of Co-operative Housekeeping, and to try to realise an ambitious co-operative housekeeping development at Ruislip for what was to have been called Melvin Park. The Ruislip proposal did not materialise, but Alice Melvin did succeed in creating a block of serviced residential flats in Golders Green, which also took her name. This was established as the Melvin Hall Co-operative Housekeeping and Service Society (Golders Green) Ltd.[317]

These experiments in forms of co-housing seemed at the time to presage a much more significant shift in the way households would be organised, driven partly by the increasing difficulties middle-class women were encountering in employing domestic servants. Writing in 1918 the Garden City advocate Frederic Osborn was convinced of a forthcoming significant growth of what he called domestic co-operation. "New types of accommodation will thus be necessary both for the families from which servants are withdrawn and for those whose women members prefer to spend the better part of their time in business or industry," he asserted. "What is wanted is a group of buildings in which the privacy of individual homes is combined with a common organisation of cooking and cleaning".

Osborn's prediction did not come true. When he revised his 1918 book, this time during the Second World War in 1942, the section on co-operative housekeeping had been completely rewritten: "Keeping house for a family is important work; and there are many signs of a new and modern re-emphasis of family idealism. The solution for most people will not be found in co-operative housekeeping but rather in the better equipment of the individual family home, coupled perhaps with group heating ... It would be a mistake to plan for a wholesale change of fundamental family habits."[318]

With only the handful of exceptions mentioned above, the pre-First World War co-partnership housing societies did indeed focus on building the 'individual family home' rather than anything more communal. Nevertheless, given the focus on the estates on social life, we might expect more informal collaboration between neighbours than would have been the case in conventional housing. To what extent did this happen?

The evidence, it has to be said, is meagre and mainly limited to Manchester Tenants at Burnage and to the very particular circum-stances of the First World War. In the Autumn of 1916 there is a report in *Co-partnership* that a shared vacuum cleaner had been acquired by some of the women in the estate, with the magazine asking aloud "One wonders if the idea could be extended to the purchase of up-to-date labour saving washing appliances, or to collective cooking of meals".[319] In fact, the following summer Burnage did go on to introduce a collective system for meals, cooked by a professional cook and a paid helper, and available for those who wanted to participate at 4d or 7d per meal. News of the scheme reached the *Manchester Guardian* in July 1917, who reported "Every family wishing to use the central kitchen takes up a £1 share; two meals a day are served ... There are at present 76 shareholders and the plan is working smoothly under a local committee." The *Manchester Guardian* added though that it expected that "those special dishes popular in individual families would still be provided by the thoughtful housewife".[320]

Quite how long the central kitchen arrangement lasted at Burnage is not clear. It was still operating in December 1917, although not without some reported difficulties linked to procuring the food.[321]

Food shortages were an increasing problem as the war dragged on, and indeed rationing was introduced by the government early in 1918, initially for sugar and then for meat, butter, margarine and cheese. Households were given ration cards and obliged to register with local grocers and butchers. It may be that these requirements caused the Burnage arrangements to fizzle out.

In one respect, though, women at Burnage demonstrated a powerful determination to act together, when in November 1916 they launched a milk boycott to protest at the price which milk had reached as a result of wartime inflation. Again the *Manchester Guardian* offers us a valuable source, in their news report on a meeting held in the estate's hall on November 14 1916 when the vast majority of the Manchester Tenants agreed not to buy milk if it cost more than 5d for a quart (two pints). Families with very young children were exempted from the boycott, which was designed to put pressure on suppliers and to bring down milk prices for all across the whole city.[322]

The boycott, proposed by a Manchester Tenant woman Mrs Dent, clearly had male support. It fell to Harry Richardson,[323] a journalist and playwright who lived at 18 East Avenue, to explain to *Manchester Guardian* readers a few days later what was behind the protest: "We of the Garden Village have decided to do without fresh milk until the price is reduced ... The boycott is not a pleasant weapon. It blesses neither him who boycotts nor him who is boycotted. But it is our only weapon ... If the farmers and dealers can sell at less than sixpence, the Government should compel them to do so. If they cannot, the Government and the municipalities should take steps to ensure that milk, which is as necessary to infants as water is to the community at large, shall be supplied to the poor at a price within their means," he wrote.[324]

The protest was not forgotten; very many years later, the 2018 Manchester Histories Festival would include a dramatisation of the 'Burnage Milk Strike', written and performed by local women.[325]

CHAPTER 11

THE EVE OF WAR

An observer looking in on the world of co-operative and co-partnership housing societies in, say, July 1914 might easily have drawn the conclusion that here was a movement accelerating towards real influence and scale.

In the short period since 1911 a whole host of new initiatives had got under way. In 1912, co-partnership societies on garden suburb lines were registered, for example, in Haslemere (where Aneurin Williams had finally managed to get something started, with the aid of the local Rector), in Knebworth (where the co-partnership would form part of a much larger development plan prepared for the landowner Earl Lytton by Edwin Lutyens), in Coventry (where the silk manufacturer Thomas Cash was the leading light), in Fairfield on the eastern outskirts of Manchester on land adjacent to the fine Moravian church and settlement (where Thomas Marr once again undertook the task of chairman), and in Didsbury (south Manchester). Plans for a co-partnership garden suburb in Sutton (Surrey), first discussed some years earlier, were now at the development stage, at the Rose Hill end of the town.[326]

In 1913 there were further initiatives, in Carlisle (Newby West)[327] and in Worcester[328], where the Dean of Worcester Cathedral, Rev. William Moore Ede had got involved (Moore Ede, something of a social reformer, had called on Christians to work to improve working-class housing in a book he had written almost two decades earlier).[329] CTL had picked up another member society (and Vivian, Litchfield and Hutchings further directorships) in the form of Rudheath Tenants, in a village close to Northwich, Cheshire. CTL was reportedly giving advice to another Cheshire initiative, in Winnington[330], as well as to a developing society in Glastonbury.[331]

CTL, and CTL's in-house architect George Lister Sutcliffe were also involved in a three-acre garden suburb development in Berkhamsted, where a local landowner A. A. Dorrien-Smith had been instrumental in establishing a co-partnership society called Berkhamsted Tenants. The building work for an initial 24 houses was well underway in the Autumn of 1912 with a new road named 'Greenway' created for the new estate. As well as working-class housing, the development included four much larger properties, described by the local newspaper at the time as 'commodious villas'. However Berkhamsted Tenants seems to have very quickly hit financial difficulties and the estate was advertised for sale by auction in 1919.[332]

More positively, there were major plans under way in Ruislip, on the outskirts of London which had been opened up to development with the arrival of the Metropolitan Line in 1904. King's College, Cambridge, which owned 1,500 acres here, were keen to develop the land on garden suburb lines and a development company Ruislip Manor Ltd was established. A separate society, Ruislip Manor Cottage Society, was set up in 1911 charged with building the 'artisan quarter' of Ruislip. The housing reformer William Thompson, the Richmond alderman and by now Surrey county councillor who had given evidence before the Select Committee in 1906, took a leading role in the early establishment of the Cottage Society, which put up housing in Ruislip Manor itself as well as in the outlying areas of Eastcote and Northwood.[333] Ruislip, Eastcote and Northwood have a significant place in town planning history as the largest of the early town plans formally prepared by a local authority using powers in the 1909 Housing and Town Planning Act.[334]

Over the preceding few years there had also been new attempts to interest a reluctant mainstream co-operative movement in the ideas of the Garden City and garden suburb movement. Following Aneurin Williams' address to the 1907 Co-operative Congress on housing issues (page 15), he and another co-operator Fred W. Rogers had been instrumental in establishing in 1908 the Co-operative Garden City Committee. In a series of articles in *Garden City* magazine in 1908, Rogers called for the movement to create its own new Co-operative Garden City. "Surely the co-operative movement of the United Kingdom, with its vast resources, its unique and closely-knit organisation, its centralised experience and accumulated knowledge of industrial possibilities could plan and carry out the creation of a co-operative city and community," Rogers had written in January 1908. "Is there enough grit in the movement to make it possible?" he added.[335]

The necessary grit was obviously not forthcoming and the Committee's idea that the co-operative movement could establish its own large-scale Garden City did not come about. (Much later, and in a very different world, there was to be a reprise of the idea when in 2005-9 the Co-operative Group tried unsuccessfully to get permission for a 20,000 home 'eco town' on agricultural land in Leicestershire.)[336] Nevertheless Williams and Rogers were able to interest a small number of established distributive co-operative societies in the idea of putting up garden suburb developments. There was talk of possible developments by a number of societies, but the only significant example was the development in 1912 of thirty houses for rent undertaken by the Woking Co-operative Society in the Horsell area to the west of the town centre. The society already owned much of the land it needed for its 'Woking Garden Suburb', land which it had previously used for grazing its horses, for allotments and for society fetes. Now the society went ahead to build on about a third of the site, borrowing part of the £9,000 or so needed from the CWS at 3¾% and arranging for Clapham Lander to be the architect. The development was based on a single road off the main Well Lane, duly given the name of Holyoake Crescent after George Jacob Holyoake (Holyoake had died in 1906). Just eight houses were built to each acre and, following best garden suburb principles, Lander included a village green in the design. The society also arranged for the occupants to have access to a shared lawn-mower and a shared long ladder. This part of Woking is now quite deservedly a Conservation Area.[337]

In other words, there was considerable activity taking place in England in the years immediately before the First World War, much of it outside the CTL orbit. There was also a new national co-partnership housing organisation operating, a top-down philanthropic initiative with the remit to bring affordable working-class housing into rural areas. This was the Rural Co-partnership Housing Association, which was set up following the 1909 Housing Act and which in a short time went through a bewildering number of name changes. It is mentioned in 1913 calling itself the Rural Co-partnership Housing and Land Council, a little later becoming the Rural Housing Organisation Society and then, by 1916, simply the Housing Organisation Society. It also set up a parallel sister organisation, the Rural Co-partnership Housing Trust, which operated as the business arm of the new movement, in a way that was directly modelled on CTL's role.

Sybella Gurney (or Mrs Branford as she was now referred to, following her marriage in December 1910 to a sociologist and businessman Victor

Branford) was certainly involved in this venture, although she and her husband were living in the United States for considerable periods at this time. The Conservative politician Lord Henry Cavendish-Bentinck took the chairmanship.[338]

The story of the Rural Co-partnership Housing Association has not attracted much attention from historians, but in a short period of time it managed to produce some significant practical achievements. By the end of 1912, it had already established six co-partnership societies in villages across southern England and the Midlands. In Datchet (then in Buckinghamshire, now Berkshire) twenty-eight cottages were close to completion and some were occupied, on 30 acres of land. In Otford (Kent), 160 acres had been acquired and building work was under way. In Petersfield (Hampshire) 33 acres were purchased and a first phase of eighteen cottages was planned. In Somersham (Huntingdonshire, now Cambridgeshire) around seventeen acres of fruit-growing land was purchased, with building work begun. In Budleigh (Devon), four acres were bought while in Hadleigh (Suffolk) the first twelve cottages were being built in Cranworth Road. There were further schemes afoot, for example in the village of St Mawes on Cornwall's south coast. Here the growth of tourism was creating exactly the same issues for housing for locals as Cornwall is facing today: "Owing to the increase in the number of visitors to this fishing village there is a danger of the poorer inhabitants having their cottage accommodation curtailed," wrote Ewart Culpin in 1913.

Culpin added, "The Council is following the true method of co-partnership and the tenants take up three £1 shares, paid for by instalments of a penny a week, with a preliminary payment of 1s. a share, and it is interesting to notice that security of tenure is given to the tenant, and this tenancy passes to his family after him so long as the conditions of membership are fulfilled. This meets one of the difficulties often raised in connection with co-partnership tenancy and does away with the fear of a tenant being victimised in consequence of some temporary difference of opinion."[339]

Rural housing (or more precisely, housing for agricultural workers) was seen at the time as a rather separate issue to that of urban working-class housing. This was in part because agricultural labourers' wages were so low that, perforce, the rents charged for their cottages were also very low. This in turn meant that there were significant challenges in building new cottages for rent in a financially sustainable way. But interest in rural housing was also very closely linked with the question of land cultivation, and the Rural Co-partnership Housing Association clearly anticipated that its tenants would be working the very considerable garden areas which were included with the cottages that were built. At Hadleigh, for example, each of the original houses had not less than a quarter of an acre attached.

Indeed, the rules for Hadleigh, and we can assume for the Association's other communities, included powers to enable the society to undertake the collective marketing of produce grown: "To carry on, if thought desirable, the business of wholesale and retail dealers in agricultural requirements, dairy, farm and garden produce, eggs and poultry".[340] In one or two cases, particularly the very large land acquisition at Otford, land usage seems to have been a more important driver than housing. A comparison with today's community-led agricultural ventures may not be inappropriate.

The broader context here is the passing in 1908 by the Liberal administration of the Small Holdings and Allotments Act, a measure which gave county councils powers to acquire land to make available for smallholdings. This legislation followed long years of campaigning for access to land as a measure to relieve rural poverty, most memorably summed up in Eli Hamshire's call for 'Three acres and a cow'. It is perhaps possible to see the Rural Co-partnership Housing Association as attempting to demonstrate, in line with co-partnership ideology, that state intervention was not the only way to achieve this end.

Quite how the Association oversaw developments in so many different villages is not clear, although the local gentry obviously played a major role. At Hadleigh, for example, it was the Rowley family holding the Baronetcy of nearby Tendring Hall who appear to have taken the lead. At Datchet, Lord Rothschild was the society's president. The Association also tried to extend its reach by establishing county-based branches, although in 1915 only two of these were functioning (Suffolk and Westmorland).

By 1916, it had reportedly established more than twenty separate societies. The Association clearly faced a demand in some areas for housing for purchase rather than rent, and it adapted its model to permit occupants to gradually purchase their homes. Although the evidence is not clear-cut, it would appear that the Association subsequently had the first right to re-acquire the properties in the case of sales.[341]

We have focused up to now almost exclusively on the developments in England but by 1914 there was co-partnership housing activity also in Scotland, where two branches of the Garden Cities and Town Planning Association (one based in Edinburgh and one operating in Glasgow and the West of Scotland) had been set up in 1908-9. It was the latter group who were responsible for progressing a significant development at Westerton, in what was then a rural area to the north-west of Glasgow city centre. The impetus appears to have come from a lecture given by Thomas Marr, who had been invited up from Manchester by the GCTPA branch in December 1910. The meeting was chaired by the Conservative politician Sir John Stirling-Maxwell, the 10th Baronet of Pollok, and after the meeting Maxwell went on to play a major role in the establishment of the Westerton development. (The Maxwell name will be a familiar one to Glaswegians: the family house for several centuries was Pollok House, now in the care of the National Trust for Scotland.)

The meeting with Marr was followed by a positive follow-up meeting in early 1911, and in 1912 a new co-partnership society, Glasgow Garden Suburb Tenants Ltd, was registered. Land had been investigated at Cathcart and Giffnock before the decision was taken to take an option to acquire land at Garscube, on land forming part of South Westerton Farm. The land was isolated, but the committee negotiated with the North British Railway Company for a new station to be built at Westerton.

The first 45 houses were ready for the opening ceremony in April 1913, and available for occupancy the following month. A further fifteen houses were completed by early 1914 and by 1915 a total of 84 houses had been built. Originally some 300 houses had been envisaged, but the war effectively stopped further progress. Raymond Unwin was brought in in an advisory capacity, and although a Glasgow-based architect was employed the houses have an English Arts and Crafts feel. Stirling-Maxwell's contribution was recorded in the naming of two of the new streets Maxwell Street and Stirling Street.

The Glasgow Tenants built in 1914 an initial village hall themselves out of corrugated iron and many of the residents also were active in establishing a co-operatively run grocery shop to serve the new housing area: Westerton Garden Suburb Co-operative Society was set up in 1915.[342] The centenary of the estate was commemorated in 2013 with, among other things, a debate in the Scottish Parliament. "The aim in building it 100 years ago, in 1913, was to create high-quality and affordable housing for the working classes," one MSP (Labour's Anne McTaggart) said at the time, before adding a more barbed political comment: "I am sad to say that that is still every bit as necessary today as it was all those years ago".[343]

Another person in the audience in 1910 for Thomas Marr's lecture had been the Conservative politician and landowner Sir Hugh Shaw-Stewart, and Shaw-Stewart subsequently became a key player in the establishment of tenant societies in Greenock and next-door Gourock, close to where his family country house was located. As the author John Boughton has pointed out, Greenock had historically suffered from appalling working-class housing conditions (the 'unhealthiest town in Scotland', according to an 1860s report) and matters were not improved by the decision of the British government to relocate around seven hundred munitions workers from the Arsenal in London to the new Royal Naval Torpedo Factory which opened in Greenock in 1910.[344] Shaw-Stewart offered land for the Greenock Garden Suburb Tenants at a below-market price, although only a small number of houses appear to have been built. A separate society, Gourock Garden Suburb Tenants, acquired land to the west of the torpedo factory and around sixty houses were built, in Caledonia Crescent and Manor Crescent.

There also was a third local initiative in the form of the Gourock and Greenock Tenants, which according to Ewart Culpin had the distinction of being the first co-partnership to be registered in Scotland. This seems for once to have been more of a self-help initiative than the top-down developments promoted by Scottish establishment figures. Culpin says that the majority of the shareholders were "artisans in the Royal Naval Torpedo Factory, who since their transfer from Woolwich have had great difficulty in obtaining suitable housing".[345] The original ambitious plan was, it would seem, for several hundred houses but only a small number of houses were eventually completed, in Reservoir Rd, Greenock.

The Glasgow, Greenock and Gourock ventures are fortunate to have had the attention of the Scottish historian Lou Rosenburg who in his recent book *Scotland's Homes Fit for Heroes* also describes the other co-partnership societies which were being developed at this time in Renfrew and Alexandria (the Vale of Leven Tenants).[346]

Turning to Wales, the situation in 1914 had changed considerably over the previous three years, mainly through the energetic activity of the Welsh Town Planning and Housing Trust which was established in

1913 and which, as we have seen, took over the Rhiwbina co-partnership estate following the unfortunate collapse of Jevons's Housing Reform Company. Much of the energy appears to have come from the top of the organisation, in the shape of its chairman David Davies MP. Davies is a significant figure in early twentieth century Welsh history, known among other things for his active support of the National Library of Wales and of University College Aberystwyth (where he endowed a professorship) and – after the First World War – for his passionate support for the League of Nations and the cause of peace. He came from a wealthy family: his grandfather, also David Davies but given the sobriquet 'top sawyer', had built up a vast industrial empire with interests in railways and coal mining as well as ownership of Barry Docks. Top Sawyer's grandson, who started out in adult life already a multimillionaire, was a director also of the Great Western Railway and the Midland Bank.

Among other things Davies relished hunting. He bagged five lions and a rhinoceros on a trip to Africa as well as, closer to home, riding with the Llandinam hunt. But he was also a strong Welsh non-conformist, a teetotaller and a committed philanthropist. He helped fund a Welsh campaign in 1911-1912 against the scourge of TB and, perhaps as a direct result, thereafter began to address housing issues. He had contracted with Raymond Unwin to work on houses for workers on his own country estate, and one of Unwin's colleagues the architect T. Alwyn Lloyd was to go on to play a significant role in the development of the Welsh Town Planning and Housing Trust.[347]

As well as the rescue at Rhiwbina, the Trust very early on embarked on a major development at Wrexham, primarily to provide housing for workers at the Gresford Colliery and other nearby pits. The Trust acquired around 100 acres of land with an option on a further hundred and put in the roads and sewers, leasing part of the land to Wrexham Tenants Ltd. The society began building work in 1913 (partly assisted by a PWLB loan), and had completed 245 houses by 1917.[348]

The Trust also turned its attention to Barry, a town where Davies had of course family business interest in the docks. Here sixteen acres were bought in 1913 on a 999 year leasehold basis with a further 146 acres held under option. Building work commenced in 1915, with 52 houses built by 1917; more were later put up in the 1920s.

Barry Garden Suburb is today one of the most immediately attractive estates of its kind, mainly as a result of its striking location on a headland overlooking the sea. The land adjacent to the sea at Cold Knap Point was left undeveloped and was passed by the Trust to the local authority. The estate was declared a Conservation Area in 1973.[349]

By early 1914, the Welsh Town Planning and Housing Trust also had three smaller ventures either under way or in planning. These were a development in Machynlleth (Machynlleth Garden Village) where nineteen houses were being built, a similar venture at Llanidloes (where another nineteen houses would shortly be built) and a prospective development just across the English border in Shropshire in the mining community of Weston Rhyn where thirteen houses would be put up during the war. Another similar plan, for the town of Newtown was also under discussion but although the Trust acquired around thirty acres here housing does not seem to have been put up and in 1917 the land was still being used for agricultural purposes.[350]

The choice of Machynlleth, Llanidloes and Newtown is hardly coincidental, given that Davies was at the time Montgomeryshire MP and therefore the MP for these towns. Davies had in fact already been sprinkling philanthropic dust in Machynlleth and Llanidloes; in 1908 he had paid the construction costs for the Town Hall in Llanidloes and in 1911 he had paid for the mediaeval Owain Glyndŵr Parliament House in Machnylleth to be restored.

Davies was not, it must be said, particularly committed to the idea of tenant empowerment; his Dictionary of National Biography entry describes him thus: "Davies was an imperious, impatient idealist who stamped his personality on Welsh, and to a degree on British, life over three decades ... He was generous and public-spirited ... But he was liable to assume that his wealth alone would decide outcomes."[351] The Trust he led, however, played a significant role in developing both the co-partnership and garden suburb movements in the Welsh context, and was to continue to do so during and after the First World War. Its final significant project was at Burry Port, west of Llanelli in Carmarthenshire, where it was asked during the war by the government to help provide housing for munitions workers.[352]

There were other organisations active in Wales at this time, including commercial ventures which adopted at least the 'co-partnership' name for some of their developments. The largest of these, Welsh Garden Cities Ltd, had by 1915 put up approaching two thousand houses in eight areas: Gorseinon, the Swansea valley, Pengam, Gilfach Goch, Fernhill (Rhondda), Hengoed, Aberaman and Highley (Shropshire). Housing in these developments was available both for rental and purchase.[353]

CHAPTER 12

HOUSING AND THE FIRST
WORLD WAR

A conference of locally based housing societies to discuss their role in a national housing policy once peace finally returned to Britain was organised in October 1916 by the Garden Cities and Town Planning Association.[354] By this stage, Britain and her allies had been fighting the Germans and their allies for over two years, and thoughts of early victory had long given way to a realisation that the war would be one of attrition. At the time of the GCTPA event, the later stages of the Battle of the Somme were taking lives on the Western Front; the Somme offensive which had begun in July that year would peter out in November with well over a million soldiers as casualties; of these about three hundred thousand were killed.

It was during the year of 1916, as the war in Europe dragged on, that the issue of post-war housing started to climb higher up the British government's agenda. Minds were being focused by the passing by Parliament at the end of 1915 of rent control legislation which had frozen the rents payable on working-class housing at the 'standard rent' level they were at on August 3 1914, the day before war was declared. As well as protecting rent levels, Parliament also froze mortgage interest rates (this was partly to protect landlords who might otherwise have defaulted on mortgages on the houses they were renting out). As is well known, this legislation, the Increase of Rent and Mortgage Interest (War Restrictions) Act, was effectively forced on the government by the working-class protests which had been erupting over rent increases, particularly on Clydeside where by the Autumn of 1915 perhaps as many as twenty thousand people were participating in rent strikes. The catalyst for the decision to pass emergency rent control legislation, pushed through hurriedly at the time by Lloyd George, was the mass demonstration outside the Glasgow Sheriff Court in mid-November, where eighteen tenants were being prosecuted for non-payment of the rent increases being demanded of them by profiteering landlords.[355]

By the time of the GCTPA event in October 1916 the language being used for the movement of independent local housing societies had changed. 'Co-partnership' had ceased to be the usual convenient catch-all term. Instead the GCTPA invitation to its conference was addressed to 'public utility societies'. This was the term which had originally come in to the British town planning movement from Germany and which had become much more widely used following the 1909 Housing Act. The Act had defined a public utility society as one which was registered under the Industrial and Provident Societies Act, and which included in its rules a restriction on interest and dividend payments to no more than 5%. The definition (and particularly the cap on interest payments) was important in the context of housing societies being able to access loan finance from the Public Works Loan Board.

We can safely conclude that by the time of the October 1916 event any suggestion that the Co-partnership Tenants Housing Council and/or the CTL spoke for the whole community housing movement had long since disappeared. In fact, the GCPTA had already established a committee (at an initial event for societies held a year earlier in November 1915) to perform the new co-ordinating role it was taking on, the GCTPA Public Utility Societies Committee.[356] Henceforth, in the sometimes fraught negotiations with government and the civil service over the future role of these societies in providing affordable working-class housing, it would be the GCTPA which would take the initiative as the lead body for the movement.

War was having its effect at home, as well as on the battlefields. *Co-partnership* magazine regularly updated its readers on some of the ways that life on the existing estates was changing. Liverpool Tenants, for example, had by the Autumn of 1914 set up a drill section for the men, while its women were being encouraged to take first aid training; the society had also established a relief fund, so that no tenants would have to leave the estate because of changed economic circumstances. Anchor Tenants reported that tenants were suffering from a fall in income from reduced working hours, while Derwentwater advised that it had lost some of its tenants to the armed forces. In Manchester, as we have seen, women began a lively campaign to protest against the high wartime cost of milk. In both Ealing and Hampstead, Belgian refugees were being housed in, respectively, the cricket pavilion and the central clubhouse.[357]

More significantly, the momentum behind the growth of most of the individual co-partnership and community housing developments was grinding to a halt. All sorts of new problems were causing significant difficulties. The cost of building materials and estate development had risen sharply following the coming of war, part of the general pattern of wartime inflation. There was a scarcity of labour as more men enlisted for the war effort. There was also a shortage of capital: in March 1915, the Treasury had pulled the plug on PWLB loans for new schemes except for those which were urgently needed for war-related housing. Funds from private investors were also proving hard to find. (There was, one report said, "shyness by those with capital" following the declaration of war.)[358]

It was not just the co-partnership and community housing societies affected by these trends but the whole building industry that sought to address working-class housing needs. Liverpool Tenants' Bryce Leicester described the industry as in a "state of stagnation" by mid-1915, with new-build completions dramatically down. The government had abandoned housing when war broke out, he said. The result, according to Leicester, would be a shortage of 250,000 working-class houses and therefore the retention of insanitary houses which should be removed from the housing stock.[359]

In fact, although war conditions exacerbated the situation, the building slump and the overall decline in new-builds pre-dated the coming of war by a number of years. CTL, for example, had complained of building material costs rising in 1912 and had found 1913 a difficult year. The war compounded its difficulties. At the start of the war, CTL claimed to be giving work to over 760 people, taking into account its two 'subsidiaries' of Woodworkers Ltd and Brick and Tile Workers as well as CTL itself. Staff were given encouragement to join the armed forces, and those remaining were hurriedly put on three-quarters time, at three-quarters pay. "The immediate concern," wrote Frederick Litchfield in September 1914, "is to secure employment, to ward off the day of privation". CTL appealed to private investors to support a new £10,000 loan stock issue.[360]

Henry Vivian later was to write, in 1918, that "The task of bringing to a standstill, without seriously injuring our interest, the developments we were proceeding with when the war broke out was difficult," but it was a task he claimed had been successfully accomplished. Certainly there was a major curtailment of CTL development plans for expansion, particularly for the most ambitious projects such as that in Wavertree, Liverpool. Other would-be CTL schemes fell through: in May 1915 it was reported that that a proposed co-partnership estate in the Walker area of Newcastle had been unexpectedly abandoned, just at the time when everything seemed set to go ahead.[361]

It was not just the CTL-associated housing societies where plans for development were severely scaled back by war conditions. This was the case at Thomas Cash's Coventry Garden Suburb, for example, and at Fairfield to the east of Manchester. As we have seen, it was also true at the Glasgow Tenants estate at Westerton.

So the 1916 GCTPA conference of the 'public utility societies' had plenty to discuss. It was attended by a total of 36 organisations, including many of the co-partnership and co-operative societies we have already encountered. Among those sending delegates were Anchor Tenants, Sevenoaks Tenants, Garden City Tenants, Bournville Tenants, Stoke-on-Trent Tenants, Manchester Tenants, Haslemere Tenants, Fairfield Tenants, Ruislip Manor Cottage Society, Rudheath Tenants, and three of the Hampstead Garden Suburb societies. The Welsh Town Planning and Housing Trust's various endeavours were represented among others by Cardiff Workers Co-operative Garden Village (Rhiwbina), Barry Garden Suburb and Weston Rhyn Tenants. Two of the Rural Co-partnership initiatives, those from Otford and Petersfield, participated. There were also other housing societies such as the Howard Cottage Society from Letchworth.[362]

Ewart Culpin, the secretary of GCTPA and there representing the host organisation, set the scene for the discussion of societies' role in post-war housing provision. There was a consensus emerging, he said, that working-class housing in the future would not be able to be provided by individuals, which left either local authorities or public utility societies to cope with the demand. The societies, he added, were in a strong position to move quickly when peace came, not least because of the thousands of acres of land they had available to them. Culpin argued, however, for local authorities to support this work, firstly by buying land for societies to develop but also by investing significant sums in societies in order to help finance the build costs. If local authorities put up 90% of the finance, he said, this would mean that only 10% had to be sought from external investors and tenants. With this sort of arrangement, Culpin went on, management committees should be eight strong, with five members representing the local authority and the remaining three being elected by tenants and investors. It was a refinement of the model which of course had been proposed before, for example by Sybella Gurney and John Nettlefold (page 89). It was also a model which, had it been implemented, would have given a very different feel to local authority engagement in housing in the remainder of the twentieth century.

Thomas Marr, by this stage a Manchester city councillor, also spoke at the conference, in his role as chairman of Fairfield Tenants. "While I am theoretically much in favour of municipal house building, I must own that the practical results achieved up to the present are disappointing," he said. The machinery of municipal government did not lend itself to economic or efficient building, he added. So Marr too called for local authorities to be persuaded to acquire the land for development and to make it available on a leasehold basis to public utility societies who, he said, would be able to undertake the actual development "with considerable economy". The red tape of the Public Works Loan Board and the Treasury needed to be tackled, and PWLB funding should be made available much earlier in the build process. But anyway, if public utility societies were to extend their role, "it is obvious that much more capital must be available", he argued.

Other participants also addressed the role of the PWLB in funding societies' work. One grouse was that, while societies were required to freeze their rents at pre-war levels, their legal obligations to the PWLB remained unchanged. Frederic Osborn of the Howard Cottage Society spelled out the dilemma: "Societies now find themselves prevented from raising their rents, while at the same time the rate of interest has risen to a point which makes temporary borrowing prohibitive," he said, adding that suspension of PWLB repayments during the rent freeze period was "imperative".[363] In fact Aneurin Williams, by now a Liberal MP, had attempted during the passing of the 1915 rent control Act to achieve something on these lines by having the concessions to landlords on mortgage interest also extended to PWLB loans, but had not been successful.[364]

There were, in other words, plenty of issues on which the public utility societies wanted government action and government concessions. But certainly in late 1916 there was no sense that the societies would not be major players in the provision of working-class housing in the brave new world of post-war Britain.

What of the government itself? The process by which Parliament and government departments debated the housing question in the period from 1916 onwards to the eventual culmination of legislation in the Addison Act (the Housing, Town Planning &c Act 1919) has attracted considerable interest from historians, and the housing historian Peter Malpass has been particularly assiduous in researching the National Archives records which reveal the tensions and disagreements, particularly between the Local Government Board and the Ministry of Reconstruction (set up in 1917), over the future role of public utility societies (PUSs). Malpass writes that "During the debate of 1917–18 the Local Government Board tended to take a pro-local authority line, and to be much less enthusiastic about the potential of the PUSs, while the Ministry of Reconstruction showed greater willingness to recognise the deficiencies of local authorities, to consider the need for strong default powers and to support the case for the PUSs".[365]

One difficulty facing the government as it pondered its eventual housing policy was that many local authorities showed very little willingness to take on the responsibility of providing housing. Malpass quotes an internal memo from Christopher Addison, at that stage the first Minister of Reconstruction, who wrote that "A certain number of Local Authorities are likely to prepare adequate schemes for meeting the shortage in their area. But it is quite clear that a large number will not ... I believe, from the evidence I have received, that a large number of Authorities are against building, quite apart from the risk to the rates."[366]

There were a number of key reports between 1916 and 1919, which fed into the government's policy-setting agenda on housing. The Local Government Board (LGB) issued a Memorandum on housing in June 1916 which strongly promoted the role of local councils in housing delivery, and a Circular to local authorities in March 1918 which gave details of proposed government financial support; public utility societies did not feature in these documents. Partly because of this, the 1918 LGB Circular immediately was strongly critiqued by the so-called group of 'nineteen eminent men'. Housing policy was proving to be contested ground.

But in the meanwhile Christopher Addison at the Ministry of Reconstruction had set up in 1917 a Housing Advisory Panel of experts, chaired by Lord Salisbury and including among its members Beatrice Webb and Seebohm Rowntree, who were given the brief to explore housing policy options. Rowntree contributed his own research to this panel which suggested that the country post-war would face a housing shortage of 300,000 houses. The Panel's report, produced in late 1917, took a markedly different approach to the LGB and was generally supportive of the contribution public utility societies could play.[367]

What sort of houses would need to be built, though? Here the significant work was being undertaken by the committee chaired by the architect and MP John Tudor Walters. The celebrated Tudor Walters Report, which came out in the Autumn of 1918, established strong standards for new housing design and construction as well as a commitment to very low density housing. By this stage Rowntree's estimate of 300,000 houses needed had been revised upwards: Tudor Walters thought the post-war housing shortfall would be 500,000 houses.

As many have observed, the report was very much the work of Raymond Unwin, who was one of the members of the committee. Unwin had left private practice in 1914 to take up the post of chief town planning inspector at the Local Government Board, and then had been seconded in July 1915 to the wartime Ministry of Munitions where he was responsible for overseeing the building of a major estate for munitions workers at Gretna and Eastriggs on the Solway Firth as well as a smaller estate at Mancot Royal in Flintshire. Given Unwin's oversight, their design was inevitably strongly garden suburb in influence.

The Tudor Walters report can be seen to mark the symbolic moment when Unwin's garden suburb approach formally made it through into mainstream thinking. The report itself was translated into official policy through the Housing Manual issued by the LGB in April 1919 and although the Tudor Walters standards were subsequently to be watered down Unwin's philosophy can be seen as directly influencing the way council housing was built over at least the twenty years up to the Second World War. The most obvious example is Manchester's enormous Wythenshawe estate to the south of the city centre which was begun in the 1920s, but very many councils also adopted in their approach to post-1919 public housing the model of the substantially built semi set in a generous garden on a winding avenue. The fact that – for better or worse – our cities (in England at least) are sprawling suburban affairs rather than more compact entities with continental-style apartment living is a direct legacy of Unwin's pioneering work. (Not everyone, incidentally, was convinced by the model. As early as 1913-4 Trystan Edwards had offered two enjoyably swashbuckling critiques of the garden suburb movement in the Town Planning Review: why plant people like vegetables in the countryside?, he argued. What's wrong anyway with city living?)[368]

The government immediately followed the Armistice on November 11 1918 by calling a snap General Election, and the Prime Minister Lloyd George ensured that housing was to be an election issue in his famous call for the country to provide 'homes fit for heroes'. (In fact, the phrase used by Lloyd George at the time has been misremembered. He used the rather less memorable sound-bite of "habitations fit for the heroes who have won the war". Nevertheless, a commitment to decent housing in adequate numbers had been clearly made.)[369]

Following the Election, which resulted in a landslide victory for Lloyd George and his Liberal and Conservative Coalition partners, the pledge had to be made good. For effectively the first time, the way that this was to be achieved was through significant state grant funding for working-class housing (Treasury housing grants had been made available in 1914 but only in extremely limited circumstances related to the war). Grants were to be made available both to local authorities and to public utility societies.

Malpass in his writings on this period is keen to correct the impression given by some historians that the focus in the run-up to the 1919 Addison Act was solely on local authority housing provision, which he argues is partly a result of a post-hoc reading of that period of history. "The PUSs [public utility societies] were seen as worthy of assistance throughout the second half of the war. This is significant in reorientating the way that the origins of 'social rented housing' in Britain are conceptualized, for it is a reminder that right from the start of subsidized housing there was what might be seen as a dual system, embracing both municipal and non-municipal providers," he writes.[370]

Nevertheless, as we have seen, the LGB was not particularly supportive of voluntary sector efforts, and the Treasury and the LGB had also previously expressed concern that some public utility societies were getting round the 5% restriction on dividends and interest payments. In fact, both Ebenezer Howard and Ewart Culpin had expressed similar concerns privately that some societies were bending the rules and risking giving the whole sector a bad name. Culpin in 1915 had said it was essential that societies were entirely free of suspicion, even if it meant a measure of extra state supervision.[371]

It also has to be recognised that the Addison Act as it was finally legislated in 1919, while supporting the idea of public utility societies as agents of affordable housing, offered significantly better funding provision to local authorities than it did to the societies. Effectively local authorities' exposure to housing costs was capped at the equivalent of just a penny on the rates, with all the remaining costs being met by central government funding. There was a strong element of realpolitik here – if the many reluctant local authorities in the country were to be cajoled into house-building then they needed to be placated with adequate financial incentives. (As it was, a significant minority of authorities still did not use the Addison Act provisions to build any housing.)

Public utility societies received help from the Act in two main ways. Firstly, the percentage of capital costs they could receive in loans from the PWLB was increased from two-thirds to three-quarters. Secondly, grant funding was made available to societies to subsidise the costs of paying interest on the capital loans. The subsidy was at the rate of 30% of the annual costs of paying interest on the loans acquired, the figure being calculated as if the PWLB had lent the full 100% of the capital.

There were other parts of the Act that were intended to help societies. Firstly, the PWLB's maximum lending term could now be fifty years, rather than forty. Secondly, there were provisions for PWLB funding to be made at a slightly earlier stage in developments than hitherto, responding to one of the demands raised at the 1916 GCTPA conference. Thirdly, the cap on interest and dividend payments for societies was raised from 5% to 6%.

There was also provision in the Act to enable local authorities to partner with societies in working-class housing construction, in a similar way to that being proposed by Ewart Culpin in 1916. Authorities were given powers to help form new public utility societies, and could also make grants and loans to societies, acquire shares and offer guarantees against societies' borrowings. But these were permissive powers rather than statutory obligations and in practice these powers would turn out to be rarely exercised. Why would local authorities take this route when they were being well rewarded for their own direct housing ventures? The alternative model of a partnership approach to social housing between councils and societies remained effectively stillborn.

One key disadvantage facing societies compared with local authorities was that they were left exposed to significant financial risk. A second problem was that they remained responsible for finding a quarter of the total funding package for each development, a not insignificant percentage. In the post-war economic climate, even the increase in permitted interest rates to 6% no longer seemed a particularly satisfactory return for what could be a risky investment. (The Bank of England base rate had increased from 5% to 6% in November 1919 and then up to 7% in April 1920 before gradually being brought down to 5% in 1921.) Even though the maximum return on societies' capital was subsequently raised in late 1921 up to 6.5% the challenge of finding sufficient capital was to be a major struggle for societies in the post-1919 period.

There was to be one further concession to public utility societies in the supplementary housing legislation (the Housing and Town Planning (Additional Powers) Act 1919) introduced shortly after the Addison Act, which increased the grant subsidy from 30% to 50% of interest on borrowings for the years up to 1927, when it was expected post-war economic pressures would have receded. But societies with existing housing developments remained caught by 1915 rent controls, the provisions of which were only liberalised to a limited extent in 1919 and 1920. Furthermore, the legal terms of past PWLB loans generally set the rent levels which societies were obliged to charge their tenants. It was not an easy time to be planning ambitious new initiatives.

The immediate period after the end of the war was in any case a very difficult time to be house-building. Partly because of the new government funding which was lubricating the system, building costs rose extremely fast. John Burnett in his history of social housing in Britain states that houses on average were costing four times their pre-war level, with each house put up following the Addison Act averaging at £1,000.[372] It meant that the economic level at which rents on new-builds would have to be set also rose significantly. Burnett suggests this meant that the economic rent was 30s in Manchester for a house which was actually bringing in rent of 12s 6d.

By the end of 1920 the GCTPA was raising concerns on behalf of public utility societies with the Ministry of Health (the Ministry with housing responsibilities) that cash-flow problems were being exacerbated by over-rigid rules from the PWLB relating to payment schedules. The government offered no redress.[373]

And then, following the immediate post-war boom of 1919-20 came the economic slump of 1921, when wage levels dropped and unemployment rose. Later in 1921 the GCTPA was again in contact with the Ministry, by which time it was definitely sounding alarm bells. Societies were encountering financial difficulties, costs were escalating, and the rents which societies were obliged to charge by their development costs were being undercut by the rents which local authorities were charging on similar properties. Another conference of public utility societies, brought together by the GCTPA at London's Olympia in March 1922, was held under dark clouds for the movement.[374]

It meant, in summary, that public utility societies' contribution to house-building after the war was very much less than its advocates had anticipated. Indeed, the figures for the houses constructed under the Addison Act (together with the later 1919 supplementary Housing Act) are extremely revealing. In total, 213,821 houses were constructed. Local authorities erected 170,090 of these. Private builders (helped by a subsidy introduced in the second 1919 Act) erected 39,186 houses. And what about the public utility societies? Their contribution was embarrassingly low: they were responsible for just 4,545 houses.[375]

CHAPTER 13

AFTERWARDS

It makes sense, I argued in the Introduction, for this account of housing initiatives to take as its end point the Addison Act of 1919, a symbolic moment in the development of Britain's housing policy. But already in the previous chapter we have ventured beyond 1919, and an abrupt conclusion now would leave too many loose ends untied and too many questions unanswered. So this chapter will carry the story forward, through the years that followed the First World War and towards the present day.

It will be appropriate to begin by recounting the later story of the Addison Act's implementation. When the centenary of the Act was celebrated in 2019 there was perhaps an impression held by some people that the path forward for council housing in Britain after Addison was a smooth affair. But in reality the measures introduced by Addison lasted only two years. Originally the government had set itself the target of building half a million of those 'homes for heroes' houses in three years. But in the summer of 1921 this target was abandoned, and as we have seen the eventual total built as a result of the 1919 Act was only a little over 200,000. Christopher Addison himself was moved from his post overseeing housing by Lloyd George in the Spring of 1921 and – following the government decision to abandon the targets – had little option but to resign from the Cabinet in July. Effectively he was sacked, a sacrificial victim.

What had happened in the two years between 1919 and 1921? One problem was that the rapid inflation in building costs had meant that the costs to the public purse were much greater than originally contemplated. The building trade had found it had a bonanza on its hands. Controls over cost inflation proved ineffective.

There were also growing pressures on the government to rein in its spending, with the Treasury and the City of London strongly supporting such an approach. The Cabinet had agreed to a balanced budget and to strict controls of public borrowing in December 1919 and there were to be increasingly vocal demands from financial interests for Britain to return to the gold standard, a direct link between the value of sterling and the value of gold. The country had been obliged to leave the gold standard at the start of the war; it was to restore the link in 1925, a controversial and ultimately unsuccessful move which was overseen by Churchill as Chancellor of the Exchequer. The country was to leave the gold standard again in 1931.

Public opinion was harnessed in the cause of a 'sound monetary policy', and the right-wing press added their voice. This was the time when the term 'squander-mania' briefly entered the language, a populist coinage to suggest profligate government expenditure.

There was another change that had happened between 1919 and 1921, however, which directly affected the fate of the Addison Act. At the end of the war the British government was responding to the fear of revolution. The Russian Revolution of 1917 had inspired many. The British Socialist Party's newspaper *The Call*, for example, marked the Armistice with a bold headline on its front page a few days later "Now for the enemy at home".[376] There were mutinies of soldiers in camps in France and a British military adventure to aid the White Russians against the Bolsheviks had to be abandoned. The aftermath of war was an uneasy time for the British establishment.

By 1921, the climate had changed completely. The Labour movement was much weakened by the economic recession and particularly by the failure of the so-called Triple Alliance between the National Transport Workers Union, the National Union of Railwaymen and the Miners' Federation. The coal mining industry, under state control during the war, had been decontrolled at the end of March 1921, with miners required to accept reduced wages. Under the informal agreement between the three powerful unions, there was an expectation that the transport and rail unions would strike in solidarity. But on April 15 the two union executives resolved not to do so.

The historian Laurence Orbach in his account of housing policy during this period summarises the government's approach to the Addison Act measures as follows: "So long as the expense was justified in terms of offsetting industrial and social unrest, it was unchallenged, if not enthusiastically endorsed. As soon as fears of industrial and social unrest disappeared, the expense became, it seems, politically and financially unsupportable."[377]

As regards the public utility societies, in hindsight it is clear that the Addison Act did not do as many favours for them as had been anticipated. Nevertheless, we should avoid following the simplistic approach which some previous histories have followed which suggests that this housing movement, so flourishing before 1914, disappeared almost without trace after 1919. Such an approach has perhaps encouraged a regrettable fracture in our historical understanding, so that later twentieth century and twenty-first century ventures into co-operative forms of housing in Britain have been unaware of their antecedents.

Despite all the challenges, there were new initiatives which we need to record. The most ambitious of these was Ebenezer Howard's decision in 1920 to bid at an auction for land at Welwyn, in order to bring about Britain's second Garden City. His collaborator Frederic Osborn was later to state rather ruefully that the decision to progress Welwyn had been taken by Howard alone, without briefing others in the Garden City movement, and at a time when Howard did not even have access for the funds for the purchase he had made.[378] Public utility societies were to play a significant role in Welwyn's development, which included a co-operative housekeeping scheme of forty flats, Guessens Court, which was developed by the New Town Housing Society in 1924-5.[379]

Another significant initiative was the garden village of Onslow outside Guildford, where a society named Onslow Village Ltd acquired over six hundred acres of land from the local landowner Lord Onslow at below market value. CTL's Frederick Litchfield was influential in this project and was chairman of the public utility society, which was registered in February 1920. Significantly, this housing scheme appears to have been the first one to have attracted financial support from the local authority, Guildford Town Council, using the 1919 Act provisions. The council invested £20,000, mostly in the form of 5% loan stock. Lord Onslow also invested £20,000 at 5%, and the vice-chairman of Surrey County Council at the time personally put in a further £5,000.

Onslow Garden Village was an ambitious venture, envisaging housing at no more than five houses per acre with the usual public buildings, allotments and open spaces familiar from the pre-war co-partnership garden suburb movement but with plans too for co-operative housekeeping flats with a communal dining room. This latter proposal did not materialise but the society had successfully built over ninety houses by March 1922 and eventually went on to develop many more.[380]

There was also a very interesting initiative for women's housing at this time in the town of Malvern, undertaken by local members of the National Council of Women of Great Britain, the organisation established in 1895 and still operating today. The development comprised three single-storey buildings each divided into six flats, and building work was commenced in April 1921. One difficulty facing the public utility society, Workers Ltd, which was created for the venture was that the PWLB questioned whether its prospective properties were sufficiently 'working-class' to qualify for PWLB funding. Nevertheless the eighteen flats were completed and occupied by May 1922. Among the tenants were two school teachers, two nurses, two cooks, a gardener, a dressmaker and three clerks.[381]

Another successful housing project run by a public utility society was the Quaker-linked community at Jordans in Buckinghamshire, in a village with long historical Quaker connections. According to Jordans Village Ltd, the society which oversaw the development, "the village was intended to be a community where artisans could ply their trades and skills in conditions that would provide a fuller opportunity for the development of character and self-expression". The community was not restricted to Quakers, although it was intended to be run on Christian principles.

Building work at Jordans began in 1919 and work continued thereafter for many years. Although the bulk of the development was completed by 1939 there has been more recent additional housing created. The society continues in operation, renting out two blocks of flats, four blocks of terraced cottages and some detached and semi-detached houses.[382]

What of the mainstream co-operative movement's approach to housing after the war? The co-operative sector had its opportunity to discuss housing provision at a special Co-operative Congress held in Blackpool in mid-February 1920. The Congress was called to discuss approval of the recommendations of an internal co-operative commission, the General Co-operative Survey, which had been meeting during the war with the aim of identifying the strategic direction of the movement in the conditions of peacetime. The Survey found that by this stage the movement had invested about £8.2m in housing, the vast bulk of this (£8.1m) coming from the distributive societies (the shops) and only about £110,000 from the CWS and Scottish CWS. The Survey's final report in 1919 indeed offers a politely-worded criticism of the CWS, pointing out that in the past when it had opened new factories the land for nearby housing had been snapped up by speculators and developed privately rather than through co-operation. The Survey suggested that the Wholesale societies should take a lead in the future in developing estates for their workers "on garden-city lines". (However, the General Co-operative Survey committee suffered somewhat in credibility in that it had been boycotted by the CWS and that the Scottish CWS also later chose to withdraw its two representatives.)

More generally, the final report suggested that the retail societies were not best placed to undertake housing, not least because of the limitations of relying on a committee of members running their societies on a spare-time basis. Instead, "we are of the opinion that special co-operative housing societies on the lines of the co-partnership-tenant societies provide the form of organisation which is best suited for developing housing under the auspices of the co-operative movement". However it also concluded that the role of these 'special co-operative housing societies' should be supplementary to the main provision of housing, which was to be undertaken by local authorities.

The Survey's housing recommendations were not discussed at the Blackpool Congress and there is little evidence that the movement as a whole after the war had any great appetite for further engagement in housing matters. For those who had pleaded with co-operators before the war to harness the large resources at their disposal in housing projects, the movement in the post-war period showed an equal lack of interest. The opportunities which perhaps might have been there were not embraced.[383]

Any review of the progress of public utility housing societies after 1919 has to focus particularly on Wales, and especially on the on-going work of David Davies' Welsh Town Planning and Housing Trust. The Trust's development at Burry Port near Llanelli was not only one of the most ambitious being attempted in the early 1920s, it was also the venture which perhaps most clearly demonstrated the great difficulties under which the societies were labouring at this time. Burry Port turned into a near-disaster which could have threatened the whole of the Trust's operations in Wales.[384]

The Burry Port scheme started promisingly enough. Early in the war the government had negotiated to locate a munitions factory at nearby Pembrey on a site which had previously had a factory manufacturing explosives for commercial use. The Trust arranged with the Ministry of Munitions to take responsibility for providing housing for the workers and it acquired land for 300 houses, the first 104 of which were started in 1917. The Trust adopted the approach it had taken elsewhere, in setting up an arms-length society which would hold the land on a leasehold basis once the development phase was completed. In practice, however, the Trust continued to exercise considerable influence over this new society, Burry Port Garden Suburb Ltd.

After the war, the Trust was intent on completing the Burry Port estate by building the remaining 196 houses. "The remaining two-thirds of the Estate is admirably suited for an after-War scheme," it told Arthur Thomas, the Housing Commissioner in Cardiff in May 1919.[385] Wheels turned slowly, however: during 1920 there were frustrating delays as the PWLB questioned aspects of the scheme, but eventually the Trust felt able to progress, although only with a further hundred houses. The build was well under way by the Spring of 1921.

It was at this point that the troubles really started. Costs rose, the build contract being increased from £78,515 to over £91,000 in early 1921 and then again to £95,000 a few weeks later. It meant that the new houses would cost almost £1,000 each, far more than the £606 build cost for the first 104 (on which in any case the Trust had been able to benefit from a government £173 subsidy under the 1914 grant funding provisions for munitions workers).[386] This in turn meant that the new houses would have to be let at rents very much higher than the first 104 houses. By May 1922, the new estate was almost complete, with 66 houses ready for occupancy and the remaining 34 very close behind. But, given the high rents, there was almost no demand for them.

The government had dropped, as one might describe it, a bomb-shell the previous year when it had taken the decision to close the Pembrey munitions factory. Late in 1921 the Burry Port society wrote to the government asking for reconsideration of the assistance it was receiving given "the complete change in the prosperity of the district resulting from the closing of the Government Factory". The new housing scheme would not have been undertaken, the society said, but for the assurance it had received that housing would be needed. "The difficulties which now face the Society are entirely the result of the scrapping of the War factory," the letter went on.[387]

Further increasingly anxious letters were fired off over the following months to different arms of the government. In March 1922, for example, the society was in touch with the Cardiff office of the Ministry of Health, complaining that local wage levels had fallen from £6-£10 pw to

£2-£3 pw. "The Society is fully aware of the result of such a financial crisis and the inevitable outcome will be a failure to meet its obligations to the PWLB, the loan stock holders and the shareholders," it stated. By this point, the society had another substantive grouse: most of its tenants in the original estate were having to travel to Llanelli for work – and Llanelli council was taking advantage of the better government funding to put up its own council housing, at only 9s a week rent. "It now appears that our scheme is to be stranded financially, having been wrecked by the rapid change in economic conditions and by the unfair and inequitable competition of the State-aided Municipal schemes," the letter added.[388]

The crisis came to head in the summer of 1922, by which time only eight of the new houses were occupied and the society was in arrears to the PWLB. The secretary of the Burry Port society Hall Williams, attending a May meeting with civil servants and the PWLB to try to thrash out a solution, urged the need for more state support. The civil servant who minuted the meeting was clearly unimpressed. Mr Hall Williams, "who by the way was very voluble, idealistic and dogmatic ... repeatedly emphasised that all public utility societies throughout the country were similarly placed and that Government MUST (sic) extend relief," read the internal memo.[389] This meeting was followed by several others, as well as correspondence directly between David Davies MP on behalf of the Trust and the Minister of Health, Sir Alfred Mond. The PWLB, trying to save its investment, attempted unsuccessfully to persuade the Trust to step in and eventually, in the Autumn of 1922, offered to increase its own lending in exchange for a second charge on the original houses. It is not clear whether this offer was accepted but in any event bankruptcy was averted. However there was a price to be paid. In April 1924 the first of a series of plaintive handwritten letters from a woman tenant at Burry Port Mrs Jane Rodham arrived at 10 Downing Street. Her long letter to the Prime Minister complained of the unsustainable rents she and her neighbours were being asked to pay: "these Garden Suburb houses were said to have been built for the working class, but prices were screwed up so high". A few weeks later she was back in touch: "With every week and month that go by the misery of our people gets more intense," she wrote this time.[390] Her letters continued regularly thereafter for several weeks. The Burry Port society had survived, but at some considerable cost.

It should be said that, despite this close shave, the Welsh Town Planning and Housing Trust continued its work. Indeed, undoubtedly facilitated by David Davies' position on the board of the GWR, from 1924 the Trust partnered on a series of housing developments with the railway company for the housing of railway workers which created societies which, at least in some places, had co-operative elements to their functioning. The developments in London, at Acton and Hayes, for example, were reported to be "fully co-operative" in character, with the management committees elected by the tenants. Elsewhere there were estates in Plymouth (in two areas of the city), in Truro, Penzance, Severn Valley Junction, Swansea, Caerphilly and at Barry, where the railway houses were built on part of the garden suburb site. Post-1945 there was also a similar scheme undertaken at Banbury.[391]

However, back in the dark days of the early 1920s Hall Williams was undoubtedly correct in trying to convince his civil servant listeners that the Burry Port problems were not unique to his society. Led by the GCTPA the public utility societies lobbied hard for greater state support for their ventures and eventually in 1923 gained a very small concession: the new Minister of Health Neville Chamberlain arranged for the grant subsidy on loan charges (due to be reduced from 50% to 30% in 1927) to be reduced instead to 40%. However, the societies' efforts continued and had the effect of alienating the key civil servants. Peter Malpass writes that "The societies pleaded their case at every opportunity, seeking more financial aid, while the civil servants expressed rising exasperation and repeated that asking Parliament to increase subsidy was out of the question". Malpass quotes a 1924 internal memo referring to the public utility societies as 'continual agitators'.[392]

Government support for local authority housing schemes was given a new fillip in the Housing Act of 1924, the Wheatley Act, shepherded through Parliament by John Wheatley the Minister of Health under the first, minority, Labour government. The Wheatley Act can be seen as establishing much more firmly than the Addison Act the role of local authority social housing in Britain and, although the Labour government soon fell, the influence of the Act in relation to housing policy continued to be felt for many years. By 1939, local authorities had built more than 1.1m council houses.[393]

The sense that the voluntary sector could play any kind of equal role to the local state in housing delivery had effectively evaporated, however. The Garden Cities and Town Planning Association continued to act as the organisation representing public utility societies into the mid-1930s, when it helped create the National Federation of Housing Societies, the precursor of today's National Housing Federation. Today what were once known as public utility societies play a much more significant role in housing provision, known to us all as housing associations.

But the question has to be asked as to what happened to those particular public utility societies we have been following in this book, the ones with roots in co-operation, co-partnership and the garden village/suburb movement.

It may be appropriate to begin with those societies which most firmly embraced the concept of co-partnership, with its suggestion of joint endeavour between tenants and investors and some sense at least of tenant empowerment. In fact, the term was already becoming rather tarnished in the period before the Addison Act. As early as 1915 Ewart Culpin had complained that "There is more than a suspicion that the only vestige of co-partnership in some societies going by that name now is to be found in the fact that they are registered under the [Industrial and Provident Societies] Act and obtain the two-thirds loan from public funds".[394] Co-partnership could certainly seem attractive to developers, if it meant that tenants could be encouraged, or indeed obliged, to contribute some of the development capital needed.

Henry Vivian continued as chairman of CTL until his death in 1930, living not in one of the CTL-affiliated estates but in a substantial villa called The Limes on Crouch End Hill, which was eventually to be demolished in the late 1960s.[395] Some of his CTL colleagues pre-deceased him: Frederick Litchfield in 1923, for example, and John Greenhalgh in 1928. Another member of the original co-partnership clan, Aneurin Williams, died in 1924.

CTL and the CTL-affiliates had moved during the 1920s well away from their original roots. CTL, for example, developed its new Hampstead Heath extension land in large measure for owner-occupation. In the process, there was a significant falling out between CTL and the Hampstead Garden Suburb Trust: "The Copartnership companies abandoned the struggle and gave up the aims which had first commended them to Mrs Barnett and her colleagues," wrote Brigid Grafton Green in her 70th anniversary history of the Suburb.[396]

The later fate of some of the CTL-affiliates has been recorded by a number of historians, including Margaret Tims, Johnston Birchall and Aileen Reid.[397] In outline, the interlocking share-ownership between

CTL societies, together with CTL's dominant position as an investor in several of the individual societies, meant that there was to be considerable scope for take-overs and acquisitions once CTL had set its path resolutely forward as a property company. CTL took over Oakwood Tenants and Hampstead Heath Extension Tenants societies in 1930, and the two earlier tenants' societies at Hampstead a few years later. It also gradually absorbed Ealing Tenants, which it sold off in 1936 to the property firm Liverpool Trust. Liverpool Trust, part of a company called Bradford Property Trust, had a short time earlier taken over Liverpool Tenants Ltd (the Wavertree Garden Village).

Garden City Tenants in Letchworth, according to Johnston Birchall, had also been taken over by CTL and then subsequently sold on (in 1934) to Bradford Property Trust. Fallings Park in Wolverhampton similarly fell into CTL ownership.

Stoke Tenants at Penkhull tried after the war to sell its existing houses to Stoke local authority, but without success. The society undertook some new building work in the late 1930s, but it too ended life by being acquired by Bradford Property Trust, in this instance in 1963.[398]

The Sealand Tenants co-partnership, or at least the bulk of the estate, was to be absorbed (in 1950) into the ownership of the steelworks company for whose workers the houses had first been put up.

At John Nettlefold's Harborne estate in Birmingham the story was a little different. The society was converted to a Companies Act company, Harborne Tenants Ltd, in 1940, but one which was still tenant controlled. However it too fell within Bradford Property Trust's empire when BPT acquired all the shares around 1995. Harborne Tenants Ltd remains today as a dormant company under the control of the international property company Grainger plc, which in turn had snapped up Bradford Property Trust. However, there remains a strong sense of community on the estate, and one welcome recent development was the successful take-over of the original meeting room and other community facilities by a newly-formed locally-run charity, Moor Pool Heritage Trust. Residents and supporters raised over £300,000 to purchase these facilities at a time when Grainger were threatening to sell them at auction.

There seem to have been at least three triggers which pushed societies towards demutualisation. The first was the passing of the Prevention of Fraud (Investment) Act of 1939. This, as its name implies, was designed to tighten on procedures for organisations appealing for investment capital, but it included very tight controls on organisations registered under the Industrial and Provident Societies Act. Henceforth, this Act could only be used for 'bona-fide co-operative societies' or for organisations which, because they were improving the well-being of the working-classes, could claim special reasons for remaining an IPS society. Otherwise, the new Act said that they should be registered under the Companies Act. The Registrar of Friendly Societies was given the power under the legislation to cancel the registration of societies unable to claim this concession.

It was for this reason that Harborne Tenants re-registered as a company in 1940, and it was also following this Act that CTL itself converted into a business registered under the Companies Act. Many of the early housing societies did not convert, however – perhaps they were small enough to avoid attention or perhaps they successfully claimed 'special reasons' for remaining IPS societies.

The second significant driver towards demutualisation was the occasion for each society when the final repayment of loans taken out with the Public Works Loan Board came to be made, generally after forty or fifty years. This certainly is what appears to have happened in the case of the large and successful Cardiff society at Rhiwbina. It would seem that the society's committee struggled to understand what its on-going role could be once all borrowings had been repaid. According to a local history of the garden suburb, "A special AGM was called in September 1968, where the chairman announced to the unsuspecting tenant holders that they could buy the leasehold to their properties on very favourable terms. His words were met with stunned silence before a rapturous round of applause."[399] By 1969 the society was reporting that all its housing stock had been disposed of.[400]

Finally, the Thatcher-era housing reforms and particularly the Right to Buy legislation for council house owners also encouraged the trend which had already been there for other societies to look to sell their houses to their tenant residents.

Over the years, societies disappeared one by one from the Mutuals Register, the most recent being the demutualisation of Sevenoaks Tenants in 2010 when the lucky members of the society shared a bonanza of around £12m. Sevenoaks Tenants, the second co-partnership after Ealing, had been in existence for over a century at this point.

And yet, against all the odds, some of the co-operative and co-partnership housing societies established before the First World War continue to operate today, providing inexpensive rental accommodation to their tenant-members. Their survival is remarkable, particularly as they have had almost no knowledge of the other remaining societies and no relationship with the mainstream co-operative housing movement. They are not necessarily easy to track down and they tend to eschew publicity. As a committee member with one society put it to a recent academic researcher, "I think ... we're the best kept secret ... we like to go under the radar a bit, don't we?"[401]

The co-operative historian Johnston Birchall, writing in 1995, called the societies which were still functioning as being "like time capsules buried away for future generations to find".[402] This book's introduction perhaps gave away a spoiler when it revealed that there are ten operating societies today which have come to light.[403] Derwentwater Tenants in Keswick has already been mentioned. It had the good sense from the 1950s until the 1980s to buy back almost all the shares from external investors and this has placed the tenants entirely in charge (the society has 25 members, one from each house).

What of the other survivors? Manchester Tenants at Burnage is one. The estate remains almost as it was in Thomas Marr's day, and the meeting room, bowling green and one of the original two tennis courts are still very much in use, at the heart of the estate. Manchester Tenants Ltd continues to act as the collective landlord for tenants of their 136 houses, the society being managed by a nine-person committee elected by the tenants. The society employs three full-time and two part-time staff and turns over not far short of half a million pounds a year.

Anchor Tenants in Leicester is another. The society remains the landlord of 143 houses as well the meeting hall (let out for dance classes) and the original church (now let to a local evangelical church). There are strong links back to the earliest residents: Ian Pawson, who is now in his early seventies and who runs the Anchor Tenants history website, was born in the house he still lives in.[404] Shares in the society are passed on by existing members to the next generation and houses are allocated when vacancies occur to those shareholders at the top of the waiting list, provided they are at least twenty-five years of age.

Bournville Tenants is another actively-run society and its current chair Liz Newman is the granddaughter of one of the original tenants. The bowling green and pavilion in the centre of the estate remain almost as they were when the estate was first built and the original meeting hall is also still there, although no longer owned by the Tenants.

Bournville Tenants has survived rocky financial times, not least the challenge to democracy caused for many years by external investors interested simply in the size of the dividend. ("As the dividend goes up so the attendance at the Annual Meeting goes down", said one past chairman of the society despairingly.) The decision in 1981 to offer tenants the right to buy meant that about a third of the houses passed into owner-occupation but stabilised the finances and the society now has effectively no debt and a strong balance sheet.[405] Unusually the society tries to integrate its owner-occupier neighbours, welcoming them when they move in and indeed enabling them to become members and serve on the six-person committee. 89 houses remain owned by the society; rents charged are well below those of comparable social housing nearby.

Two more functioning societies can trace their roots back to the Rural Co-partnership Housing Association. Hadleigh Co-partnership Housing Society in Cranworth Rd in the village has sold off some of its properties into private ownership but is currently actively looking to build new infill housing on the very large plots of land which were left between the original houses. St Mawes Co-partnership Housing Society also continues, owning ten semi-detached houses above the village. Each tenant is both a member of the society and a member of the committee.

Knebworth Tenants Ltd is another society which is operating effectively, as the landlord of thirty-three houses which it lets on what are (by Home Counties standards) very affordable rents. As at Bournville, some houses were sold off in the past, partly to bring finance into the society at a time when money was not readily available, but recently Knebworth Tenants has taken the opportunity to buy back one of these properties when it came on to the market again. There is a committee of seven which meets once a month, currently comprising five tenants and two non-tenants; the committee's view is that it is sometimes useful to bring in external expertise.

Hereford Co-operative Housing is also actively interested in increasing its housing stock. The society's balance sheet is strong and in recent years its committee have adopted a policy of acquiring houses close to the original estate as they come on the market. The nine-person committee, which meets every quarter, perhaps continues Fred Bulmer's original philanthropic impulse by including five local non-tenants with appropriate professional skills as well as four committee members who are tenants. The committee meets every quarter and a further twenty or so tenant-members typically attend the AGMs.

Thomas Marr's second housing society in Manchester, Fairfield Tenants, is also still operating on land immediately adjacent to the Moravian church and community, a really remarkable Georgian area in an otherwise run-down area of Tameside which now, quite rightly, is designated a Conservation Area. Fairfield Tenants today continues to hold 32 houses and is managed by an eight-strong management committee of tenants.

Ruislip Manor Cottage Society also continues strongly today and has been looking to expand its housing stock. It perhaps comes the closest of the ten societies to operating as a conventional housing association, although it has chosen to remain unregistered with the Regulator of Social Housing. Today the society has around 200 properties, an increase from 155 in 1961.

These ten societies have survived more than a century of social change. They have survived the ideological push towards owner-occupation and the wave of demutualisations which swept away so many building societies and mutual insurers in the later years of the twentieth century. As independent societies their future is in their own hands and they will undoubtedly evolve and change (although it should be added that the vast majority now have strong asset locks written into their constitutions which should help prevent any repeat of a Sevenoaks-style demutualisation). Long may they continue! [406]

CHAPTER 14

CONCLUSION

If interpreting the past can be a challenging occupation for historians, it is also true that anticipating the future can be an exercise open to error.

In 1912, tenants at the Wavertree Garden Suburb put on a dramatic sketch in their estate's club house. The theme of the sketch was *2001 AD or the Suburb of the Future,* and according to a report of the show some 'startling contrasts' emerged between life in the garden suburb in 1912 and that enjoyed by the tenants' descendants. Fortunately the estate was thriving economically at the start of the twenty-first century: according to the Wavertree playscript, news had just come through via "the mega-telephone", that "the Garden Suburb Thrift Committee had secured the contract for supplying the City Council with coal".[407]

In hindsight perhaps this wasn't quite spot-on. But nevertheless those who live today in Wavertree remain aware of their roots. An active Wavertree Society ensures that the area's heritage and history is remembered. A commemorative tea-towel was produced for the estate's centenary in 2010 and sold for the very modest sum of £2.

It is the same elsewhere. For example there is a comprehensive archive on the Ealing Tenants run by Alan Henderson, the archivist with the local Brentham Society. Copious records of the early days at Hampstead are held by the Hampstead Garden Suburb Archives Trust, who have helpfully deposited them in the London Metropolitan Archives. There are active community-run websites and Facebook groups for very many of the estates featured in this book. The societies which established them may have gone, but what they achieved is remembered as something special and worth preserving.

Many, too, have gained official recognition for their heritage and history in being designated as Conservation Areas by their local authorities. Estate agents are not averse to stressing the 'garden village' legacy when writing their advertising copy for houses on the estates coming back on the market.

We should not necessarily undervalue the original importance of all this housing activity and of all these societies, therefore, even in the case of those societies that later on did demutualise or were taken over by commercial property companies. While it is gratifying that some societies have stood the test of time, those that are no longer functioning may also in their day have made a valuable difference to their members' lives – and to have made their mark more generally on the development of working-class housing in Britain.

So the usual caveat applies: we should not allow our histories when we write them to be influenced too excessively by what happened later. In Britain, council housing became the dominant form of social housing for much of the last century, but that does not mean that we should not also give appropriate attention to the early co-operative and co-partnership housing movement.

In any analysis of these societies the first observation to make is that the movement in its heyday was by no means a marginal one. It was certainly larger than the present-day community-led housing movement, which as we have seen has been growing rapidly in recent years. Today's CLT volunteers are finding that it takes hard work, often for considerable periods of time, in order to achieve relatively small developments of affordable homes. By contrast, the pre-1919 housing societies found it possible to build significantly sized estates in relatively short periods of time. Johnston Birchall estimated that by 1912 fourteen societies had built 6,595 houses for a population of 30,000-35,000.[408] He also suggested that around 10,000 houses in total were built by 40+ societies before the movement ran out of steam after the First World War.[409] As the Gazetteer at the end of this book makes clear, there were well over a hundred towns and villages in Great Britain where co-operative and co-partnership tenant societies were at least considered, even if not finally brought to fruition. This was a widely based movement.

It was one which was embraced only tangentially, however, by the mainstream co-operative movement. Aneurin Williams and his colleagues in the Co-operative Garden City Committee would have wished otherwise, and so perhaps would others who led the movement at the time. J.C. Gray, the general secretary of the Co-operative Union in the early years of the century, argued in 1902 that co-operation was not doing very much to help those in real social need: "The truth is that

Co-operators generally do not show that genuine enthusiasm for 'social reform' which characterised the early pioneers," he said.[410]

Had the co-operative movement engaged more actively, it is possible that there would have been a much stronger co-operative housing tradition to build on in Britain later in the twentieth century. Perhaps that much-repeated call for a model where local authorities funded and tenant societies ran social housing might have had a better chance of success – although we do need to recognise that the Labour Party was moving increasingly in the direction of a stateist approach to policy by the time it first took power in 1923, discarding some of the working-class self-help tendencies which had been there in the labour movement at an earlier period.

The opportunity of having a stronger co-operative input into housing reform in the latter years of the nineteenth century was in any case compromised by the bitter dispute within the movement, of which (as we saw in Chapter 3) Henry Vivian and the Labour Association represented one side of the argument. Given the antagonism which could be engendered both by and towards those advocating co-partnership the fact that many of the early housing societies were so closely linked to co-partnership was not particularly helpful. Certainly it may have discouraged the Co-operative Wholesale Society and the Scottish CWS from considering more engagement in the provision of housing.[411]

Henry Vivian's role in building the co-partnership tenants' movement has been rightly acknowledged as an important one and he was a tireless advocate for the model which he was promoting. His energy and his vision achieved much. However his powerful position at CTL was not without a downside and his legacy can be seen as problematic. Certainly the after-life of CTL was unfortunate for many of the CTL-affiliated societies who found themselves caught up in the various property company deals which were undertaken later on. (The three former CTL-affiliated societies which are operating today – Anchor Tenants, Derwentwater Tenants and Manchester Tenants – did well to escape this fate.)

Vivian's burgeoning career as a politician and his growing disenchantment with tenant engagement (one might even say, with democratic governance) was also unhelpful. As we have seen, in several cases it engendered a resentment among tenants. It also had a long-term effect: by giving institutional power via the voting procedures in the rule books to external investors, it created the future opportunity for societies to be asset-stripped by those with the capital.

Johnston Birchall in his 1995 assessment of co-partnership housing maintained that "co-partnership had always been an unstable mix of outside investors and tenants". The pact implied by co-partnership ideology, that investor interests and the interests of tenant members of their societies could be satisfactorily united, could not hold, he argued. It was not necessarily always the investors who won out: Birchall also pointed out that in some instances societies were "asset-stripped from the other direction, when the tenants themselves decided to wind up the companies".[412] The most recent demutualisation, at Sevenoaks, could be seen as falling into this category.

Demutualisation is often opposed by co-operators instinctively, on sentimental grounds. It is rightly seen as one-way process from which there is no coming back. However, much more fundamentally, demutualisation is an inequitable process. It involves the distribution of collectively-held assets which have been built up usually over many generations to those individuals who happen to be members of a society at the time of demutualisation. There remain significant questions to be addressed by the co-operative movement as to how inter-generational equity can be better integrated within long-term co-operative structures, and this issue has not received the attention it might have done from co-operative theorists and practitioners. Nevertheless demutualisation is self-evidently not a way to achieve this.

However there is something of a conundrum at the heart of the life of some of the ten remaining pre-1919 societies, and that is the extent to which they should be run simply to maximise short-term financial benefits for current individual members rather than advancing the longer-term interests of the society as a collective entity. Tenant members of some societies have argued that their organisation's resources and reserves should simply be used to keep rent levels as low as possible. The corollary has been that some tenants have opposed moves by their societies to acquire further properties or to buy back houses previously sold off: why squander financial resources on acquisitions when these could be used to subsidise rents?

This is a complex issue, and it focuses attention on the challenge in a co-operatively run housing society of seeking a balance between individual interests and the good of the whole organisation. To an extent the question hinges on whether the societies believe themselves to be simply co-operatives being run for the benefit just of their co-op members, or community benefit societies, there to play a wider role in meeting the need for affordable housing. The answer is not always clear-cut. Both models are possible under the Co-operative and Community Benefit Societies Act, the legislation which in 2014 replaced the old Industrial and Provident Societies Acts.

Given the way that the human need for a home to live in has been successfully commodified by market forces in our society, capital is another issue that demands our consideration. Capital – the need for it, the shortage of it – was an issue for tenant housing societies before the First World War and it is also something today's community-led housing sector has to confront. By its nature, building houses requires significant short-term expenditure in exchange for a long-term asset on which the short-term returns are usually lower than would be obtained elsewhere. There is, after all, a reason why building society returns to their savers tend to be lower than those obtainable from the equity markets.

As we have seen, the CTL and its affiliates (as well as several of the non-CTL societies) tapped in to the supply of what we would now call 'ethical investment' funds. CTL's claim of having raised in excess of £300,000 by 1914 is a significant achievement, perhaps equivalent to around £40m today. Nevertheless CTL still found itself unable to break out from its niche to appeal to mainstream investors, and it also failed to develop the necessary investment infrastructure to enable its investors to easily realise their assets when they needed their funds returned. Despite considerable endeavour in recent years, some of these problems still remain unresolved for those promoting 'community shares' today.

Thomas Marr was undoubtedly right to declare in 1916 that it was "obvious that much more capital must be available" for societies if they were to be able to blossom in the post-1919 conditions faced by Britain. Government grant subsidy was absolutely necessary then (as it is today for those engaged in building social housing), but the arrangements established by the Addison Act did not in the end solve societies' funding problems. The residual 25% gap between maximum PWLB lending and total capital costs proved very challenging to bridge. Ironically – ironic, given that back in 1884 Ben Jones had been trying to find a new way of creating decent housing which did not rely on traditional philanthropy – those ventures which did progress were often those where a philanthropist or a well-intentioned landowner stepped in: David

Davies for the garden suburbs in Wales, the Earl of Onslow at Onslow village, and so on. And this in turn affected the outcome: there was little chance of much of a co-operative form of tenancy developing in those societies where a well-heeled investor held the purse-strings.

The theory, of course, was that over time the external investors would withdraw from the scene. As Ernest Betham (writing as E.B.) put it in 1910, "As the years pass and the Society's borrowed capital is gradually repaid the time will approach when the estate will become the property of the tenant-shareholders".[413] If we examine the societies which *have* continued to the present day, it does seem that the chief element to their survival has been that they have over the years managed to repay the original borrowings from external investors. The key period appears to have been the decades following the Second World War, and the process seems often to have been promoted by one or more influential individuals who understood the importance of removing power from non-resident members of their society. (It is significant that, where these societies today do continue to have shares or loans held by non-members, these are almost entirely residual and the holders have little or no financial reward or decision-making entitlement.)

How much of a distinction should we draw between those early societies which were clearly top-down in their development and those such as Anchor Tenants and Manchester Tenants which, at least initially, were much more the result of direct working-class endeavour? It is perhaps relevant that, although in both Leicester and Manchester the societies had to bring in external capital, these latter two societies have survived while others have disappeared.

But working-class-led societies proved to be the exception. The regrettable conclusion in relation to the issue of capital probably has to be that, in the period we have been considering, a widespread independent and fully democratic co-operative housing sector comparable to the member-run distributive co-operative societies that flourished in so many towns and villages simply could not be easily established. Unlike co-operative grocery stores, the challenge of finding the necessary finance to build a large and vibrant housing sector based on working-class self-help was just too great.

What then about the linked issue of tenant engagement? According to Henry Aldridge, one of the original founders of the National Housing Reform Council, future success for housing societies would depend on getting this right: "Tenants must be brought into more real co-partnership in the future," he maintained in 1915 (the trend, of course, had been in the opposite direction).[414] Here, too, we can see parallels with our own times, for what Aldridge was calling for is now a live issue in housing policy. For example, the Regulator of Social Housing, the body which oversees housing associations and the social housing sector in most of England, has produced its Tenant Involvement and Empowerment Standard which it requires its regulated housing providers to adhere to. The issue relates among other things to housing association governance, as associations (and for that matter Community Land Trusts) do not have the accountability provided for council housing – in theory at least – through local government democratic procedures. Other forms of democracy have to be created. This is an area where, it would be good to think, today's Community Land Trusts may be well-placed to take a lead.

The growth of community-led housing, mentioned at the start of this book's Introduction, does indeed suggest that there is another opportunity today to explore innovative collective solutions to the housing crisis, of the kind which Ben Jones, Sybella Gurney, John Nettlefold, Thomas Marr, Henry Vivian and all their colleagues and collaborators were trying to pursue more than a century ago. Municipal housing provision has been cut back, both by the Thatcher government's Right to Buy legislation and more recently by asset stock transfers to housing associations, and while some councils continue to run directly-controlled housing departments and a small number are actively trying to build new affordable homes for rent the hegemony that council housing enjoyed in social housing provision for much of the last century is over.

John Nettlefold, committed Liberal that he was, would probably have welcomed the decline in councils' engagement in housing. Writing in 1914, he asserted that "The great advantage of co-partnership housing over municipal house building is that in the former case people are helped to help themselves whereas in the latter everything is done for them".[415] But there is also a latent, and much more radical, current to be tapped into when it comes to collective forms of housing provision, one which goes back to nineteenth-century working-class self-organisation. Holyoake's title for his Rochdale Pioneers book, *Self-help by the People*, perhaps says it all.

The academic Michael Harloe, in an appraisal of the different theories behind social housing provision, talks of the early co-operative model which, he says, was based on self-organisation and self-management and which he argues could have provided the basis for an alternative to the "mass, bureaucratised welfare-state housing provision" offered by social-democratic parties in Europe.[416] Matthew Thompson, in his recent book on Liverpool's history of co-operative housing endeavour, also locates what he calls collective housing alternatives within the "relatively hidden traditions of utopian socialism, libertarian communism and democratic socialism" in Britain.[417]

So it is time to think again creatively about how we can bring about most effectively the affordable housing that our country still today desperately needs. In this context the pre-1919 efforts that so many people voluntarily put in to developing working-class housing through those pioneer housing societies deserve both remembering and studying. That there were problems and disagreements is clear. But there were also achievements to celebrate, together with a sense of shared purpose.

"Though Government can and ought to help in these matters, there is no need to wait for that Governmental action before work of a good kind can be accomplished," said Leicester's Amos Mann in 1914.[418] One of Mann's Anchor Tenants neighbours, a contributor to the estate's newspaper who simply used the pen-name 'Forward', can have the last word:

"We are all I hope ambitious enough to desire that it may with truth be said concerning us, that not only did we build a Garden Suburb where we and ours might enjoy the pure air, the song of the birds, the fragrance of the flowers, and the beauty of field and hedgerow, but also did what we could to make life brighter, happier and more joyous".[419]

GAZETTEER

This A-Z Gazetteer lists those cities and towns where a co-operative/co-partnership housing society was either established or was at least discussed. This should be treated very much as a provisional list, and more research into individual initiatives – particularly more research in local archives by local historians – would be valuable. For each entry I try to identify one or more potentially helpful starting point(s) for research, including where relevant reference to publications listed in the bibliography. I have tended to omit developments which were entirely commercial in nature even if they followed garden village/suburb principles of design, although a few borderline cases are included (Shirehampton, Glyn Cory, Welsh Garden Cities Ltd, etc). I have also included some societies established after 1919.

More than elsewhere in this book I am conscious that there are likely to be omissions and errors in this list. There is much scope for others to refine what is here.

Websites referenced have been accessed during late 2022. For abbreviations used, see below.

Aberaman
Development by Welsh Garden Cities Ltd, including co-partnership element. GCTP, Feb. 1915.

Abercarn
Development by Welsh Garden Cities Ltd, for sale rather than tenancy. GCTP, Feb. 1915.

Aberdaron (N Wales)
Aberdaron Co-operative Housing Society registered 1908. Links to co-operatively run granite quarries. See article by Michael Statham in *Journal of Co-operative Studies*, Winter 2020, Vol. 53, No. 3 (No. 160).

Acton
Welsh TPHT and GWR. See above, chapter 13.

Alexandria
Vale of Leven Tenants. For workers of the Argyll Motor Works. Culpin (1913); GCTP, Oct. 1913; Rosenburg (2016).

Alkrington (Middleton)
Alkrington Housing Society (Alkrington Garden Village) reportedly included some co-partnership housing within a larger–scale development. Culpin (1913); GCTP May 1911, Sep. 1911, July 1913.

Barry
Major development of Welsh Town Planning & Housing Trust. GCTP Oct. 1914, Oct.-Nov. 1915; Lloyd (1952), See above, chapters 11, 12. Later Welsh TPHT/GWR development on same land. Barry Garden Suburb Residents Facebook group; Vale of Glamorgan: Barry Garden Suburb Conservation Area, Appraisal and Management Plan (2009); https://coflein.gov.uk/en/site/407670/.

Berkhamsted
Early attempt (LCP, May 1906), later reports of Berkhamsted Tenants initiative to build 24 houses in Cross Oak Rd (CP, Dec. 1912, Jan. 1913, Mar. 1914). See Shepherd (2019).

Bournville
Bournville Tenants. LCP, July 1906; Dale (1907); Abercrombie (1910); Cadbury Brothers (1922, 1928); Henslowe (1984); Harrison (1999); Taylor (2004); Bournville Tenants (2006); Bridgman (2021); Bibby (2022); https://bournvil-letenants.blogspot.com/2018/05/welcome.html See above, chapters 5, 8, 13. Continuing today.
Separately in Bournville: St George's Court (co-operative housekeeping flats) from Residential Flats Ltd (Pearson, 1988).

Brent
Brent Garden Village (Finchley) Society, formed 1910 by co-operative housekeeping advocate Alice Melvin (Pearson, 1988). See also Golders Green, Hampstead. See above, chapter 10.

Bridge of Weir
Proposed society under auspices of Rural Co-partnership Housing Association. Culpin (1913), GCTP, June 1913. Assume did not progress.

Brighton
Brighton and Sussex Tenants. Early mention LCP, Jan. 1906; also mentioned in Labour Co-partnership Association annual report year ending Aug. 31 1906; CP, Aug. 1908. Did not progress. See above, chapter 5.

Bristol – see Shirehampton

Brockenhurst
Early mention LCP, Aug. 1905; mentioned also in Appendix of Labour Co-partnership Association annual report year ending June 30 1905. Reference to registration of New Forest Tenants, CP, Aug. 1908. Did not progress. See above, chapter 5.

Bromley
Bromley Tenants. Early mention LCP, Dec. 1905; Gurney (1906); Labour Co-partnership Association annual report 1906-7. Did not progress.

Budleigh (Devon)
Rural Co-partnership Housing Association venture on 4 acres. Culpin (1913). Few other references.

Burnage (Manchester)
Manchester Tenants Ltd. Frequently reported in LCP/CP, GC/GCTP.
Manchester Tenants (1956), Harrison (1976), Jackson and Nadin (2006);
Burnage Garden Village Facebook group. Minute books held by current society
secretary. See above, chapters 5-7, 9, 10, 13. Continuing today.

Burry Port
Welsh TPHT development, initially during First World War for Ministry of
Munitions. See above, chapter 13.

Bury – see Pilsworth and Unsworth

Byfleet
Birchwood Tenants Ltd successful development. CP, June 1911; Wakeford (2012)
and website www.wokinghistory.org; Woking Borough Council, The Heritage of
Woking (2000). See above, chapter 8.

Caerphilly
Welsh TPHT and GWR. See above, chapter 13.

Camberwell – see Tenant Co-operators

Cardiff: Glyn Cory (Coryndon, Peterston-super-Ely)
Garden village progressed by Wales businessmen John and Reginald Cory,
probably conventional in organisation. https://coflein.gov.uk/en/site/302107/

Cardiff: Rhiwbina
Cardiff Workers' Co-operative Garden Village Society, later name changed to
Rhiwbina Garden Village Ltd. Housing Reform Company project, taken over by
Welsh TPHT. See Davies (2011). See above, chapters 6, 11, 13.

Carlisle (Newby West)
Few references found. Reported by Culpin (1913); society represented at
GCTPA event in 1916. See above, chapter 11.

Chipping Norton
Mention of co-operative society proposal for housing, Culpin (1913).

Clydebank
Early mention, GCTP May 1911 (West of Scotland GCTPA branch involved);
Culpin (1913). Problems raising finance, appears not to have progressed.

Coventry
Early mention GCTP, June 1911; Culpin (1913). Plans curtailed by First World
War. Deregistered 1992. See above, chapters 11, 12.

Cuffley (Herts)
Culpin (1913); delegate at GCTPA event 1916; Birchall (Planning Perspectives,
1995) describes the society as Cuffley Co-operative Freeholders.

Datchet
Development by Rural Co-partnership Housing Association. Culpin (1913),
GCTP, Jan. 1915. See above, chapter 11. Deregistered 1999.

Didsbury
Surprisingly little recorded. First mention GC Dec. 1907; Culpin (1913);
Harrison (1976). Two small Didsbury Garden Suburb societies formed.

Ealing
Ealing Tenants (1912); Tims (1966); Reid (2000). See above, particularly chapter 3.

East Grinstead
No information, except for deregistration record of East Grinstead Tenants on Mutuals Register 2011. A much later society?

Eastbourne
Culpin (1913) mentions Hampden Park, Eastbourne as a charitable venture.

Eastcote
Housing built here by Ruislip Manor Cottage Society. Bowlt (2011). See above, chapter 11.

Eccles (nr. Maidstone)
Proposed co-partnership mentioned CP Aug. 1905, did not progress.

Edlington (Yorks)
Colliery village built between 1909 and 1922. Edlington Co-operative Tenants purchased ten acres to develop part of site in 1914. Not clear that the society was independent of the colliery company. Records at Doncaster Archives (not consulted).

Epsom – see Tenant Co-operators

Fairfield (Manchester)
GCTP June 1913; Harrison (1976); Harrison in Sutcliffe (ed)(1981); 1913 Prospectus held by current society secretary. See above, chapters 11, 12. Continuing today.

Fallings Park (Wolverhampton)
CP April, July 1907; Nettlefold (1908); Abercrombie (1910), Tims (1966); Wolverhampton History and Heritage website, http://www.historywebsite. co.uk/articles/FallingsPark/gardensuburb.htm. See above, chapters 5, 8.

Fernhill (Rhondda)
Development by Welsh Garden Cities Ltd, including co-partnership element. GCTP, Feb. 1915.

Fishguard
Birchall (Planning Perspectives, 1995) reports a Welsh TPHT/GWR development here (see above, chapter 13); however there is no mention of a Fishguard development in Lloyd (1952).

Gilfach Goch
Development by Welsh Garden Cities Ltd, including co-partnership element. GCTP, Feb. 1915.

Glasgow – see Westerton

Glastonbury
Mention of new society being advised by CTL in CP, March 1914; delegate at GCTPA conference in 1919. Little other documentation appears to be available. See also Street.

Golders Green (Melvin Hall)
Melvin Hall Co-operative Housekeeping and Service Society (Golders Green) Ltd: Pearson (1988). See also Brent, Hampstead. See above, chapter 10.

Gorseinon
Development by Welsh Garden Cities Ltd, including co-partnership element. GCTP, Feb. 1915.

Gourock
Gourock Garden Suburb Tenants Ltd, Gourock & Greenock Tenants Ltd. Rosenburg (2016). See above, chapter 11.

Greenock
Greenock Garden Suburb Tenants Ltd, Gourock & Greenock Tenants Ltd. Rosenburg (2016). See above, chapter 11.

Gwauncaergurwen
Proposed development of Housing Reform Company mentioned GCTP May 1913.

Hadleigh, Suffolk
Development by Rural Co-partnership Housing Association in Cranworth Rd. See above, chapter 11. Continuing today.

Hampstead
Second Melvin Hall Cooperative Housekeeping Society, later Priory Residential Society Ltd. Initiative of Alice Melvin for co-operative housekeeping venture (five houses in Priory Rd). Pearson (1988). See also Golders Green, Brent.

Hampstead Garden Suburb
Hampstead Tenants, Second Hampstead Tenants, Oakwood Tenants, Hampstead Heath Extension Tenants; also Third Hampstead Tenants (appears to have not developed). Closely linked to CTL. Green (1977). See above, chapters 3, 7-9, 11.

Harborne (Birmingham)
Culpin (1913); Nettlefold (1914); Harborne Tenants (1980); Hippisley-Cox (2009). Much useful information on two websites: http://www.moorpoolgardensuburb.co.uk/index.html;
http://www.moorpoolheritagetrust.org.uk/heritage/history.html

Haslemere
Haslemere Tenants Ltd. Early references in GCTP May 1911, CP Nov. 1911; delegate at 1916 GCTPA event. See also Hindhead.

Hayes (Middx)
Welsh TPHT and GWR. See above, chapter 13.

Hebden Bridge
Proposed garden village as part of Eaves Bottom Self-Help Manufacturers Society, an unsuccessful productive co-operative 1907-9. Bibby (2015).

Hengoed
Development by Welsh Garden Cities Ltd, including co-partnership element. GCTP, Feb. 1915.

Hereford
Hereford Co-operative Housing Society. Culpin (1913); Nettlefold (1914). See above, chapters 8, 9. Continuing today.

Highley (Shropshire)
Development by Welsh Garden Cities Ltd, including co-partnership element. GCTP, Feb. 1915.

Hindhead (Beacon Hill)
Reference to society being formed in 1905 (LCP, Aug. 1905), presumably by Aneurin Williams. Gurney (1906). Appears not to have taken off. See also Haslemere.

Horsforth (Leeds)
Horsforth Co-partnership Tenants Society registered 1919, deregistered 1991 (information from Mutuals Register). No other information has come to light.

Ilford
Early mention in GCTP, July 1910. GCTP July 1911 reports of a co-partnership scheme for Ilford Garden Suburb, by members of East London Garden Suburbs Association who would hold land jointly and own their houses individually.

Keswick
Derwentwater Tenants Ltd. Frequent mentions in GCTP and CP, including CP Sep. 1909; Wilkinson (2005). See above, Introduction and chapter 8. Continuing today.

Kings Norton (Birmingham)
Report of meeting with H. Vivian (LCP, July 1906); King's Norton Tenants registered 1908 (CP Aug. 1908). Appears not to have progressed.

Knebworth
Knebworth Tenants Ltd. Culpin (1913). See above, chapters 11, 13. Continuing today.

Leeds – see Horsforth

Leicester: Humberstone Garden Suburb
Anchor Tenants Ltd. Mann (1914); Forrester (1984); Pawson n.d., [c. 2008]. See https://anchorhistory.uk/index.php. See above, chapters 4-8, 12-13. Continuing today.

Letchworth
Garden City Tenants. Gurney (1906). Frequent references in LCP/CP, GC/GCTP. See above, chapters 4-6, 8.
Letchworth Co-operative Homes Ltd (Homesgarth). CN Oct. 12 1907. Pearson (1988). See above, chapter 10.

Liverpool (Wavertree)
Liverpool Tenants. CP, Aug. 1910, and many references in CP in following years; Chitty (1999), Wavertree Society website at http://wavsoc.awardspace.info/wgs/. See above, chapters 6, 7, 13.

Llanelli
Mention of proposal linked to co-op society (GCTP, June 1911).
Development by Welsh Garden Cities Ltd, for sale rather than tenancy. GCTP, Feb. 1915.

Llanidloes
Llanidloes Garden Suburb, developed by the Welsh TPHT. GCTP, Oct. 1914; Lloyd (1952). Archive records 1913-1927 held by the National Library of Wales, ref. GB 210 1997 Donation E2. See above, chapter 11.

Machynlleth
Machynlleth Garden Village, developed by the Welsh TPHT. Culpin (1913); GCTP, Jan. 1914, Oct. 1914; Lloyd (1952). https://coflein.gov.uk/en/site/409332/details/machynlleth-garden-village-tregerddi-machynlleth-newtown-road-machynlleth. See above, chapter 11.

Malvern
Development by Malvern branch of National Council of Women. Sayle (1924), Tims (1966). See above, chapter 13.

Manchester – see Burnage, Fairfield, Didsbury

Margam (Port Talbot)
Birchall (Planning Perspectives, 1995) mentions Margam Co-operative Homes Ltd as being established in 1922, as a GWR initiative.

Merthyr (Gellifaelog/Pen-y-darren)
Merthyr Co-operative Garden Village. Formed under auspices of Trades and Labour Council (GCTP, May 1912). Culpin (1913). https://coflein.gov.uk/en/site/409904/details/merthyr-co-operative-garden-village-garden-city-gelli-faeloggellyfaelog-merthyr-tydfil. In addition, GCTP, Aug. 1913 mentions plans drawn up by R. Unwin for a development near Dowlais; this may be a separate venture.

Newark
Single mention (GCTP, June 1911) of proposal.

Newcastle-upon-Tyne (Walker)
Plans for co-partnership estate abandoned 1915 (GCTP May 1915).

Newport (Mon.)
Reference to proposed development by Housing Reform Company, GCTP, Aug. 1913.

Newtown (Powys)
Proposed development by Welsh TPHT. See above, chapter 11.

Northwood, Middx
Housing built here by Ruislip Manor Cottage Society. Bowlt (2011). See above, chapter 11.

Ogmore Vale
Reference to proposed development by Housing Reform Company, GCTP, Aug. 1913.

Oldham
LCP, July 1906, Sep. 1906; CP, Jan. 1907; Culpin (1913). See above, chapters 5, 8.

Onslow (near Guildford)
GCTP, Dec. 1920; Onslow Village Conservation Area, Study and Character Appraisal, Guildford Borough Council, 2003. See above, chapter 13.

Otford (Kent)
Otford Small Holders Ltd. Development by Rural Co-partnership Housing Association. Culpin (1913), GCTP, Jan. 1915; delegate at GCTPA conference 1916. See above, chapter 11.

Oxford
Discussions 1906-7 (CP, May 1906, CP Jan. 1907). Did not progress.

Pengam (Rhymney Valley)
Development by Welsh Garden Cities Ltd, including co-partnership element. GCTP, Feb. 1915.

Penge – see Tenant Co-operators

Penkhull – see Stoke-on-Trent

Penzance
Welsh TPHT and GWR. See above, chapter 13.

Petersfield
Development by Rural Co-partnership Housing Association. Culpin (1913). See above, chapter 11.

Pilsworth & Unsworth (Bury)
Pilsworth and Unsworth Garden Village Ltd. Mutuals Register: registered 1919, deregistered 1997. Tims (1966).

Plashet (East Ham) – see Tenant Co-operators

Plymouth
Welsh TPHT and GWR. See above, chapter 13.

Pontardulais
Development by Welsh Garden Cities Ltd, for sale rather than tenancy. GCTP, Feb. 1915.

Pontymoile
Development by Welsh Garden Cities Ltd, for sale rather than tenancy. GCTP, Feb. 1915.

Renfrew
Renfrew Garden Suburb Tenants. Details in Rosenburg (2016).

Ruabon
Report in LCP, May 1906 of co-partnership society being contemplated. Not progressed.

Rubery (nr Bromsgrove)
Very little information. Rubery and Eachway Tenants reportedly registered 1908 (CP Aug. 1908); Tims (1966) says the society disaffiliated from CTL.

Rudheath (Ches)
Rudheath Tenants. Henry Vivian director. Represented at GCTPA event in 1916. See also Winnington.

Ruislip
Ruislip Manor Cottage Society. Bowlt (2011). See above, chapter 11. Continuing today.

Rushden
Mention of proposal linked to co-operative society, perhaps a productive co-operative (GCTP, June 1911).

Sealand (Flint)
CP, Aug. 1910; Culpin (1913). See above, chapters 8, 9, 13.

Sevenoaks
Culpin (1913); Reid (2001). See above, chapters 4, 5, 8, 13.

Severn Tunnel
Welsh TPHT and GWR. See above, chapter 13.

Sheffield
Report in LCP, Oct. 1905 of co-partnership society being contemplated. Not progressed.

Shilbottle
CWS owned colliery. Redfern (1938, p. 271) says CWS created a village of 170 houses.

Shirehampton
Brief mentions in GCTP 1911 and 1918, Culpin (1913). Appears to have been commercial development. Dockers' Union reportedly involved.

Sidmouth
Public meeting, co-partnership proposed by Medical Officer of Health, see CP, Aug. 1912. Did not progress.

Snowdown and Betteshanger (Kent)
Snowdown and Betteshanger Tenants. Housing for colliery workers in the East Kent coalfield, 1928 (Brading, 1973).

Somerdale (near Keynsham)
Tims (1966) mentions tenant-shareholders at Somerdale Village Housing Society Ltd (1925).

Somersham (Hunts)
Development by Rural Co-partnership Housing Association. See above, chapter 11. Allotment and smallholding society also formed 1920, and continuing today.

St Mawes
Development by Rural Co-partnership Housing Association. See above, chapter 11. Continuing today.

Stirling Homesteads
Culpin (1913); Aitken et al (1984); Smyth and Robertson (2017). See above, chapter 8.

Stoke on Trent (Penkhull)
Culpin (1913); Taylor (1997). See above, chapters 6, 7, 8, 9, 13.

Street (Som.)
Street Tenants. Considerable archive material held by the Alfred Gillett Trust in Street, including a minute book dated 1914–1934 (ref: CJC/211/4), prospectuses, rules of the society, loan stock and share certificate (ref No1/31/4), and a small bundle of correspondence relating to the society (ref: BC/309/3). See also Glastonbury.

Sutton
'Rose Hill estate'. Meetings in Sutton, Carshalton, Wallington reported 1909 (CP Aug. 1909); GCTP July 1913; London Borough of Sutton, Sutton Garden Suburb Conservation Area Character Appraisal (2006).

Swansea
Welsh TPHT and GWR. See above, chapter 13.

Swansea Valley
Development by Welsh Garden Cities Ltd, including co-partnership element. GCTP, Feb. 1915.

Tenant Co-operators Ltd
Hodgkin (1901), Yerbury (1913). See above, chapter 2.

Thorne (near Doncaster)
Darlington Grove Garden Suburb, Moorends: Culpin (1913) mentions an initiative by a group of working builders to build 26 houses.

Toddington (Cotswolds)
CP, May 1918 reports that "Mr E. Bent of Morning Star Sundries Society has taken over a fruit farm in the Cotswolds" where he hopes to grow a "rural commonwealth with co-partnership village". See also CP, July 1919.

Truro
Welsh TPHT and GWR. See above, chapter 13.

Upton Park – see Tenant Co-operators

Vauxhall
Reference to Vauxhall Tenant Co-operators in papers held in the National Archives, ref. BT 31/5600/38992. Incorporated 1893, dissolved before 1916. (Not consulted.)

Vale of Leven – see Alexandria

Warrington
CP, Mar. 1907, Sep. 1907; CP Nov. 1908; Culpin (1913), Tims (1966). See above, chapter 8. Separately, CP, Mar. 1911 reports that Warrington Co-operative Society has plans for a Garden Suburb, has erected three bungalows for members of the society to live in rent free, tenants being selected on length of service to society.

Wavertree – see Liverpool

Wayford (Norfolk)
Reference to Wayford Tenants, CP, Nov. 1909; GCTP Nov. 1909. See above, chapter 6.

Welwyn
Second 'Garden City'. Co-operative housekeeping scheme Guessens Court, 1924-5 (Pearson, 1988). See above, chapter 13.

Westerton (Garscube)
Glasgow Garden Suburb Tenants: CP, Jan. 1912; Whitelaw (1992); Rosenburg (2016). See above, chapter 11.

Weston Rhyn (Shropshire)
Weston Rhyn Tenants. Development of Welsh Town Planning and Housing Trust. GCTP Oct. 1914; Welsh TPHT Fourth Annual Report (1917); Lloyd (1952). See above, chapter 11.

Wigton (Cumberland)
Report in GC, Jan. 1908 of proposed garden suburb at Brackenlands. Appears not to have been progressed.

Winchester
Report in LCP, May 1906 of co-partnership society being contemplated. Not progressed. Separate report, CP, Feb. 1911, of offer of land from the Ecclesiastical Commissioners, "a number of gentlemen had formed themselves into a Working Men's Housing Society".

Wingland (Lincs)
Co-partnership Farms: farm of 110 acres acquired 1908 (CP, Feb. 1908; GCTP May-June 1908). Henry Vivian was director. No housing believed to have been associated with this venture.

Winnington (Ches)
Proposed society, worked with CTL (CP, March 1914). See also Rudheath.

Woking
Woking Garden Suburb, initiative of Woking Co-operative Society. CP, July 1912, Aug. 1913; Culpin (1913), p. 60; Woking Borough Council, The Heritage of Woking (2000); Pictorial Souvenir of Twenty-One Years' Work of the Woking Co-operative Society 1899-1920. See above, chapter 11.

Worcester
Worcester Tenants. Culpin (1913); GCTP, Sep. 1913. Society shown on Mutuals Register as having deregistered in 1986. See above, chapter 11.

Wrexham
Wrexham Tenants. Major development of Welsh Town Planning and Housing Trust. CP, Oct. 1914, June 1917; Lloyd (1952). See above, chapter 11.

Wrotham (near Sevenoaks)
Mutuals Register shows Wrotham Tenants Ltd established 1913, deregistered 1999. Linked to Sevenoaks Tenants' initiatives?

Ynysybwl
Ynysybwl Co-operative Garden Village Society established by Miners' Lodge 1913, but did not progress. Culpin (1913).

ABBREVIATIONS

The following abbreviations have been used:

CIU: Club and Institute Union

CLT: Community Land Trust

CN: Co-operative News

CP: Co-partnership magazine (Labour Co-partnership before 1907)

CPF: Co-operative Productive Federation

CTL: Co-partnership Tenants Ltd

CWS: Co-operative Wholesale Society

GC: Garden City magazine (renamed Garden Cities and Town Planning in March 1908) (A first 'New series' launched in 1906)

GCA: Garden City Association (became GCTPA, Aug. 1909)

GCTP: Garden Cities and Town Planning magazine. (Garden City before March 1908. A second 'New series' launched in 1911)

GCTPA: Garden Cities and Town Planning Association (later Town and Country Planning Association)

GWR: Great Western Railway

ILP: Independent Labour Party

KCHT: Keswick Community Housing Trust

LCP: Labour Co-Partnership magazine (renamed Co-partnership in 1907)

LGB: Local Government Board

LNS: Land Nationalisation Society

PUS: Public Utility Society

PWLB: Public Works Loan Board

RACS: Royal Arsenal Co-operative Society

TUC: Trades Union Congress

WCG: Women's Co-operative Guild

Welsh TPHT: Welsh Town Planning and Housing Trust

WFL: Women's Freedom League

ACKNOWLEDGEMENTS

I am grateful for the help and encouragement many people have given me during the preparation of this book. A particular thank you needs to go to Gillian Lonergan, for so many years the co-operative movement's much-respected Archivist, for the painstaking attention she has given in undertaking the copy-editing of the text for me.

I received a warm welcome when I visited many of the still thriving pre-1919 housing societies during the course of my research. Thanks to Liz Newman, Lizzy Quinan, Hannah Pryce (Bournville), Alison McCarten, Ali Ronan, Amanda Wait, Antonette Hunter (Burnage), Stephen Williams, John Penlington (Fairfield), Malcolm Self, Steven Grimpsey (Hadleigh), Tim Reed (Hereford), Philip Pridmore (Keswick), Lynne Farr, Pat Lee, Peter Calver (Knebworth), John Whitford (St Mawes), Simon Brown, Felicity Holt (Ruislip Manor). My thanks also to Alan Henderson (Brentham Society Archivist), Christine Rafferty (Hampstead Garden Suburb Archives Trust), Ian Pawson (Anchor Tenants history), Mike Chitty (Wavertree Society), Julie Mather (Alfred Gillett Trust, Street, Somerset), Stoke-on-Trent Museums, and Jenny Sherwood (Berkhamsted Local History and Museum Society). Particular thanks to Bill and Wendy Bewley (Keswick CHT), Tom Chance and his colleagues at the Community Land Trust Network, and my good friends and former colleagues at Calder Valley CLT.

Finally, a thank you to my fellow members of Gritstone Publishing Co-operative Chiz Dakin, Chris Goddard, Eileen Jones, Andrew McCloy, Laurence Rose and Colin Speakman for their support.

BIBLIOGRAPHY

(Websites included in the bibliography and endnotes were accessed during late 2022)

Archives and online databases
Derwentwater Tenants (minute and share books)
Financial Conduct Authority, Mutuals Register (online)
Hereford Tenants (minute books)
Herefordshire Archive and Records Centre
Knebworth Tenants (minute books)
Manchester Tenants (minute books)
National Archives
Warwick Modern Records Centre (Labour Co-partnership Association)
Women's Co-operative Guild (Women's Library, British Library of Political and Economic Science)

Books and journal articles up to 1918
Abercrombie, P., 'Modern Town Planning in England: A Comparative Review of "Garden City" Schemes in England' in *Town Planning Review*, Vol. 1, No. 1 (Apr. 1910), pp. 18-38
---, 'Modern Town Planning in England: A Comparative Review of "Garden City" Schemes in England Part II' in *Town Planning Review*, Vol. 1, No. 2 (July 1910), pp. 111-128
Allan, J. and Gray, J.C., *The Co-operative Union: its necessity and its advantages*, Manchester: Co-operative Union, 1892
Aves, E., *Co-operative Industry*, London: Methuen, 1907
Barnett, H., 'A Garden Suburb at Hampstead' in *The Contemporary Review*, No. 87, Jan. 1 1905, pp. 231-237
E.B., (Betham, Ernest) *Co-partnership in Housing*, London: Co-partnership Publishers, 1910
---, 'Practical Housing and Town Planning' in *Charity Organisation Review*, New Series, Vol. 23, No. 138 (June 1908), pp. 325-331
Board of Trade, *The Cost of Living of the Working Classes, Report of an Enquiry by the Board of Trade into Working Class Rents, Housing and Retail Prices*, London: H.M.S.O., 1908

Brabrook, E.W., 'Friendly Societies and Similar Institutions' in *Journal of the Statistical Society of London*, Vol. 38, No. 2 (June 1875), pp. 185-214

Bournville Tenants Ltd, *Bournville Tenants Ltd* (pamphlet), Bournville: Bournville Tenants, n.d., [1909 or 1910]

Carpenter, E., *My Days and Dreams*, London: G. Allen and Unwin, 1916

Champion, H.H. and Jones, B., *Co-operation versus Socialism*, Manchester: Central Board, Co-operative Union, 1887

Cheap Cottages Exhibition, *Book of the Cheap Cottages Exhibition*, London: The County Gentleman and Land and Water, 1905

Co-partnership Tenants Housing Council, *Garden Suburbs, Villages and Homes*, London: Co-partnership Tenants Housing Council, 1906

---, *Garden Suburbs, Villages and Homes, Vol. 2* (Summer 1912), London: Co-operative Tenants Housing Council, 1912

Cochrane, C., 'The Letchworth Housing Exhibition' in *Charity Organisation Review*, New Series, Vol. 18, No. 107 (Nov. 1905)

Crotch, W.W., *The Cottage Homes of England*, London: P. S. King & Son, 1901

Culpin, E.G., *The Garden City Movement Up to Date*, London: Garden Cities & Town Planning Association, 1913

Dale, J.A., 'Bournville' in *The Economic Review*, Vol. XVII, (Jan. 1907), pp. 13-27

Dickson-Poynder, Sir J.P., *The Housing Question*, London: Political Committee of the National Liberal Club, 1908

Ealing Tenants Ltd, *The Pioneer Co-Partnership Society*, London: Co-Partnership Publishers, 1912

Ede, W.M., *The attitude of the church to some of the social problems of town life*, Lecture 3, Cambridge: Cambridge University Press, 1896

Edwards, A.T., 'A Criticism of the Garden City Movement' in *Town Planning Review*, Vol. 4 (2), (July 1913) pp.150-157

---, 'A Further Criticism of the Garden City Movement' in *Town Planning Review*, Vol. 4, (4), (Jan. 1914), pp. 312-318

Fay, C.R., *Copartnership in Industry*, Cambridge: Cambridge University Press, 1913

George, W.I., *Engines of Social Progress*, London: A. and C. Black, 1907

Gilzean-Reid, H., *Housing the People: an example in cooperation*, London: Alexander Gardner, 1895

Gray, J.C., 'Co-operation and the poor', in *The Co-operative Wholesale Societies, England and Scotland, Annual for 1902*, Manchester: Co-operative Printing Society, 1902

Gurney, S., 'Co-Partnership in Housing' in *Charity Organisation Review*, New Series, Vol. 19, No. 109 (Jan. 1906), pp. 5-12

---, *Co-partnership in Housing in Town and Country* [written for Christian Social Union, reprinted in British Labour History Ephemera 1900-1926, World Microfilms 1973], n.d.

---, 'Housing Reform' in *Charity Organisation Review*, New Series, Vol. 21, No. 123 (Mar. 1907), pp. 131-140

Harborne Tenants Ltd, *Harborne Tenants*, Birmingham: Harborne Tenants, 1909

Hodgkin, H., 'Tenant Co-operators' in *Friends' Quarterly Examiner*, Vol. 35, No.137 (First Month 1901), pp. 53-63 [wrongly catalogued on JSTOR as 1890]

Hole, J., *The homes of the working classes*, London: Longmans Green, 1866

Howard, E., *Garden Cities of To-morrow*, London: Swan Sonnenschein, 1902 [rev. ed. of *To-morrow, a peaceful path to real reform*]

Johnston, J., *How to obtain healthy houses: municipal, co-operative, tenant co-operators, garden cities, private enterprise*, Manchester: Co-operative Printing Society, 1908

Jones, B., *Co-operative Production*, Oxford: The Clarendon Press, 1894

London County Council, *Housing of the Working Classes 1855-1912*, London: London County Council, 1913

Leppington, d'E, 'The Tenant's Point of View' in *Charity Organisation Review*, New Series, Vol. 25, No. 148 (Apr. 1909), pp. 179-195

Lloyd, H.D., *Labor Copartnership*, New York; London: Harper Brothers, 1898

Lumsden, M. [attrib.], 'Octavia Hill and the Housing Problem' in *Edinburgh Review*, Vol. 217, No. 444, Apr. 1913, pp. 452-465

McInnes, D, *How Co-operative Societies can supply their members with dwelling homes*, Manchester: Co-operative Union, 1899

Maddison, F., 'The Labour Co-partnership Association' in *The Economic Review*, Vol. XX, (July 1910) pp. 314-317

Mann, A., *Democracy in Industry, The Story of Twenty-One Years' Work of the Leicester Anchor Boot and Shoe Productive Society Ltd*, Leicester: Co-operative Printing Society, 1914

Mayo, C., *Co-operative House-building*, Kirkby Lonsdale: Women's Co-operative Guild, 1898

Mearns, A., *The Bitter Cry of Outcast London*, London: James Clarke, 1883

Napier-Clavering, C., *The History of Harborne Tenants Ltd*, n.d. [1908] [available from https://www.moorpoolhall.org.uk/heritage/history.html]

Nettlefold, J., *Practical Housing*, Letchworth: Garden City Press, 1908

---, *Practical Town Planning*, London: St Catherine Press, 1914

New Townsmen [Osborn, F.J., et al] *New Towns after the War*, London: J.M. Dent and Sons, 1918

Parker B. and Unwin, R., *The art of building a home*, London: Longmans, 1901

Potter, B., *The Diary of Beatrice Webb* [Typewritten transcript of Vols. 13-16, accessed at digital.library.lse.ac.uk]

Purdom, C.B., *The Garden City*, London: J.M. Dent and Sons, 1913

Reade, C. C., 'A Defence of the Garden City Movement' in *Town Planning Review*, Vol. 4, No. 3, Oct. 1913, pp. 245-251

Redfern, P., *The Story of the C.W.S., 1863-1913*, Manchester: Co-operative Wholesale Society, n.d. [1913]

Royal Commission on Housing of the Working Classes *Vol. II., Minutes of Evidence and Appendix as to England and Wales [Twenty-Sixth Day, Tuesday 1st July 1884]*, London: Eyre and Spottiswood, 1885 [Benjamin Jones evidence] (XXX Qs 13760-13847)

Royal Commission on Labour, *Fourth Report, Minutes of Evidence, Digest of Evidence, Indexes, Vol. IV, Appendix to Minutes of Evidence*, London: H.M.S.O., 1894 [Henry Vivian evidence]

Royal Select Committee on Town Holdings *Report from the Select Committee on Town Holdings, Together with the Proceedings of the Committee, Minutes of Evidence and Appendix*, London: Henry Hansard, 1887 [Benjamin Jones evidence] (XIII Qs 10635-11208)

Select Committee on Housing of the Working Classes Acts Amendment Bill, *Report and Special Report from the Select Committee on Housing of the Working Classes Acts Amendment Bill*, London: H.M.S.O., 1906

Solly, H., *Home Colonisation. Rehousing of the industrial classes; or Village Communities v. Town Rookeries*, London: Sonnenschein, 1884

Unwin, R., *Town Planning in Practice*, London; Leipsic: T. Fisher Unwin, 1909

Vivian, H., 'An Interesting Co-operative Housing Experiment' in *Co-operators Year Book 1902* [reproduced in Forrester (1984)]

---, 'A Novel Attempt at Co-operative Production in the Building Trades' in *The Economic Journal*, Vol. 6, No. 22 (June 1896), pp. 270-272

---, 'Co-partnership in Housing' in *The Economic Journal*, Vol. 15, No. 58 (June 1905), pp. 254-257

---, 'Co-partnership in Housing' in *The Economic Review*, Vol. XVI, pp. 76-81 (Jan. 1906)

---, 'Co-partnership in Housing' in *The Economic Review*, Vol. XVII, pp.199-202 (Apr. 1907)

---, *Co-partnership in Housing*, London: Co-partnership Tenants Ltd, n.d. [1910]

---, 'Co-partnership in Housing' in *Westminster Review*, Vol. 168, Dec. 1907, pp. 615-621

---, *Co-partnership in practice*, London: Labour Co-partnership Association, 1914

---, 'Garden Cities, Housing and Town Planning' in *Quarterly Review*, No. 431, Apr. 1912, pp. 493-515

---, *How Co-operative Production may be successfully applied to the building trades*, London: Labour Association, n.d. [1897?] [Held in the Modern Records Centre, MRC 310/4/2/1/12]

---, *(Some Experiments in) Community Making*, London: Co-partnership Publishers, n.d. [1912?]

Webb, C., *Co-operation as applied to domestic work*, Women's Co-operative Guild paper for Annual Meeting, Leicester, June 1893 [available British Library of Political and Economic Science, ref. Microfilm 69, Reel No. 3, coll. Misc. 258, Item 6, folio 11]

Webb, C. (ed.), *Industrial Co-operation*, 3rd Edition, Manchester: Co-operative Union, 1907

Williams, A., *Government by the Fit*, London: Labour Association, n.d. [1898?]

---, 'Co-operation in Housing and Town-Building' in *Co-operative Congress report*, Manchester: Co-operative Union, 1907

Wood, A., *Co-partnership housing, A Manual of Accounting*, London: Co-partnership Tenants Ltd, 1913

Yerbury, J. E., *A Short History of the Pioneer Society in Co-operative Housing*, London: The Committee of the Tenant Co-operators, 1913

Books and journal articles after 1918: local housing initiatives

Ackers, P., 'Experiments in Industrial Democracy: An Historical Assessment of the Leicestershire Boot and Shoe Co-operative Co-partnership Movement' in *Labor History*, Vol. 57, No. 4, 2016

Aitken, P., Cunningham, C. & McCutcheon, B., *The Homesteads: Stirling's Garden Suburb*, Stirling: the authors, 1984

Atkinson, S., 'Idealism, secrets and paranoia' in *The Mill* [online newspaper], Nov. 21 2020

Bournville Tenants, *100 years of Bournville Tenants Ltd 1906-2006*, Bournville: Bournville Tenants, 2006

Bowlt, E. M., *Ruislip Manor Cottage Society, The first hundred years*, Ruislip: Ruislip Manor Cottage Society, 2011

Cadbury Brothers, *Bournville Housing, a Description of the Housing Schemes of Cadbury Brothers Ltd and the Bournville Village Trust*, Bournville: Cadbury, 1922

---, *Bournville Housing, a Description of the Housing Schemes of the Bournville Village Trust and Cadbury Brothers Ltd, Sixth edition*, Bournville: Cadbury, n.d. [1928]

Chitty, M., *Discovering Historic Wavertree*, Liverpool: The Wavertree Society, 1999

Daunton, M., *Coal Metropolis: Cardiff 1870-1914*, Leicester: Leicester University Press, 1977

Davies, W., *Rhiwbina Garden Village: A history of Cardiff's Garden Suburb*, Cardiff: Rhiwbina Civic Society, 2011 [reprint of 1985 self-published book]

Dodge, M. and Ronan, A., *Celebrating Burnage Garden Village, Resource Booklet and Exhibition Catalogue*, Manchester, 2019

Green, B.G., *Hampstead Garden Suburb 1907-1977, A History*, London: Hampstead Garden Suburb Residents' Association, 1977

Greening, E.O., *A Pioneer Co-partnership*, London; Manchester; Leicester: Labour Co-Partnership Association; Co-operative Union; Leicester Co-operative Printing Society, 1923

Harborne Tenants, *Into the 1980s at Moor Pool*, 1980 [accessed http://www.moorpool.com/moorpool.ra/history/Into%20the%201980s.pdf]

Harrison, M., *Bournville: Model Village to Garden Suburb*, Chichester: Phillimore, 1999

---, 'Burnage Garden Village' in *Town Planning Review*, Vol. 47, No. 3 (July 1976), pp. 256-268

Henslowe, P., *Ninety Years On, An Account of the Bournville Village Trust*, Bournville: Bournville Village Trust, 1984

Hippisley-Cox, C., 'The Secret Garden Suburb' in *Context* (110), 2009, pp. 34-35

Jackson, K. and Nadin, D., *Burnage Garden Village*, Manchester: Burnage Heritage, 2006

Lancaster, B., *Radicalism, Co-operation and Socialism, Leicester Working-class Politics 1860-1906*, Leicester: Leicester University Press, 1987

Lloyd, R.A., 'The Welsh Town Planning and Housing Trust and its Affiliated Societies' in *Town Planning Review*, Vol. 23, No. 1 (Apr. 1952), pp. 40-51

Malpass, P., *The Howard Cottage Society*, Letchworth: Howard Cottage Society, 2001

Manchester Tenants Ltd, *Burnage Garden Village Jubilee booklet*, Manchester: Manchester Tenants Ltd, 1956

Miller, M., *Letchworth, the first Garden City*, Chichester: Phillimore, 1989

Parker, B., *The Fallings Park Garden Suburb* [accessed http://www.history-website.co.uk/articles/FallingsPark/gardensuburb.htm]

Piper, H.W., 'The Work of Co-partnership Tenants Ltd' in *Town and Country Planning*, July 1957, pp. 302-304

Reid, A., *Brentham: a history of the pioneer garden suburb*, London: Brentham Heritage Society, 2000

---, 'Survival of the Smallest, The Sevenoaks Tenants Estate' in *Architectural History*, Vol. 44, Essays in Architectural History Presented to John Newman (2001), pp. 401-410

Rooksby, D. A., *And Sometime Upon the Hills (the Quakers in North-West England, 3)*, self-published, 1998

Shepherd, B., 'Berkhamsted's Garden Suburb' in *The Chronicle*, Vol. XVI, Mar. 2019, Berkhamsted: Berkhamsted Local History and Museum Society

Slack, K.M., *Henrietta's Dream: A chronicle of the Hampstead Garden Suburb 1905-1982*, self-published, 1982

Spence, M., *Lucas Rd, Britain's first co-operative street*, London: self-published, 2015

--- , 'Tenant Co-operators' in *Journal of Co-operative Studies*, Vol. 53, No. 2 (No. 159) Autumn 2020 pp. 5-15

Statham, M., 'Charles Sheridan Jones – the Co-operative Granite Quarries Limited and the Aberdaron Co-operative Housing Society' in *Journal of Co-operative Studies*, Vol. 53, No. 3 (No. 160) Winter 2020, pp. 30-35

Taylor, A., 'The garden cities movement in a local context: the Development and Decline of the Penkhull Garden Village Estate' in *The Local Historian*, Vol. 27, No. 1 (Feb. 1997), pp. 30-47

Tims, M., *Ealing Tenants Ltd*, London: Ealing Local History Society, 1966

Wakeford, I., *West Byfleet and Sheerwater: a self-guided heritage walk*, Woking: Alfred Arthur Wakeford, 2012 [accessed www.wokinghistory.org]

Whitelaw, M., *A Garden Suburb for Glasgow: The Story of Westerton*, Glasgow: self-published, 1992

Woking Co-operative Society, *Pictorial Souvenir of Twenty-One Years' Work of the Woking Co-operative Society 1899-1920*, Woking: Woking Co-operative Society, n.d. [1921]

Books and journal articles after 1918: housing generally

Adams, J.W.R., *Modern Town and Country Planning*, London: J. and A. Churchill, 1952

Ashworth, W., *The Genesis of Modern British Town Planning*, London: Routledge and Kegan Paul, 1954

Beevers, R., *The Garden City Utopia, a critical biography of Ebenezer Howard*, London: Macmillan, 1987

Boughton, J., *A History of Council Housing in 100 Estates*, London: RIBA Publishing, 2022

---, *Municipal Dreams: The Rise and Fall of Council Housing*, London; Brooklyn: Verso, 2018

Burnett, J., *Social History of Housing*, Newton Abbot: David and Charles, 1978

Byrne, D. and Damer, S., 'The State, the Balance of Class Forces, and Early Working Class Housing Legislation', *in Housing Construction and the State*, London: Political Economy of Housing Workshop, Conference of Socialist Economists, 1980

Clapp, B.W., 'Henry Percival Bulmer' in *Oxford Dictionary of National Biography*, Oxford: Oxford University Press, 2004

Cleary, E.J., *The Building Society Movement*, London: Elek Books, 1965

Creese, W.L., *The Search for Environment, The Garden City Before and After*, New Haven; London: Yale University Press, 1966, rev. ed. 1992

Creese, W.L. (ed.), *The Legacy of Raymond Unwin*, Cambridge (Mass.); London: M.I.T. Press, 1967

Darley, G., *Octavia Hill*, London: Constable, 1990

---, *Villages of Vision*, London: Architectural Press, 1975

Daunton, M., *A Property Owning Democracy? Housing in Britain*, London: Faber, 1987

Drury, M., *Wandering Architects*, Stamford: Shaun Tyas, 2000

Englander, D., *Landlord and Tenant in Urban Britain 1838-1918*, Oxford: The Clarendon Press, 1983

Fishman, R., *Urban Utopias of the 20th Century*, New York: Basic Books, 1977

Gauldie, E., *Cruel Habitations, A History of Working-Class Housing 1780-1918*, London: Allen and Unwin, 1974

Hall, P., *Cities of Tomorrow*, Oxford: Basil Blackwell, 1988

Hardy, D., *From Garden Cities to New Towns*, London: Chapman and Hall, 1991

Harloe, M., *Social Construction of Social Housing*, Canberra: Australian National University, 1993

---, *The People's Home? Social Rented Housing in Europe and America*, Oxford: Blackwell, 1995

James, M.F., 'John Sutton Nettlefold' in *Oxford Dictionary of National Biography*, online edition, 2013

Keable, G., *Tomorrow Slowly Comes*, London: Town and Country Planning Association, 1963

---, *Towns of Tomorrow*, London: S.C.M. Press, 1946

Lowe S. and Hughes D. (eds.), *A New Century of Social Housing*, [includes Richard Best, 'Housing Associations 1890-1990'], Leicester: Leicester University Press, 1991

Malpass, P., *Housing and the Welfare State*, Basingstoke: Palgrave Macmillan, 2005

---, *Housing associations and housing policy: a historical perspective*, Basingstoke: Macmillan, 2000

---, 'Public Utility Societies and the Housing and Town Planning Act 1919: A re-examination of the Introduction of State-Subsizised Housing in Britain' in *Planning Perspectives*, Vol. 15, (2000), pp. 377-392

---, 'The discontinuous history of housing associations in England' in *Housing Studies*, Vol. 15, No. 2, 2000, pp. 195-212

---, 'The uneven development of social rented housing: Explaining the historically marginal position of Housing Associations in Britain' in *Housing Studies*, Vol. 18, No. 2, 2001, pp. 225-242

Malpass, P. and Cairncross, L. (eds), *Building on the Past: Visions of housing futures*, Bristol: Policy Press, 2006

Morgan, K., 'David Davies' in *Oxford Dictionary of National Biography*, online edition, rev. 2008

Orbach, L., *Homes for Heroes: A Study of the Evolution of British Public Housing 1915-1921*, London: Seeley, 1977

Osborn, F.J., *New Towns after the War*, London: J.M. Dent, 1942

Parsons K.C. and Schuyler D. (eds.), *From Garden City to Green City*, [includes Steven V. Ward, 'The Howard Legacy'], Baltimore; London: Johns Hopkins University Press, 2002

Pevsner, N., 'Model Houses for the Labouring Classes' in *Architectural Review*, Vol. XCIII, No. 557, May 1943

Power, A., *Hovels to High Rise: State Housing in Europe since 1850*, London: Routledge, 1993

Sayle, A., *The Houses of the Workers*, London: T. Fisher Unwin, 1924

Skilleter, K.J., 'The role of public utility societies in early British town planning and housing reform 1901-1936' in *Planning Perspectives*, Vol. 8 (1993), pp. 125-165

Smyth, J. J., and Robertson, D. S., 'Lost Alternatives to Council Housing? An examination of Stirling's alternative housing initiatives c 1906-1939' in *Journal of Scottish Historical Studies*, Nov. 2017, Vol. 37, No. 2, pp. 117-135

Sutcliffe, A. (ed), *British Town Planning: the Formative Years* [includes M. Harrison, 'Housing and Town Planning in Manchester'], Leicester: Leicester University Press, 1981

Swenarton, M., *Homes Fit for Heroes*, London: Heinemann Educational, 1981

Tarn, J.N., *Five Per Cent Philanthropy*, London: Cambridge University Press, 1973

---, *Working Class Housing in the Nineteenth Century*, London: Lund Humphries, 1971

Thompson, F.M.L. (ed.), *The Rise of Suburbia*, Leicester: Leicester University Press, 1982

Wilding, P., 'The Housing and Town Planning Act 1919 – A Study in the Making of Social Policy' in *Journal of Social Policy*, Vol. 2, 4 (1972), pp. 317-34

---, 'Towards Exchequer Subsidies for Housing 1906-1914' in *Social & Economic Administration*, Vol. 6, No. 1, Jan. 1972, pp. 3-18

Books and journal articles after 1918: the co-operative movement

Ackers, P. and Reid, A.J. (eds.), *Alternatives to State-Socialism in Britain: Other Worlds of Labour in the Twentieth Century*, London: Palgrave Macmillan, 2016

Bellamy, J., 'Benjamin Jones' in *Dictionary of Labour Biography Vol. 1*, London: Macmillan, 1972

Bibby, A., *All Our Own* Work, London: Merlin, 2015

---, 'Flying below the radar: England's early co-operative and co-partnership tenant societies today' in *Journal of Co-operative Studies*, Vol. 55, No. 1 (No. 164), Summer 2022

Bing, H.F., 'Amos Mann' in *Dictionary of Labour Biography Vol. 1*, London: Macmillan, 1972

Birchall, J., *Building communities the co-operative way*, London: Routledge and Kegan Paul, 1988

---, 'Co-partnership Housing and the Garden City Movement' in *Planning Perspectives*, Vol. 10:44 (1995), pp. 329-358

---, 'Managing the co-partnership way' in *Town and Country Planning*, LXIV/1 (Dec. 1995), pp. 333-335

---, *People-Centred Businesses: co-operatives, mutuals and the idea of membership*, Basingstoke: Palgrave Macmillan, 2011

---, *The hidden history of co-operative housing in Britain*, Uxbridge: Brunel University, 1991

Blaszak, B. J., *The Matriarchs of England's Cooperative Movement*, Westport: Greenwood Press, 2000

Brading, K., 'Housing Societies – A Special Report' in *Report of the Registrar of Friendly Societies 1972*, London: H.M.S.O., 1973

Brown, J. (ed.), *Co-operative Capital: A New Approach to Investment in Co-operatives*, Co-operative Action, 2004

Coates, C., *Utopia Britannica*, London: Diggers and Dreamers, 2001

Cole, G.D.H., *A Century of Co-operation*, Manchester: Co-operative Union, 1944

Crimes, T., *Edward Owen Greening*, Manchester: Co-operative Union, 1923

Dackombe, B., 'A Fine and Disinterested Spirit: the life and activities of Aneurin Williams' in *Journal of Liberal History*, No. 57 (Winter 2007-8)

General Co-operative Survey, *Fourth and Final Report*, Manchester: Co-operative Union, 1919

---, *Third Interim Report*, Manchester: Co-operative Union, 1919

Greening, E.O., *A Pioneer Co-partnership: being the history of the Leicester Co-operative Boot and Shoe Manufacturing Society Ltd*, London: Labour Co-partnership Association; Manchester: Co-operative Union, 1923

Gurney, P., *Co-operative culture and the politics of consumption in England 1870-1930*, Manchester: Manchester University Press, 1996

Hands, J., *Housing Co-operatives*, London: Society for Co-operative Dwellings, 1975

Hardy, D., *Alternative communities in nineteenth century England*, London: Longman, 1979

---, *Utopian England*, London: E. and F.N. Spon, 2000

Jones, H., *Ben Jones, A Great Co-operator*, London: Co-operative Printing Society, 1946

Mansbridge, A., *Brick upon Brick*, London: Dent, 1934

Ospina, J., *Housing Ourselves*, London: Shipman, 1987

Pearson, L.F., *The Architectural and Social History of Co-operative Living*, Basingstoke: Macmillan, 1988

Pottle, M., 'Henry Vivian' in *Oxford Dictionary of National Biography*, Oxford: Oxford University Press, 2007

Purvis, M., 'Benjamin Jones' in *Oxford Dictionary of National Biography*, Oxford: Oxford University Press, 2004

Redfern, P., *The New History of the C.W.S.*, London: Dent; Co-operative Wholesale Society, 1938

Robertson, N., *The Co-operative Movement and Communities in Britain, 1914-1960: Minding Their Own Business*, Farnham: Ashgate, 2010

Rosenberg, L., *Scotland's Homes fit for Heroes: Garden City Influences on the Development of Scottish Working Class Housing, 1900-1939*, Edinburgh: Scottish Centre for Conservation Studies; The Word Bank, 2016

Rowlands, R., *Forging Mutual Futures*, Birmingham: Centre for Urban and Regional Studies, University of Birmingham, 2009

Scott, J., 'Victor Verasis Branford' in *Oxford Dictionary of National Biography*, online edition, 2015

Thompson, M., *Reconstructing Public Housing*, Liverpool: Liverpool University Press, 2020

Newspapers, magazines, annuals
A.T. Forerunner (Anchor Tenants) 1910-1912
The Call (1918)
Co-operative Congress reports (1880-1920)
Co-operative News (1871-1909)
Daily Mail (1913)
Daily News (1904)
Garden City/Garden Cities and Town Planning (1904-21)
Hansard, (1906-1909) [Henry Vivian MP]
Housing Reformer (Cardiff) (1912)
International Co-operative Alliance, report of 1902 conference
Keswick Reminder (2020)
Labour Co-partnership/Co-Partnership (1894-1919)
Labour Co-partnership Association Annual Reports (1904-1911)
Manchester Courier (1913)
Manchester Guardian (1908-1917)
Wolverhampton Journal (1907)

Unpublished
Bridgman, J., *A Suitable Housing Model? A Case Study of Bournville Tenants Ltd*, Masters' dissertation, Leeds Beckett University, 2021
Butler, J. H., *The origins and development of the retail co-operative movement in Yorkshire during the nineteenth century*, (Ph.D thesis, University of York), July 1986
Forrester, M.D., *An Examination of the Origins and Sources of Humberstone Garden Suburb, Leicester (1907-1914)*, MA Dissertation, Leicester Polytechnic, 1984
Owen, C., *David Davies 75: International 'Father' of the Temple of Peace*, [accessed https://www.wcia.org.uk/wcia-news/wcia-history/david-davies-75-father-of-the-temple-of-peace/?print=print]
Pawson, I., *Anchor Tenants Limited, A Brief History*, n.d. [c. 2008] [accessed https://anchorhistory.uk/booklet/brief_history.pdf]
Smith, S., *Co-Partnership Housing – creating places: Co-operative housing development of the Garden Suburbs 1900-1914*, 1998 [accessed http://www.moorpool.com/moorpool.ra/history/Co-Partnership%20Housing%20Creating%20Places%20by%20Stephen%20Smith.pdf]
Taylor, C., *Co-operative Housing in the West Midlands*, MBA Thesis, University of Birmingham, 2004
Tennyson, Sir C., *Biography of Lord Davies*, unpublished, n.d. [c. 1953?] [accessed https://viewer.library.wales/4683286#?c=&m=&s=&cv=&manifest=https%3A%2F%2Fdamsssl.llgc.org.uk%2Fiiif%2F2.0%2F4683286%2Fmanifest.json&xywh=-931%2C-398%2C5658%2C5933]
Wilkinson, B., *Greta Hamlet: A short history of Keswick's 'Garden Suburb'*, unpublished, 2005

ENDNOTES

Abbreviations used in the Endnotes:
CN: Co-operative News; CP: Co-partnership magazine (Labour Co-partnership before 1907); CTL: Co-partnership Tenants Ltd; GC: Garden City magazine (a first 'New series' launched in 1906; renamed Garden Cities and Town Planning in March 1908); GCTP: Garden Cities and Town Planning magazine (Garden City before March 1908; a second 'New series' launched in 1911); LCP: Labour Co-partnership (became Co-partnership in 1907); WCG: Women's Co-operative Guild

Full details of publications referenced in the Endnotes can be found in the Bibliography.

1   Keswick Reminder, Oct. 5 2020.
2   Allerdale District Council, *Housing Study 2016*, p. 65.
3   www.keswickcommunityhousingtrust.co.uk
4   www.communitylandtrusts.org.uk
5   Brian Wilkinson, *Greta Hamlet: A short history of Keswick's 'Garden Suburb'*, 2005.
6   Andrew Bibby, *All Our Own Work*, 2015.
7   There had also been earlier attempts at organising regular co-operative congresses, for example in the years between 1831-1835 and again (under the auspices of the Christian Socialists) in the early 1850s.
8   See in particular the writings of the co-operative historian Johnston Birchall.
9   Aileen Reid, *Brentham: A history of the pioneer garden suburb*, 2000.
10 CN, Dec. 1 1894, p. 314.
11 CN, July 5 1902, p. 817.
12 E.W. Brabrook, *Friendly Societies and Similar Institutions*, 1875, p. 205.
13 Percy Redfern, *The Story of the C.W.S., The Jubilee History of the Co-operative Wholesale Society 1863-1913*, n.d., [1913], p. 418.
14 CN, Sep. 1 1871, p. 3; Percy Redfern, *The Story of the C.W.S., The Jubilee History of the Co-operative Wholesale Society 1863-1913*, n.d. [1913], p. 66.
15 G.D.H. Cole, *A Century of Co-operation*, 1944, p. 75.
16 G.D.H. Cole, *A Century of Co-operation*, 1944, p. 92.
17 Johnston Birchall, *Co-partnership Housing and the Garden City Movement*, 1995, pp. 331-332.
18 CN, Mar. 14 1908, p. 293; the 1868 start date is confirmed by the centenary history of the Bacup society written in 1947.

19 CN, Mar. 18 1876, p. 135; CN, Mar. 22 1873, p.122.

20 CN, Mar. 28 1891, p. 302.

21 CN, Dec. 1 1894, p. 1314.

22 CN, June 16 1900, p. 648ff.

23 Aneurin Williams, *Co-operation in Housing and Town-Building*, 1907.

24 CN, Jan. 27 1900, p. 95.

25 Aneurin Williams, *Co-operation in Housing and Town-Building*, 1907.

26 LCP, Sep. 1904.

27 CN, July 26 1902, pp. 904ff.

28 Ben Jones evidence, *Royal Select Committee on Town Holdings*, 1887.

29 The rent was set at 3s 2d for every £100 of cost, and the houses were reportedly built for around £250. Rates were extra. CN, July 5 1902 pp. 817ff; Co-operative Congress report 1907.

30 CN, July 5 1902, pp. 817ff.

31 Co-operative Congress report 1907; CP, Apr. 1915, p47; Martin Gaskell *The Suburb Salubrious* in Anthony Sutcliffe (ed.), *British Town Planning: the Formative Years*, 1981, p. 30.

32 K. Brading, *Housing Societies – A Special Report*, 1973.

33 CN, Mar. 9 1901, p. 273.

34 *Royal Commission on Housing of the Working Classes, Vol. II.*, 1885.

35 Joyce Bellamy, 'Benjamin Jones' in *Dictionary of Labour Biography Vol. 1.*, 1972; Martin Purvis, 'Benjamin Jones' in *Oxford Dictionary of National Biography*, 2004.

36 *Royal Commission on Housing of the Working Classes, Vol. II.*, 1885.

37 John E. Yerbury, *A Short History of the Pioneer Society in Co-operative Housing*, 1913.

38 John E. Yerbury, *A Short History of the Pioneer Society in Co-operative Housing*, 1913.

39 Andrew Mearns, *The Bitter Cry of Outcast London*, 1883.

40 Gillian Darley, *Octavia Hill*, 1990, pp. 224-225.

41 Edward Vansittart Neale's translation of Jean-Baptiste André Godin's book on Le Familistère was published by the Co-operative Union in 1881.

42 CN, Feb. 12 1881, p. 99.

43 *Royal Commission on Housing of the Working Classes, Vol. II.*, 1885.

44 Henry H. Champion and Benjamin Jones, *Co-operation versus Socialism*, 1887. (As an aside, Jones also took the opportunity to say how he thought a co-operative railway could be structured: one "where the public and the employees had both the right to elect a part of the management as well as the capitalists, then there would be less necessity for State Control").

45 *Royal Select Committee on Town Holdings*, 1887.

46 John E. Yerbury, *A Short History of the Pioneer Society in Co-operative Housing*, 1913.

47 Martin Spence, *Tenant Co-operators*, 2020.

48 John E. Yerbury, *A Short History of the Pioneer Society in Co-operative Housing*, 1913.

49 John E. Yerbury, *A Short History of the Pioneer Society in Co-operative Housing*, 1913.

50 John E. Yerbury, *A Short History of the Pioneer Society in Co-operative Housing*, 1913.

51 CN, Apr. 28 1888, p. 392.

52   CN, Feb. 23 1889, p. 277; CN, Aug. 31 1889, p. 929.

53   CN, Aug. 31 1889, p. 929; CN, Feb. 15 1890, p. 153.

54   Benjamin Jones, *Co-operative Production*, 1894, pp. 556-561; the progress of Co-operative Builders can be followed (including data on trade, profit and employee numbers) in Co-operative Congress reports from 1890 to 1907. The co-op is not mentioned thereafter.

55   Co-operative Congress annual reports; also Henry D. Lloyd, *Labor Copartnership*, 1898, p. 147.

56   Martin Spence, *Lucas Rd, Britain's first co-operative street*, 2015.

57   Beatrice Potter, *The Diary of Beatrice Webb*, entry for June 4 1889.

58   CN, Aug. 24 1895, p. 877.

59   John E. Yerbury, *A Short History of the Pioneer Society in Co-operative Housing*, 1913.

60   Howard Hodgkin, *Tenant Co-operators*, 1901.

61   Epsom was probably chosen because of the support of the local co-operative society. CP, Vol. XII, 1905, p. 45.

62   Howard Hodgkin, *Tenant Co-operators*, 1901; John E. Yerbury, *A Short History of the Pioneer Society in Co-operative Housing*, 1913.

63   John E. Yerbury, *A Short History of the Pioneer Society in Co-operative Housing*, 1913.

64   W. H. Brown, *The Story of Co-partnership Housing*, in Co-partnership Tenants Housing Council, *Garden Suburbs, Villages and Homes Vol. 2*, 1912.

65   Joyce Bellamy, 'Benjamin Jones' in Dictionary of Labour Biography Vol. 1., 1972; Mark Pottle, 'Henry Vivian' in Oxford Dictionary of National Biography, 2007.

66   Joyce Bellamy, 'Benjamin Jones' in Dictionary of Labour Biography Vol. 1., 1972; Tom Crimes, *Edward Owen Greening*, 1923.

67   Andrew Bibby, *All Our Own Work*, 2015, especially chapters 3, 8 and 9.

68   The separate Scottish Co-operative Wholesale Society had a somewhat different approach from the CWS and retained the bonus to labour for longer.

69   Andrew Bibby, *All Our Own Work*, 2015, chapter 8.

70   *Royal Commission on Labour, Fourth Report, Minutes of Evidence, Digest of Evidence, Indexes, Vol. IV, Appendix to Minutes of Evidence*, 1894.

71   LCP, Vol. I, 1896, p. 180.

72   Henry Vivian, *How Co-operative Production may be successfully applied to the building trades*, n.d. [1897?].

73   Aileen Reid, *Brentham: a history of the pioneer garden suburb*, 2000, pp. 60-62.

74   LCP, Vol. XI, Apr. 1905.

75   Henry Vivian, *The Co-partnership Tenants' Movement* in Co-partnership Tenants Housing Council, *Garden Suburbs Villages and Homes Vol. 2*, 1912.

76   LCP, Vol. XI, Apr. 1905.

77   Daily News, Aug. 9 1904.

78   Margaret Tims, *Ealing Tenants Ltd.*, 1966, p. 12.

79   Aileen Reid, *Brentham: a history of the pioneer garden suburb*, 2000, p. 67.

80   CP, Vol. XI, Apr. 1905.

81   See for example Henry Vivian, *Co-partnership in Housing*, Economic Review, Jan. 1906.

82   Aileen Reid, *Brentham: a history of the pioneer garden suburb*, 2000, p. 86.

83   Aileen Reid, *Brentham: a history of the pioneer garden suburb*, 2000, p. 135.

84   Ebenezer Howard, *Garden Cities of To-morrow*, 1902, p. 28.

85 Ebenezer Howard, *Garden Cities of To-morrow,* 1902, p. 50.

86 Ebenezer Howard, *Garden Cities of To-morrow,* 1902, p. 39.

87 LCP, Vol. V, Jan., Dec. 1899.

88 LCP, Vol. VII, Mar. 1901.

89 Neville is included in the list of Labour Association members, as at 1893, supplied by Vivian to the Royal Commission on Labour: *Appendix CXXVIII to the Fourth Volume of the Royal Commission on Labour report,* 1894.

90 Edward Carpenter, *My Days and Dreams,* 1916, p. 131.

91 Barry Parker and Raymond Unwin, *The Art of Building a Home,* 1901, pp. 91-107.

92 Raymond Unwin, *Co-partnership in Housing,* in Co-partnership Tenants Housing Council, *Garden Suburbs, Villages and Homes Vol. 2,* 1912.

93 Aileen Reid, *Brentham: a history of the pioneer garden suburb,* 2000, p. 40; Fishman, *Urban Utopias of the 20th Century,* 1977, p. 66.

94 Barry Dackombe, *A Fine and Disinterested Spirit,* 2007-8, pp. 34-41.

95 CP, Vol. XV, June 1909.

96 LCP, Vol. X, Nov. 1904; LCP, Vol. XII (Aug. 1906), CN, July 14 1906, p. 828.

97 LCP, Vol. X, Dec .1904.

98 GC, Vol. I, No. 11, Dec. 1906, p. 242.

99 CN, May 20 1905, pp. 580-581.

100 CN, Aug. 5 1905, p. 946.

101 LCP, Vol. XI, June 1905; CN, July 20 1907, p. 898.

102 Raymond Unwin, *Town Planning in Practice,* 1909, pp. 346-349.

103 Raymond Unwin, *Town Planning in Practice,* 1909, p. 376.

104 Amos Mann, *Democracy in Industry,* 1914.

105 H.F. Bing, 'Amos Mann' in *Dictionary of Labour Biography, Vol. 1,* 1972; Amos Mann, *Democracy in Industry,* 1914.

106 Bill Lancaster, *Radicalism, Co-operation and Socialism,* 1987.

107 It changed its name again in 1928 to the Industrial Co-partnership Association, again in 1972 to the Industrial Participation Association and finally in 1989 to the Involvement and Participation Association, under which name it continues today.

108 Amos Mann, *Democracy in Industry,* 1914, chapter 8.

109 The A.T. Forerunner, No. 10a, July 1911.

110 LCP, Vol. X, Nov. 1904.

111 Aileen Reid, *Survival of the Smallest, The Sevenoaks Tenants' Estate,* 2001, pp. 401-402. 'Mrs Percy Thompson' was included as a member of the Labour Association in *Appendix CXXVIII to the Fourth Volume of the Royal Commission on Labour report,* 1894.

112 Aileen Reid, *Survival of the Smallest, The Sevenoaks Tenants' Estate,* 2001.

113 LCP, Vol XI, Apr. 1905.

114 A list of Labour Association members, as at 1893, is included as *Appendix CXXVIII to the Fourth Volume of the Royal Commission on Labour report,* 1894.

115 New Statesman, *Special Supplement on Co-operative Production and Profit-sharing,* Sat. Feb. 14 1914, Vol. II, No. 45.

116 GC, New Series, Vol. 1, No. 9, Oct. 1906, p. 196.

117 Anchor Tenants rules 1902, 1910.

118 Henry Vivian, *The Pioneer Co-partnership Village (Appendix E)* in John Nettlefold, *Practical Housing,* 1908, p. 192.

119 Henry Vivian, *Co-partnership in Housing,* n.d. [1910].

120 Henry Vivian, *Co-partnership in Housing,* n.d. [1910].

121 Ewart Culpin, *The Garden City Movement Up to Date,* 1913, p. 2.

122 Labour Co-partnership Association, executive committee minutes MSS 310/1/2/7 Apr. 11 1907.

123 Labour Co-partnership Association, executive committee minutes MSS 310/1/2/6 Dec. 5 1904; Aug. 1 1905; Oct. 3 1905.

124 Labour Co-Partnership Association *20th Annual Report (year ending June 30 1905), Appendix*; held at Modern Records Centre, Warwick, MSS 310/4/1/1.

125 John Scott, 'Victor Verasis Branford' in *Oxford Dictionary of National Biography,* 2015. Sybella Gurney married Victor Branford in 1910 and Sybella's own biography is included in her husband's entry in the DNB!

126 LCP, Vol. XI, May and June 1905.

127 Sybella Gurney, *Co-partnership in Housing,* 1906, pp. 5-12.

128 Labour Co-partnership Association *20th Annual Report (year ending June 30 1905), Appendix*; held at Modern Records Centre, Warwick, MSS 310/4/1/1. Gurney was thanked for her 'practical sympathy' in making it possible for the Housing Council to participate in the exhibition.

129 Cheap Cottages Exhibition, *Book of the Cheap Cottages Exhibition,* 1905.

130 LCP, Vol. XI, Aug., Oct., Dec. 1905, Vol. XII, Jan., May 1906.

131 LCP, Vol. XII, Jan. 1906.

132 Data included in Co-operative Congress reports, 1904-1907.

133 CP, Vol. XIII, June 1907.

134 Labour Association, executive committee minutes MSS 310/1/2/6 July 5 1902.

135 Michael Harrison, *Bournville: Model Village to Garden Suburb,* 1999, pp. 71ff.

136 CP, Vol. XIII, Jan. 1907, Vol. XIV, Apr. 1908.

137 LCP, Vol. XII, July, Oct. 1906.

138 CP, Vol. XIV, Oct. 1908.

139 Henry Vivian, *Co-partnership in Housing,* n.d. [1910].

140 E.B. [Ernest Betham], *Practical Housing and Town Planning,* 1908, pp. 330-331.

141 CTL Prospectus, 1907.

142 CTL Rules 1907 as amended March 1908 (available in Herefordshire Archive and Records Centre, ref. J35/1132).

143 CP, Vol. XIV, May 1908.

144 The General Election was excellent news for Garden City Press, which reported that it was running its presses day and night to meet the demand for election material.

145 Hansard, Feb. 12 1907.

146 Joyce Bellamy, 'Henry Vivian' in the *Dictionary of Labour Biography, Vol. 1,* 1972.

147 Labour Co-partnership Association, executive committee minutes MSS 310/1/2/7 Apr. 11 1906, Apr. 2 1907.

148 *Royal Commission on Labour, Fourth Report, Minutes of Evidence, Digest of Evidence, Indexes, Vol. IV, Appendix to Minutes of Evidence,* 1894.

149 Michael F. James, 'John Sutton Nettlefold' in *Oxford Dictionary of National Biography,* 2013.

150 Minutes of Evidence taken before the Select Committee on the Housing of the Working Classes Amendment Bill, pp. 122-140, in the *Report and Special Report from the Select Committee on Housing of the Working Classes Acts Amendment Bill,* 1906. Bournville is spelled Bourneville in the transcription of the evidence.

151 Minute books from January 8 1907 are retained at the Manchester Tenants' office.

152 LCP, Vol. XII, Oct. 1906.

153 Manchester Tenants committee minutes Jan. 8 1907.

154 Manchester Tenants committee minutes, May 1 1907, May 8 1907.

155 Manchester Tenants committee minutes, Sep. 6 1907, Oct. 16 1907.

156 Michael Harrison, *Burnage Garden Village*, 1976, pp. 256-257; Michael Harrison, *Housing and Town Planning in Manchester before 1914* in Anthony Sutcliffe (ed.), *British Town Planning: The Formative Years*, 1981, pp. 116-118.

157 Manchester Tenants committee minutes, Mar. 18 1908.

158 Manchester Tenants committee minutes, July 15 1908.

159 Manchester Tenants committee minutes Sep. 14 1908.

160 CP, Vol. XIV, Nov. 1908.

161 CP, Vol. XXII, Nov. 1916.

162 Letter to Frederick Litchfield, July 17 1908, included in Manchester Tenants committee minute book.

163 *Report and Special Report of the Select Committee on the Housing of the Working Classes Acts Amendment Bill, Appendix 12, 1906.*

164 Keith Skilleter, *The Role of Public Utility Societies in early British Town Planning and Housing Reform 1901-1936*, 1993, pp. 137ff.

165 *Report and Special Report from the Select Committee on Housing of the Working Classes Acts Amendment Bill, 1906.*

166 Manchester Tenants committee minutes May 18 1908.

167 Manchester Tenants committee minutes, Jan. 8 1907.

168 Andrew Bibby, *All Our Own Work*, 2015, pp. 115-116.

169 GCTP, New Series, Vol. IV, No. 35, Nov. 1909.

170 Gillian Darley, *Octavia Hill*, 1990, p. 92.

171 CP, Vol. XIII, Dec. 1907.

172 GCTP, New Series, Vol. XI, No. 4, Apr. 1921, p. 89.

173 Frederic Osborn, *New Towns After the War*, 1942, p. 15.

174 Walter. L. Creese, *The Search for Environment, The Garden City Before and After*, 1992, p. 141.

175 Robert Beevers, *The Garden City Utopia*, 1987, p. 78; Peter Malpass, *The Howard Cottage Society*, 2011, p.2, p. 13; Aileen Reid, *Brentham: a history of the pioneer garden suburb*, 2000, p. 80.

176 CP issues for 1909-1914.

177 Rhubina, the English spelling, is also used at this period.

178 Quoted in Wynford Davies, *Rhiwbina Garden Village*, 2011, pp. 10-12.

179 Housing Reformer, Vol. 1, No. 4, Mar.-Apr. 1912, pp. 51ff.

180 Wynford Davies, *Rhiwbina Garden Village*, 2011, p. 13.

181 National Archives, BT 31/20364/119171.

182 National Archives, BT 31/ 3719/119171.

183 GCTP, New Series, Vol. IV, No. 12, Dec. 1914, p. 264.

184 Herefordshire Archive and Records Centre, archive ref. BH28/2/17.

185 GCTP, New Series, Vol. VI, No. 8, Nov. 1916, pp. 141ff.

186 Sir Richard Winfrey, Commons debate, July 24 1914.

187 GCTP, New Series, Vol. V, No. 2, Feb. 1915, p. 42.

188 GCTP, New Series, Vol. VI, No. 8, Nov. 1916, pp. 141ff.

189 Jim Brown (ed.), *Co-operative Capital*, 2004.

190 LCP, Vol. XII, Mar. 1906.

191 CP, Vol. XIX, Jan. 1913.

192 CP, Vol. XVI, Aug 1910.

193 CP, Vol. XVII, June 1911.

194 Bryce Leicester, *Life in a Garden Suburb,* in Co-partnership Tenants Housing Council, *Garden Suburbs, Villages and Homes Vol. 2,* 1912.

195 Bryce Leicester, *Life in a Garden Suburb,* in Co-partnership Tenants Housing Council, *Garden Suburbs, Villages and Homes Vol. 2,* 1912.

196 CP, Vol. XVIII, Mar. 1912, Nov. 1912; Bryce Leicester, *Life in a Garden Suburb,* in Co-partnership Tenants Housing Council, *Garden Suburbs, Villages and Homes Vol. 2,* 1912.

197 CP, Vol. XIX, Jan. 1913.

198 CP, Vol. XVIII, Oct. 1912.

199 CP, Vol. XV, Jan. 1909, Mar. 1909; CP, Vol. XVI, July 1910.

200 CP, Vol. XVII, Mar. 1911; Burnage Garden Village Amateur Players, *Coming-of-age commemorative booklet,* included in Martin Dodge and Alison Ronan, *Celebrating Burnage Garden Village,* 2019.

201 CP, Vol. XVII, Mar. 1911.

202 The A.T. Forerunner, No. 10a, July 1911.

203 The A.T. Forerunner can be consulted at http://anchorhistory.uk

204 The A.T. Forerunner, Feb. 1911.

205 The A.T. Forerunner, Dec. 1910; CP, Vol. XVII, Sep. 1911.

206 CP, Vol. XIV, Aug. 1908.

207 The A.T. Forerunner, May 1911; M.D. Forrester, *An Examination of the Origins and Sources of Humberstone Garden Suburb, Leicester (1907-1914),* 1984, p. 20.

208 The A.T. Forerunner, Oct. 1910, Nov. 1910.

209 This was, for example, the title given to the booklet produced in 1912 and published by Co-partnership Publishers.

210 Quoted in Aileen Reid, *Brentham: a history of the pioneer garden suburb,* 2000, p. 97.

211 CP, Vol. XV, July 1909.

212 Michael Harrison, *Burnage Garden Village,* 1976.

213 Antony Taylor, *The Garden Cities Movement in a Local Context,* 1997, pp. 41-43.

214 Ewart Culpin, *The Garden City Movement Up to Date,* 1913, pp. 215ff.

215 Board of Trade, *The Cost of Living of the Working Classes,* 1908.

216 John H. Butler, *The origins and development of the retail co-operative movement in Yorkshire during the nineteenth century,* 1986, p. 209.

217 Quoted in Michael Harrison, *Burnage Garden Village,* 1976, p. 264.

218 GC, Vol. III, No. 30, Sep. 1908, p. 115.

219 CP, Vol. XVII, Feb. 1911.

220 My grateful thanks to Ali Ronan for passing on to me her speaker's notes from the heritage walks.

221 Information communicated to the author.

222 B.W. Clapp, 'Henry Percival Bulmer' in *Oxford Dictionary of National Biography,* 2004 (includes information on Fred Bulmer); see also E.F. Bulmer Trust website, https://www.efbulmer.co.uk/fred-bulmer

223 Very much later, in 1938, Bulmer was to pass a tenth of his wealth into an employee welfare fund, now the local charity the E.F. Bulmer Trust.

224 Letter from John Nettlefold to Henry Vivian, Nov. 15 1908, held at Herefordshire Archive and Records Centre, archive ref. J65/1180.

225 Letter from John Nettlefold to Henry Vivian, Nov. 15 1908, held at Herefordshire Archive and Records Centre, archive ref. J65/1180.

226 Information on the Mutuals Register, https://mutuals.fca.org.uk/

227 Ewart Culpin, *The Garden City Movement Up to Date*, 1913, p. 33.

228 Letter from John Nettlefold to Henry Vivian, Nov. 15 1908, held at Herefordshire Archive and Records Centre, archive ref. J65/1180.

229 Sybella Gurney, *Co-partnership in Housing*, 1906, p. 10.

230 GCTP, New Series, Vol. IV, No. 35, Nov. 1909, p. 264; *Report of Hereford Co-operative Housing Society, year ending December 31 1909*, at Herefordshire Archive and Records Centre, archive ref. BH28/2/17.

231 Herefordshire Archive and Records Centre, archive ref. AB23/37.

232 *Report of Hereford Co-operative Housing Society, year ending December 31 1909*, at Herefordshire Archive and Records Centre, archive ref. BH28/2/17.

233 Herefordshire Archive and Records Centre, archive ref. AE38/127.

234 John Nettlefold, *Practical Town Planning*, 1914, pp. 102ff; Patrick Abercrombie, *Modern Town Planning in England Part II*, July 1910, p. 124.

235 GCTP, New Series, Vol. IV, No. 35, Nov. 1909, p. 264.

236 Ewart Culpin, *The Garden City Movement Up to Date*, 1913, pp. 45-46.

237 CP, Vol. XVII, June 1911; John Burns MP, speech, Second Reading, Housing of the Working Classes Bill, Mar. 15 1912; Iain Wakeford, *West Byfleet and Sheerwater*, 2012 and see also Iain Wakeford's website www.wokinghistory,org; Woking Borough Council, *The Heritage of Woking*, 2000.

238 Peter Aitken et al, *The Homesteads: Stirling's Garden Suburb*, 1984; James J. Smyth and Douglas S. Robertson, *Lost Alternatives to Council Housing?*, 2017; see also Ewart Culpin, *The Garden City Movement Up to Date*, 1913, p. 43.

239 James J. Smyth and Douglas S. Robertson, *Lost Alternatives to Council Housing?*, 2017.

240 James J. Smyth and Douglas S. Robertson, *Lost Alternatives to Council Housing?*, 2017.

241 Lou Rosenburg, *Scotland's Homes Fit for Heroes*, 2016, pp. 130-131.

242 Aileen Reid, *Brentham: a history of the pioneer garden suburb*, 2000, chapter 3.

243 Aileen Reid, *Survival of the Smallest, The Sevenoaks Tenants' Estate*, 2001.

244 CP, Vol. XV, Feb. 1909; Ewart Culpin *The Garden City Movement Up to Date*, 1913, pp. 215ff; Peter Malpass, *The Howard Cottage Society*, 2001.

245 CP, Vol. XVIII, Dec. 1912; The A.T. Forerunner, Jan., Apr., May 1911; M.D. Forrester, *An Examination of the Origins and Sources of Humberstone Garden Suburb*, 1984.

246 Ewart Culpin, *The Garden City Movement Up to Date*, 1913, pp. 215ff.

247 Keith Jackson and Dennis L. Nadin, *Burnage Garden Village*, 2006, p. 9.

248 CP, Vol. XVII, July 1911.

249 Raymond Unwin, *Town Planning in Practice*, 1909, p. 387.

250 John Nettlefold, *Practical Housing*, 1908, p. 12.

251 C. Napier-Clavering, *The History of Harborne Tenants Ltd*, n.d. [1908].

252 C. Napier-Clavering, *The History of Harborne Tenants Ltd*, n.d. [1908].

253 John Nettlefold, *Practical Town Planning*, 1914, p.98; GCTP, New Series, Vol. I, No.2, Mar. 1911, p. 44.

254 Wolverhampton Journal, Feb. 1907, at http://www.historywebsite.co.uk/articles/FallingsPark/article.htm

255 CP, Vol. XVI, May 1910.

256 Martin Hawtree, *The Emergence of the Town Planning Profession*, in Anthony Sutcliffe (ed.), *British Town Planning: The Formative Years*, 1981, pp. 82-84; Dennis Hardy, *From Garden Cities to New Towns*, 1991, pp. 39ff.

257 Bev Parker, *The Fallings Park Garden Suburb*, article at http://www.history-website.co.uk/articles/FallingsPark/gardensuburb.htm

258 CP, Vol. XV, Mar. 1909.

259 Antony Taylor, *The Garden Cities Movement in a Local Context*, 1997, p. 34.

260 In the custody of the society's secretary.

261 CP, Vol. XVII, July 1911.

262 Information from Shotton Steel history website, https://shottonsteel.co.uk/year/1909

263 Margaret Tims, *Ealing Tenants Ltd,* 1966.

264 Later the Hampstead Garden Suburb Trust.

265 Henrietta Barnett, *A Garden Suburb at Hampstead,* 1905.

266 E.B. [Ernest Betham], *Co-partnership in Housing,* 1910 p. 12.

267 Ewart Culpin, *The Garden City Movement Up to Date,* 1913.

268 CP, Vol. XV, Apr. 1909.

269 CP, Vol. XVI, Apr. 1910.

270 Vivian again stood unsuccessfully for Parliament at Edmonton in 1918 and Northampton in 1922. He was successful in 1923 at Totnes, standing as a Liberal, but lost his seat the following year.

271 Labour Co-partnership Association, executive committee minutes, MSS 310/1/2/7, Mar. 30 1911.

272 CP, Vol. XVIII, Jan. 1912.

273 Joyce Bellamy, 'Henry Vivian' in the *Dictionary of Labour Biography, Vol. 1,* 1972.

274 National Archives, archive ref. BT 31/20425/119799.

275 CP, Vol. XVIII, Oct. 1912.

276 Brigid G. Green, *Hampstead Garden Suburb 1907-1977,* 1977, p. 17.

277 John Yerbury, *A Short History of the Pioneer Society in Co-operative Housing,* 1913, p. 57.

278 Hereford Archive and Records Centre, archive ref. J65/1184.

279 C. Napier-Clavering, *The History of Harborne Tenants Ltd,* n.d. [1908].

280 Margaret Tims, *Ealing Tenants Ltd,* 1966; Keith Skilleter, *The Role of Public Utility Societies in early British Town Planning and Housing Reform 1901-1936,* 1993, p. 132.

281 Manchester Tenants minute book, July 21 1908.

282 Manchester Guardian, Sep. 9 1908.

283 Manchester Tenants minute book, entries for May 18 1908, July 29 1908, Sep. 14 1908, Sep. 28 1908, and letter from William Hutchings to CTL Board July 26 1908 included in minute book.

284 Keith Skilleter, *The Role of Public Utility Societies in early British Town Planning and Housing Reform 1901-1936,* 1993, p. 143; Aileen Reid, *Brentham: a history of the pioneer garden suburb,* 2000, pp. 77-78.

285 Manchester Tenants and Leicester Anchor rulebooks from this period may be consulted on the Mutuals Register; Anchor Tenants rulebooks at http://anchorhistory.uk

286 https://www.ica.coop/en/cooperatives/cooperative-identity

287 Labour Co-partnership Association, executive committee minutes, MSS 310/1/2/7, Jan. 8 1907.

288 Aneurin Williams, *Government by the Fit*, n.d., [1898?].

289 John Nettlefold, *Practical Town Planning*, 1914.

290 GCTP, New Series, Vol. IV, No. 3, Mar. 1914, p. 72.

291 Keith Skilleter, *The Role of Public Utility Societies in early British Town Planning and Housing Reform 1901-1936*, 1993, p. 143; Aileen Reid, *Brentham: a history of the pioneer garden suburb*, 2000, pp. 87-88.

292 Association of Hampstead Tenants, Leaflet No. 1, Leaflet No. 2, quoted in Keith Skilleter, *The Role of Public Utility Societies in early British Town Planning and Housing Reform 1901-1936*, 1993, p. 145.

293 National Archives, archive ref. T 1/11416/9116.

294 See Johnston Birchall, *Co-partnership Housing and the Garden City Movement*, 1995, p. 352.

295 The A.T. Forerunner, No. 10a, July 1911; CP, Vol. XVII, Aug. 1911; CP, Vol. XVI, May 1910.

296 *Garden Villagers' Troubles*, Manchester Courier, 1913.

297 GCTP, New Series, Vol. IV, No. 3, Mar. 1914.

298 Catherine Mayo, *Co-operative House-building*, 1898.

299 LCP, Vol. XII, July 1906.

300 National Archives, archive ref. RECO 1/620.

301 In 1892 J.C. Gray, Co-operative Union general secretary at this time, reported that 932 societies with 1,020,291 individual members were affiliates of the Union and a further 718 (primarily smaller) societies were not. See John Allan and J.C. Gray, *The Co-operative union: its necessity and its advantages*, 1892.

302 Barbara Blaszak, *The Matriarchs of England's Cooperative Movement*, 2000, p. 72.

303 GC, Vol. I, No. 8, Sep. 1906, p. 170.

304 GCTP, New Series, Vol. III, No. 6, June 1913, p. 156.

305 Catherine Webb, *Co-operation as applied to Domestic Work*, 1893.

306 WCG Circular number 24 (undated, c 1899?), in British Library of Political and Economic Science, microfilm 69, Reel No. 3, coll. Misc. 258, item 53, folio 165.

307 Lynn Pearson, *The Architectural and Social History of Co-operative Living*, 1988, chapters 1,2.

308 Lynn Pearson, *The Architectural and Social History of Co-operative Living*, 1988, chapters 1-5.

309 Barry Parker/Raymond Unwin, *The Art of Building a Home*, 1901, pp. 91-107.

310 GCTP, New Series, Vol. I, No. 3, Apr. 1911, p. 71.

311 Daily Mail, Mar. 27 1913.

312 C.B. Purdom, *The Garden City*, 1913, chapter 6; Lynn Pearson, *The Architectural and Social History of Co-operative Living*, 1988, chapter 6.

313 Lynn Pearson, *The Architectural and Social History of Co-operative Living*, 1988, pp. 94-102.

314 Lynn Pearson, *The Architectural and Social History of Co-operative Living*, 1988, pp. 110-114.

315 CP, Vol. XXIII, Mar. 1917.

316 Lynn Pearson, *The Architectural and Social History of Co-operative Living*, 1988, pp. 103-110.

317 Lynn Pearson, *The Architectural and Social History of Co-operative Living*, 1988, chapter 7.

318 New Townsmen, *New Towns After the War*, 1918, pp. 73ff; Frederic Osborn, *New Towns After the War*, 1942, pp. 63ff.

319 CP, Vol. XXII, Nov. 1916.

320 CP, Vol. XXIII, May 1917; Manchester Guardian, July 24 1917.

321 CP, Vol. XXIII, Dec. 1917.

322 Manchester Guardian, Nov. 15 1916.

323 Richardson was active in the National Union of Journalists and a few weeks later was to be appointed the union's general secretary.

324 Manchester Guardian, Nov. 17 1916.

325 The event was filmed and can be watched at https://www.youtube.com/watch?v=jcU9230gJNM

326 Hazlemere: Ewart Culpin, *The Garden City Movement Up to Date*, 1913, p. 33; CP, Vol. XVII, Nov. 1911; GCTP, New Series Vol. I, No. 4, May 1911, p. 81. Knebworth: Culpin (as above), p. 35; GCTP, New Series, Vol. IV, No. 5, May 1909, p. 206; GCTP, New Series, Vol. I, No. 4, May 1911, p 97; GCTP, New Series Vol. II, No. 5, May 1912, p. 107. Coventry: Culpin, p. 26; GCTP, New Series Vol. I, No. 5, June 1911, facing p. 125; GCTP, New Series Vol. II, No. 10, Oct. 1912, p. 227. Fairfield: Culpin, p. 28; Martin Gaskill *The Suburb Salubrious* in Anthony Sutcliffe, *British Town Planning: The Formative Years*, 1981, p. 34; CP, Vol. XIX, June 1913; GCTP, New Series, Vol. III, No. 3, June 1913, p. 144. Sutton: Culpin, p. 45; GCTP, New Series, Vol. III, July 1913, p. 179, p. 191.

327 Ewart Culpin, *The Garden City Movement Up to Date*, 1913, p. 26; GCTP, New Series, Vol. III, No. 11, Nov. 1913, p. 283.

328 Ewart Culpin, *The Garden City Movement Up to Date*, 1913, p. 47; GCTP, New Series, Vol. III, No. 9, Sep. 1913, p. 219.

329 William Moore Ede, *The attitude of the church to some of the social problems of town life*, 1896.

330 It is possible that Rudheath and Winnington were a single venture.

331 CP, Vol. XX, Mar. 1914.

332 Brian Shepherd, *Berkhamsted's Garden Suburb*, 2019.

333 Eileen Bowlt, *Ruislip Manor Cottage Society*, 2011.

334 Peter Hall, *Cities of Tomorrow*, 1988, p. 57; GCTP, New Series, Vol. IV, No. 10, Oct. 1914, p. 235.

335 GC, New Series, Vol. II, No. 23, Jan. 1908.

336 CN, *Eco-town project fails approval*, July 24 2009.

337 CP, Vol. XVIII, July 1912; CP, Vol. XIX, Aug. 1913; GCTP, New Series, Vol. III, No. 7 July 1913, p. 172; Ewart Culpin, *The Garden City Movement Up to Date*, 1913, p. 60; Woking Borough Council, *The Heritage of Woking* (2000); *Pictorial Souvenir of Twenty-One Years' Work of the Woking Co-operative Society 1899-1920*, n.d. [1921].

338 John Scott, 'Victor Verasis Branford' in Oxford Dictionary of National Biography, 2015.

339 Ewart Culpin, *The Garden City Movement Up to Date*, 1913, pp. 57-58.

340 Hadleigh Co-partnership Housing Society Ltd 1933 rulebook, based on 1912 rulebook, made available to the author by a former tenant.

341 GCTP, New Series, Vol. V, No. 1, Jan. 1915, p. 17.

342 Ewart Culpin, *The Garden City Movement Up to Date*, 1913, p. 30; CP, Vol. XVIII, Dec. 1912; CP, Vol. XIX, May 1913; GCTP, New Series, Vol. 3, May 1913, p. 138; Lou Rosenburg, *Scotland's Homes Fit for Heroes*, 2016, pp. 125ff; material from East

Dunbartonshire council at https://www.edlc.co.uk/heritage-arts/exhibitions/online-exhibitions/westerton-garden-suburb

343 Available at https://www.theyworkforyou.com/sp/?id=2013-10-01.5.0

344 John Boughton, *Municipal Dreams*, 2018, see also Municipal Dreams blog, Aug. 25 2020, available at https://municipaldreams.wordpress.com/2020/08/25/part_i_to_1918/

345 Ewart Culpin, *The Garden City Movement Up to Date*, 1913, p. 31.

346 Lou Rosenburg, *Scotland's Homes Fit for Heroes*, 2016, chapter 4.

347 Kenneth O. Morgan, 'David Davies' in *Oxford Dictionary of National Biography* (online edition revised Jan. 3 2008); Sir Charles Tennyson (attrib.), *Biography of Lord Davies*, n.d. [c. 1953].

348 Ewart Culpin, *The Garden City Movement Up to Date*, 1913, p. 47; T. Alwyn Lloyd, *The Welsh Town Planning and Housing Trust and its Affiliated Societies*, 1952, p. 41. For information both on Wrexham and other Welsh Town Planning and Housing Trust estates, see also Welsh TPHA *Fourth Annual Report*, available in National Archives, archive ref. RECO1/611 ; GCTP, New Series Vol. IV, No. 10, Oct. 1914, p. 229; GCTP, New Series, Vol. V, Oct./Nov. 1915, p. 188.

349 T. Alwyn Lloyd, *The Welsh Town Planning and Housing Trust and its Affiliated Societies*, 1952, p. 43.

350 Ewart Culpin, *The Garden City Movement Up to Date*, 1913, p. 35, p. 38; T. Alwyn Lloyd, *The Welsh Town Planning and Housing Trust and its Affiliated Societies*, 1952, pp. 43ff; GCTP, New Series, Vol. IV, No. 1, Jan. 1914, p. 21.

351 Kenneth O. Morgan, 'David Davies' in *Oxford Dictionary of National Biography* (online edition revised Jan. 3 2008).

352 T. Alwyn Lloyd, *The Welsh Town Planning and Housing Trust and its Affiliated Societies*, 1952, p. 47.

353 GCTP, New Series, Vol. V, No. 2, Feb. 1915 p.38.

354 GCTP, New Series, Vol. VI, No. 8, Nov. 1916, pp. 141ff.

355 See among other sources Peter Malpass, *Housing Associations and Housing Policy*, 2000, p. 73; Laurence Orbach, *Homes for Heroes*, 1977, pp. 24-26.

356 GCTP, Vol. V, No 10, Oct.-Nov. 1915, p. 194; No. 11, Dec. 1915, pp. 215ff.

357 CP, Vol. XX, Oct. 1914, Nov. 1914.

358 CP, Vol. XX, Nov. 1914; GCTP, New Series, Vol. V, No. 6, June 1915, p. 114.

359 GCTP, New Series, Vol. V, No. 6, June 1915 p. 114.

360 CP, Vol. XX, Mar. 1914; GCTP, New Series, Vol. IV, No. 11, Nov. 1914, p. 247; No. 9, Sep. 1914, pp. 201ff

361 GCTP, New Series, Vol. VIII, No. 2, May 1918, p. 21; Vol. V, No. 5, May 1915, p. 85.

362 GCTP, New Series, Vol. VI, Nov. 1916, pp. 141ff. It is highly likely that Ealing Tenants were also represented.

363 GCTP, New Series, Vol. VI, Nov. 1916, pp. 141ff.

364 GCTP, New Series, Vol. V, No. 11, Dec. 1915, p. 219.

365 Peter Malpass, *The Uneven Development of Social Rented Housing*, 2001, p. 232.

366 Peter Malpass, *Public Utility Societies and the Housing and Town Planning Act 1919*, 2000, p. 384.

367 For the background see Laurence Orbach, *Homes for Heroes*, 1977; Mark Swenarton, *Homes Fit for Heroes*, 1981; Keith Skilleter, *The Role of Public Utility Societies in early British Town Planning and Housing Reform 1901-1936*, 1993; Peter Malpass, *Housing Associations and Housing Policy*, 2000, pp. 70-81; Peter Malpass *Public Utility Societies and the Housing and Town Planning Act 1919*, 2000; Peter Malpass, *The Uneven Development of Social Rented Housing*, 2001.

368   A. Trystan Edwards, *A Criticism of the Garden City Movement,* 1913; A. Trystan Edwards, *A Further Criticism of the Garden City Movement,* 1914.

369   Mark Swenarton, *Homes Fit for Heroes,* 1981; Peter Hall, *Cities of Tomorrow,* 1988, p. 73.

370   Peter Malpass, *Public Utility Societies and the Housing and Town Planning Act 1919,* 2000, p. 389.

371   Ebenezer Howard letter to Frederic Osborn 1 Sep. 1914, quoted in Peter Malpass, *Public Utility Societies and the Housing and Town Planning Act 1919,* 2000, p. 380; GCTP, New Series, Vol. V, No. 10, Oct.-Nov. 1915, p. 194.

372   John Burnett, *A Social History of Housing,* 1978, p. 222; GCTP, New Series, Vol. XI, No. 3, Mar. 1921, p. 68.

373   GCTP, New Series, Vol. XI, No. 3, Mar. 1921, p. 76.

374   Peter Malpass, *Public Utility Societies and the Housing and Town Planning Act 1919,* 2000, p. 387; the conference was on March 11 1922, during the Ideal Home Exhibition at London's Olympia.

375   Ministry of Health *Annual Report, 1924–25* (London: HMSO, 1925, Cmd. 2450) p. 52, quoted in Laurence Orbach, *Homes for Heroes,* 1977, p. 139 and Peter Malpass, *Public Utility Societies and the Housing and Town Planning Act 1919,* 2000, p. 385.

376   The Call, Nov. 21 1918.

377   Laurence Orbach, *Homes for Heroes,* 1977, p. 8; see also Mark Swenarton, *Homes Fit for Heroes,* 1981, chapter 6.

378   Frederic Osborn, *New Towns After the War,* 1942, p. 9.

379   Lynn Pearson, *The Architectural and Social History of Co-operative Living,* 1988, pp. 168-171.

380   GCTP, New Series, Vol. X, No. 12, Dec. 1920, pp. 243-245; Guildford Borough Council, *Onslow Village Conservation Area, Study and Character Appraisal,* 2003.

381   Amy Sayle, *The Houses of the Workers,* 1924, p. 93.

382   Information about Jordans has been taken primarily from the society's website, http://jordansvillage.co.uk/about.html

383   General Co-operative Survey, *Fourth and Final Report,* 1919; The Co-operative Union Ltd, *Report of the First Special Co-operative Congress, held at Blackpool 12-13 Feb. 1920,* 1920. However, according to Percy Redfern, *The New History of the C.W.S.,* 1938, p. 271, CWS built a village for their Shilbottle colliery in Northumberland. See Gazetteer.

384   The relevant Burry Port papers in the National Archives are in BD11/1258-BD 11/1264 and BD 11/1492-1496.

385   Letter to Arthur Thomas, Housing Commissioner, Cardiff, May 8 1919, National Archives, archive ref. BS 11/1259.

386   Valuation Office memorandum from the Supervising Valuer (Wales), May 16 1922, National Archives, archive ref. BD 11/1492.

387   Letter Nov. 24 1921 from Burry Port Garden Suburb Ltd to Disposal and Liquidation Commissioners, National Archives, archive ref. BD 11/1260.

388   Letter Mar. 2 1922 from Burry Port Garden suburb Ltd to Finance Officer, Ministry of Health, Cardiff, National Archives, archive ref. BD 11/1260.

389   Minute sheet, conference May 10 1922, National Archives, archive ref. BD 11/1492.

390   Letters to the Prime Minister from Mrs Jane Rodham, received Apr. 14 1924, May 16 1924. National Archives, archive ref. BD 11/1492.

391 T. Alwyn Lloyd, *The Welsh Town Planning and Housing Trust and its Affiliated Societies*, 1952, pp. 48-49.

392 Peter Malpass, *Public Utility Societies and the Housing and Town Planning Act 1919*, 2000, pp. 387-388.

393 Ann Power, *Hovels to High Rise*, 1993, p. 213.

394 GCTP, New Series, Vol. V, No. 10, Oct.- Nov. 1915, p. 194.

395 A photograph of The Limes before demolition is available at https://harringay-online.com/photo/60-crouch-end-hill-before-demolition-1969

396 Brigid G. Green, *Hampstead Garden Suburb 1907-1977*, 1977, p. 17.

397 Margaret Tims, *Ealing Tenants Ltd.* 1966; Johnson Birchall, *Co-partnership Housing and the Garden City Movement*, 1995; Aileen Reid, *Brentham: a history of the pioneer garden suburb*, 2000.

398 Antony Taylor, *The Garden Cities Movement in a Local Context*, 1997, p. 44.

399 Wynford Davies, *Rhiwbina Garden Village*, 2011, p. 23.

400 National Archives, archive ref. BD 11/1499.

401 James Bridgman, *A Suitable Housing Model?*, 2021, p. 39.

402 Johnston Birchall, *Managing the Co-partnership Way*, 1995, p. 334.

403 And others may come to light!

404 Ian Pawson, *Anchor Tenants Limited, A Brief History*, n.d. [c. 2008].

405 Bournville Tenants, *100 Years of Bournville Tenants Ltd 1906-2006*, 2006.

406 For more details of the remaining ten societies see Andrew Bibby, *Flying Below the Radar*, 2022.

407 CP, Vol. XIX, Jan. 1913.

408 Johnston Birchall, *Building Communities the Co-operative Way*, 1988, p. 97.

409 Johnston Birchall, *Co-partnership Housing and the Garden City Movement*, 1995, Table 1, pp. 337-339.

410 J. C. Gray, *Co-operation and the Poor*, 1902.

411 But see the entry for Shilbottle in the Gazetteer.

412 Johnston Birchall, *Co-partnership Housing and the Garden City Movement*, 1995; Johnston Birchall, *Managing the Co-partnership Way*, 1995.

413 E.B. [Ernest Betham], *Co-partnership in Housing*, 1910, p. 22.

414 GCTP, New Series, Vol. V, No. 11, Dec. 1915, pp. 215ff.

415 John Nettlefold, *Practical Town Planning*, 1914, p. 200.

416 Michael Harloe, *Social Construction of Social Housing*, 1993.

417 Matthew Thompson, *Reconstructing Public Housing*, 2020.

418 Amos Mann, *Democracy in Industry*, 1914.

419 The A.T. Forerunner, Nov. 1910.

INDEX

Aberaman 126, 160

Abercarn 160

Aberdare 10

Aberdaron 160

Acland, A.H.D. 24

Acton 145, 160

Adams, Thomas 95-96

Addison Act 1919 – see Housing,
    Town Planning &c Act (1919)

Addison, Christopher 7, 132, 138

Affordable Homes programme 2-3

Agricultural and Horticultural
    Association 32

Aldridge, Henry 157-158

Alexandria 124, 160

Alkrington 161

allotments 6, 47, 120, 122, 140

Amalgamated Society of Carpenters
    and Joiners 31

Anchor Boot and Shoe Co-operative
    47-48, 80-81

Anchor Tenants 48, 51, 53-54, 59, 64,
    69, 77, 80-85, 92-93, 99, 104, 108,
    128, 130, 149, 154, 157, 159, 165

Artisans' Dwellings Act (1882) 21

Arts and Crafts Movement 39, 42, 56,
    92, 123

Bacup 12-13

Banbury 145

Barnett, Canon Samuel 23, 44, 97

Barnett, Henrietta 23, 97-98, 101, 146

Barnoldswick 10

Barry Docks 125

Barry Garden Suburb 125-126, 130, 145,
    161

Bellamy, Edward 40

Berkhamsted 56, 118-119, 161

Betham, Ernest 157

Bingley 11

Birchwood Tenants 91, 162

Birkenhead 59-60, 100, 105

Birmingham 6, 30, 42, 51, 54, 56, 61-63,
    69, 80, 88, 92, 94, 147, 164, 165

Blackpool 11, 141-142

Blandford, Thomas 34

Bolton 10

bonus to labour 26, 32-34, 49

Bostall 16-17

Bournville 42-43, 56-57, 63, 72, 87, 161

Bournville Tenants 56-57, 59, 63, 84,
    87-88, 130, 149-150, 161

Bournville Village Trust 57, 161

bowling greens 6, 47, 57, 78, 79-80, 95,
    149

Bradford Property Trust 147

Brampton, Hubert 35

Branford, Victor 120-121

Brent Garden Village 115, 161, 163

Brentham Garden Suburb – see Ealing
    Tenants

Brick and Tile Workers Ltd 101, 129

Brickhill, Annie 86

Bridge of Weir 161

Brighouse 10
Brighton 56, 161
Bristol 10, 161
British Association for the
    Advancement of Science 112
British Socialist Party 139
Brixton 26
Broadhempston 3
Broadhurst, Henry 19-20, 22
Brockenhurst 56, 161
Bromley 56, 161
Brunner, Sir John 59, 71, 78
Budleigh 121, 161
building societies 14, 16, 19, 37, 95, 151, 156
Bulmer, Fred 88-90, 102, 150
Bulmer, Percy 88
Burnage – see Manchester Tenants
Burnage Milk Strike 117
Burnhope 10
Burnley 11
Burns, John 91
Burry Port 126, 142-145, 162
Bury 162
Bury, Mrs 15
Buxton 42
bye-laws 94, 98
Byfleet 91, 162

Cadbury, Edward 46
Cadbury, George 42, 46, 56-57
Caerphilly 145, 162
Caerphilly Co-operative Garden
    Village 74, 162
Calder Valley 4
Camberwell 24, 26, 27, 29, 162
Cambridge 27, 44, 54, 88, 119
capital for housing 3, 5, 23, 25, 26,
    35-37, 46, 48-49, 52-53, 55, 57-59,
    65-76, 87, 89-90, 98, 129, 130-131,
    134-137, 140, 142-145, 156-157
Cardiff 56, 73, 74, 130, 143, 148, 162
Cardiff Workers Co-operative Garden
    Village – see Rhiwbina
Carlisle 118, 162
Carpenter, Edward 43, 85

Cash, Thomas 118, 130
Cathy Come Home 21
Cavendish-Bentinck, Lord Henry 121
Chamberlain, Joseph 21, 61
Chamberlain, Neville 61, 145
Champion, H.H. 23
Chartist movement 11, 12
Cheap Cottages Exhibition 55, 96
Chelsea 25
Chester-le-Street 10
Chicago 40
children's participation 78, 80, 97, 110,
    114, 117
children's playgrounds 6-7, 62, 78
Chipping Norton 162
Church of Christ 81
Churchill, Winston 139
Churton, Annette 54
City Beautiful movement 57, 90
Cleckheaton 10
Club and Institute Union (CIU) 24
Clydebank 162
co-housing 91, 111-117, 140
community agriculture 91, 122
Community Land Trusts 2-4, 7, 153,
    158
community shares 3, 5, 25, 28, 36, 46,
    52-53, 70-76, 89-90, 98, 156
conscientious objectors 86
Conservation areas 8, 91, 120, 126, 151,
    152-153
Co-operative and Community Benefit
    Societies Act (2014) 156
Co-operative Builders Ltd 26-27, 28,
    34, 56
co-operative building firms 26-27,
    34, 56, 101 (see also Co-operative
    Builders, General Builders)
Co-operative Congress 8-9, 11, 13-14,
    15, 32, 34, 110, 119, 141-142
co-operative dividends for housing 20,
    24, 25, 29, 35-36, 51-52
Co-operative Festivals, National 32
Co-operative Garden City Committee
    119-120, 153

Co-operative Group 120
co-operative housekeeping 111-117, 140
co-operative printing societies 27, 45, 70
co-operative production 19, 32-33, 34, 45, 47-48, 50, 70, 81
Co-operative Productive Federation 33-34, 47, 48, 70
co-operative societies and members' savings 13-14
co-operative societies and mortgage lending 14-16
co-operative societies' engagement with housing 7, 8-9, 12-17, 19-30, 43, 46-47, 49, 120, 141-142, 153-154, 169
Co-operative Survey, General 141-142
Co-operative Union 8, 11, 14, 19, 24, 32, 65, 101, 110-111, 153
Co-operative Wholesale Society (CWS) 11, 12, 17, 18-19, 23, 25, 32-33, 57, 65, 70, 105, 120, 141-142, 154, 168
Co-operatives UK 8
Co-partnership Farms 170
Co-partnership Tenants Housing Council 6, 49, 53-56, 58-59, 66, 87, 128
Co-partnership Tenants Ltd (CTL) 8, 58-59, 61, 63-64, 66-74, 78-79, 81, 83, 87, 92-99, 100-109, 114-115, 118-120, 128, 129-130, 140, 146-148, 154, 156, 163-164, 167, 170
Coryndon 162
council acquisition of land for housing 62-63, 88-89, 130-131, 135, 140, 154
council housing 5, 7, 62, 88-89, 91-92, 94, 130-135, 138, 142, 144, 145, 148, 153, 158
Coventry 10, 118, 130, 162
Cross, Sir Richard 22
Cuffley 162
Culpin, Ewart 53, 121, 124, 130, 134-135, 146
Curran, Pete 60

Darwen 15
Datchet 121-122, 162

Davies, David 75, 125-126, 142, 144-145, 156-157
Dean, Maud 86
demutualisation 146-148, 151, 153-155
Dent, J.J. 24
Dent, Mrs 117
Derby 10, 16, 32, 55
Derwentwater Tenants 4-6, 87, 92, 96-97, 99, 128, 149, 154, 165
Dewe, S.E. 114
Didsbury 118, 162
Dilke, Sir Charles 22
Doncaster 163, 169
Dorrien-Smith, A.A. 118-119
Doughty, Clara 86
Droylsden 11

Ealing Tenants 6, 8, 30, 31, 35-38, 39, 43, 46, 48, 49, 50, 52, 53-54, 59, 61, 66, 69, 71-73, 82-85, 87, 90, 92, 98-99, 100, 104, 107-108, 128, 147, 148, 152, 163
East Grinstead 163
East Ham 25, 28, 29
Eastbourne 163
Eastcote 119, 163
Eastriggs 133
Eccles (Kent) 56, 163
Edinburgh 67, 123
Edlington 163
Edwards, Trystan 134
Eltham 17
Epsom 29, 87, 162
Equity Shoes 47
Ethex 76
eugenics 108

Facebook 8, 154
Fairfield Tenants 118, 130-131, 151, 163
Fallings Park Tenants 63-64, 92, 95-96, 99, 147, 163
Familistère, Le 22
Fenwick, Pascoe 24, 25
Fernhill 126, 163
Ferryhill 11

First Garden City Ltd 44-45, 46, 72, 90, 93, 95
First World War 5, 7-8, 17, 26, 72, 77, 86, 110, 116-117, 120, 126, 127-134, 153, 162
Fishguard 163
Friendly Societies, Registrar of 107-108, 148

Garden Cities and Town Planning Association (GCTPA) 53, 92, 123, 127-128, 130-131, 135-137, 145-146
Garden City Association (GCA) 42, 51, 53, 95
Garden City movement 6, 39-49, 53, 92, 110, 113, 119-120, 140
Garden City Press 45, 47, 59, 70
Garden City Tenants 6, 45-47, 48, 49, 53-54, 55, 59, 61, 69, 70-71, 72-73, 83-84, 85, 92-93, 99, 130, 147, 165
Garden Suburb Builders Ltd 101
garden suburbs and villages 6, 8, 39-49, 53, 56, 62, 74, 79-80, 85, 87, 92, 94-95, 97-99, 119-120, 133-134
Garrard, R.P. 104
Garscube – see Glasgow Garden Suburb Tenants
Gateshead 16
Geddes, Patrick 67
Gellifaelog 166
General Builders 27, 34, 37, 53, 56, 58, 61, 85, 101
General Election (1906) 59-60
General Election (1918) 134
General Elections (1910) 100
George, Henry 42
Germany town planning 62, 67, 128
Gilfach Goch 126, 162
Gladstone, William 21-22
Glasgow 92, 123-124, 127-128, 130, 163
Glasgow Garden Suburb Tenants 123, 130, 163, 169
Glastonbury 118, 163, 168
Glyn Cory 160, 162
Godin, Jean-Baptiste André 22

Golders Green 115, 161, 163
Gorseinon 126, 164
Gourock 124, 164
Gower – see Gŵyr
Grappenhall Tenants 90, 169
Gray, J.C. 24, 65, 153
Great Western Railway (GWR) 125, 145, 160-164, 166-169
Greenhalgh, J.H. 36, 59, 146
Greening, Edward Owen 22, 31-32, 33
Greenock 124, 164
Greenwood, Crossley 6, 33, 58, 70
Greenwood, J.W. 65-66
Greenwood, Joseph 6, 33, 70
Greta Hamlet – see Derwentwater Tenants
Gretna 133
Grey, Earl 53, 78, 97, 98, 100
Guessens Court 140, 169
Guildford 140, 166
Guise 22
Gurney, Sybella 54-56, 57, 65-66, 71, 75-76, 77, 80, 89, 93, 105, 110, 120-121, 131, 158
Gwauncaergurwen 164
Gŵyr 3-4

Hadleigh 121-122, 150, 164
Halifax 13
Hampstead 161, 163-164 (see also Hampstead Garden Suburb)
Hampstead Garden Suburb 30, 37, 56, 72, 84, 92, 97-99, 101, 107-108, 114-115, 128, 130, 146-147, 152, 164
Hampstead Heath Extension 97, 101, 146
Hampstead Heath Extension Tenants 101, 114-115, 146-147, 164
Hamshire, Eli 122
Harborne Tenants 63, 69, 88, 92, 94-95, 96, 99, 102, 104, 147-148, 164
Hardie, Keir 60
Harmony Hall 112
Haslemere 56, 118, 130, 164

Hayes 145, 164

Hebden Bridge 6, 11, 33, 58, 70, 164

Hengoed 126, 164

Heptonstall 10

Hereford Co-operative Housing 75, 88-90, 91, 102, 150-151, 164

Highley 126, 165

Hill, Octavia 23, 71

Hindhead 44, 56, 165

Hodgkin, Howard 28, 29

holiday homes 1, 121

Holyoake, George Jacob 11, 32, 33, 49, 54, 56, 120, 158

Holyoake-Marsh, Emilie 56

Homes England 2-3

Homesgarth 113-114, 165

Horsfall, Thomas 62, 67

Horsforth 165

Houghton le Springs 10

housework 111-112

Housing Act (1924) 145

housing associations 146, 151, 158 (see also public utility societies)

Housing of the Working Classes Act (1890) 61, 62

Housing Organisation Society - see Rural Co-partnership Housing Association

Housing Reform Company 73-75, 76, 125, 162, 164, 166

Housing, Town Planning &c Act (1909) 63, 69, 119, 120, 128

Housing, Town Planning &c Acts (1919) 7, 132, 134-137, 138-140, 145-146, 156

Howard Cottage Society 72, 93, 114, 130-131

Howard, Ebenezer 6, 40-44, 65, 72, 85, 92, 111-114, 134, 140

Howick, Viscount 78

Hucknall 10

Huddersfield 10, 16, 110

Humberstone – see Anchor Tenants

Hutchings, William 54, 59, 78, 100, 101, 104, 107, 118

Ilford 165

Improved Industrial Dwellings Company 115

Independent Labour Party (ILP) 47, 60, 67, 85, 91-92

Industrial and Provident Societies Acts 12, 24, 76, 107-108, 128, 146, 148, 156

International Cooperative Alliance 15, 105

Jarrow 60

Jevons, Stanley 73-75, 125

Jones, Benjamin 18-20, 22-25, 27-29, 32, 156, 158

Jordans 141

Keighley 10

Kemsing 93

Keswick 1-7, 33, 70, 87, 92, 96-97, 99, 149, 165

Keswick Community Housing Trust 2-3, 5-6

Kettering 27, 81

King, Elizabeth Moss 112

Kings Norton 165

Knebworth 118, 150, 165

Labour Association (Labour Co-partnership Association) 32-34, 36, 42, 44, 46, 48, 49, 50-53, 55, 56, 60-61, 72, 97, 100, 105, 108, 154

Labour Party 60, 154 (see also Independent Labour Party)

Ladies' Dwelling Company 112

Ladies' Residential Chambers Ltd 112

Lancashire 8, 11, 12, 32, 57

Land Nationalisation Society 42

land values 41-42, 62-63

Lander, H. Clapham 111, 113-114, 120

Leeds 4, 10, 13, 16, 165

Lees, Sarah 57, 88, 90

Leicester 6, 11, 27, 30, 45, 47-48, 49, 70, 80, 81, 84-85, 159, 165 (see also Anchor Tenants)

Leicester Printers 45

Leicester, Bryce 79, 129

Leicestershire 120

Letchworth 6, 15, 30, 44-49, 55, 70, 72, 85, 90, 93, 95, 96, 98, 101, 113-114, 130, 147, 165 (see also Garden City Tenants)

Letchworth Co-operative Homes 113-114, 165

Lever, William 46, 60

Lib-Lab MPs 19, 60, 100

Lincoln 27

Litchfield, Frederick 56, 57, 58, 66-67, 101, 103, 118, 129, 140, 146

Liverpool 4, 30, 42, 56, 62, 69, 77, 84, 97, 159 (see also Liverpool Garden Suburb Tenants)

Liverpool Garden Suburb Tenants 69, 77-80, 82-84, 92-93, 99, 128-130, 147, 152, 165

Llanelli 126, 142, 144, 165

Llanidloes 126, 166

Lloyd George, David 41, 100, 127, 134, 138

Lloyd, T. Alwyn 125

local authority housing – see council housing

Local Government Board 91, 132-134

London County Council 7, 62, 97

London Trades Council 20, 23

Lutyens, Edwin 98, 118

Lyme Regis 3

Lytton, Earl 118

Machynlleth Garden Village 126, 166

Maclaurin, Robert 92

Maddison, Fred 54, 57, 60

Maidstone 56, 163

Malvern 141, 166

Manchester 6, 8, 9, 10, 16, 18-19, 30, 42, 56, 57, 62, 65-68, 84-86, 93, 116-117, 118, 123, 131, 133, 136, 151, 166 (see also Manchester Tenants)

Manchester and Salford Co-operative Society 16

Manchester Tenants 57, 59, 64, 65-70, 77, 79-80, 82-86, 92-94, 99, 102-104, 108-109, 116-117, 128, 130, 149, 154, 157, 162

Mancot Royal 133

Mann, Amos 47-48, 54, 77, 81, 85, 105, 159

Margam 166

Marr, Thomas 67-68, 75-76, 77, 79, 86, 102-103, 108, 118, 123-124, 131, 149, 151, 156, 158

Marshall, Alfred 54

Maryport 10

Mauchline 10

Mayo, Catherine 110-111

Meadow Way Green 114

Meadway Court 114-115

Mearns, Andrew 21, 44

meeting halls 6, 47, 57, 78, 79-80, 82, 93, 95, 117, 123, 147, 149

Melvin, Alice 115, 161, 163-164

Merrill, George 43

Merthyr 166

Middlesbrough 44

Middleton 10, 161

Millthorpe 43, 85

Minet, William 24, 26, 27-28

Ministry of Health 136-137, 143-144

Ministry of Munitions 133, 142, 162

Ministry of Reconstruction 132

Mitchell, J.T.W. 11, 33

Mond, Sir Alfred 144

Moor Pool – see Harborne Tenants

Moor Pool Heritage Trust 147

Moore Ede, Rev. William 118

Morris, William 40, 42

Mytholmroyd 13, 84

National Council of Women of Great Britain 141, 166

National Federation of Housing Societies 146

National Housing Federation 146

National Housing Reform Council 54, 157

Neale, Edward Vansittart 11, 24, 29, 32, 33, 70, 112

Neale, H.J. Vansittart 24

Nettlefold, John 51, 54, 61-63, 67, 69, 71, 80, 88, 89, 94-95, 102, 106, 131, 147, 158

Neville, Ralph 42, 44, 46, 71

New Earswick 43

New Forest Tenants 161

New Lanark 22

New Town Housing Society 140

new towns 40

Newark 166

Newby West 118, 162

Newcastle-upon-Tyne 130, 166

Newport (Mon.) 166

Newtown (Powys) 126, 166

Northwich 118

Northwood 119, 166

Oakwood Tenants 101, 147, 164

Ogmore Vale 166

older people's housing 98, 115

Oldham 6, 13, 56, 57, 90, 166 (see also Oldham Garden Suburb Tenants)

Oldham Garden Suburb Tenants 56-57, 59, 84, 87-88, 90, 166

Onslow Garden Village 140, 157, 166

Onslow, Lord 140, 157

Orbiston 112

Osborn, Frederic 72, 115-116, 131, 140

Otford (Kent) 121-122, 130, 167

Owen, Robert 22

Owenite communities 112

owner occupation 5, 14-16, 19-20, 31, 122, 126, 146, 150

Oxford 24, 27, 55, 56, 111, 167

Paget, Arthur 95-96

Paget, Sir Richard 64, 95-96

Parker, Barry 42-43, 91, 98, 112, 115

Peirce, Melusina Fay 112

Pengam 126, 167

Penge 25-26, 28, 29, 167

Penkhull – see Stoke-on-Trent Tenants

Pen-y-darren 166

Penzance 145, 167

Perry, Harry 36-37, 54

Petersfield 121, 130, 167

Peterston-super-Ely 74, 162

Pilsworth and Unsworth 162, 167

Pimlico 31

Plashet 28, 29, 37, 167

Plymouth 31, 145, 167

Pontardulais 167

Pontymoile 167

Pontypool 10

Port Sunlight 46

Port Talbot 166

Post Office Savings Bank 13

Potter, Beatrice – see Webb, Beatrice

Powerstock 3

Prevention of Fraud (Investment) Act (1939) 147-148

private rental housing 5, 28, 62

public utility societies 62-63, 76, 128-137, 140-142, 144-146, 156

Public Works Loan Board (PWLB) and Commissioners 26, 28, 29, 63, 66-71, 75, 81, 82, 87, 89, 93-95, 125, 128, 129, 131, 135-136, 141, 143-144, 148, 156

Public Works Loans Act (1875) 26

Pumphrey, Henry 17

Pym, Ruth 114

Quakers 2, 5, 29, 42, 43, 141

Queenwood 112

Renfrew 124, 167

Rent and Mortgage Interest (War Restrictions) Act (1916) 127, 136

rent levels 52, 83-84, 90, 97, 98, 114, 127-128, 131, 136, 143-144, 155-156

Residential Flats Ltd 161

Rhiwbina 73-75, 125, 130, 148, 162

Rhondda 126, 163

Richardson, Harry 117

Right to Buy legislation 148, 150, 158

Roberts, John 107

Rochdale Pioneers 11, 12-13, 48, 82, 158

Rogers, Fred W. 119-120

Rothschild, (Lord) Nathaniel Mayer 122

Rothschild, Leopold de 71

Rowntree brothers 43

Rowntree, Seebohm 132-133

Royal Arsenal Co-operative Society 16-17, 27

Royal Commission on Labour 34, 61

Royal Commission on the Housing of the Working Classes 18-20, 22-23

Royal Holloway College 55

Ruabon 56, 167

Rubery and Eachway Tenants 167

Rudheath Tenants 118, 130, 167

Ruislip 115, 119 (see also Ruislip Manor Cottage Society)

Ruislip Manor Cottage Society 119, 130, 151, 163, 166, 167

Rural Co-partnership Housing Association 120-122, 130, 150, 161, 164, 167-168

Rural Co-partnership Housing Trust 120

rural housing 49, 54, 120-122, 150

Rural Housing and Sanitation Association 54

Rural Housing Organisation Society – see Rural Co-partnership Housing Association

Rushden 168

Ruskin, John 71, 81

Russian Revolution 139

Salford 18, 67 (see also Manchester and Salford Co-operative Society)

Salisbury, (Lord) 4th Marquess 21, 22

Salisbury, 5th Marquess 77-78, 132

Scotland 4, 91-92, 123-124

Scottish CWS 32, 141-142, 154

Scottish Guild of Handicrafts 92

Scottish Parliament 123

Sealand Tenants 92, 97, 102, 147, 168

second homes 1, 121

Select Committee debates, housing 23, 61-63, 69, 89, 94, 119

Sevenoaks Tenants 6, 30, 49, 53, 54, 59, 69, 71, 83-84, 87, 92-93, 99, 130, 148, 151, 155, 168

Severn Valley Junction 145, 168

shared ownership 3

Shaw, G. Bernard 40, 46, 71-72, 75

Shaw-Stewart, Sir Hugh 124

Sheerness 27

Sheffield 43, 56, 168

Shilbottle 168

Shirehampton 160, 168

Shoreham (Kent) 93

Sidmouth 168

slum housing 15, 21, 62, 67, 72, 84

Small Holdings and Allotments Act (1908) 122

smallholdings 91, 122, 168, 169

Snowdown and Betteshanger Tenants 168

Social Democratic Federation 43

Social Housing, Regulator of 151, 158

socialism 23, 40, 42-43, 47, 50, 60, 85-86, 92, 139, 159

Socialist League 42-43

Society for the Promotion of Co-operative Housekeeping 115

Somerdale 168

Somersham 121, 168

South Metropolitan Gas 50

Sowerby Bridge 13

Spitalfields 22, 44, 97

St Ives 3, 4

St Mawes 121, 150, 168

Stevenson, Canon Morley 90

Stirling Homesteads 91-92, 168

Stirling-Maxwell, Sir John 123

Stoke-on-Trent 19, 30, 69, 101, 147 (see also Stoke-on-Trent Tenants)

Stoke-on-Trent Tenants 69, 83-84, 92, 96, 99, 108, 130, 147, 168

Stoop, F.C. 91

Street (Som.) 168
Sunderland 84
Sutcliffe, George Lister 58, 114, 118-119
Sutton 118, 169
Swansea 126, 145, 169
Swanzy, Francis 49, 54, 59

Tameside 151
Taylor, J.T. 47, 54, 81, 85
tenancy conditions 51, 52, 90
Tenant Co-operators 17, 23-30, 35, 37,
    49, 51, 54, 59, 69, 87, 101-102, 169
tenant shareholdings 35-37, 48, 51-52,
    74, 90, 98, 106-107, 121, 146, 155
tenant social life 77-86, 96
tennis courts 6, 57, 78, 79-80, 82, 95,
    115, 149
Thompson, Laura Gilchrist 49, 71
Thompson, Rev. Percy 49
Thompson, William 54, 61, 119
Thorne 169
Toddington 169
Todmorden 10, 13
Torrens, William 22
Tottenham 25
Town and Country Planning
    Association 42 (see also Garden
    City Association; Garden Cities
    and Town Planning Association)
town planning 40-41, 62, 77, 119 (see
    also Garden City movement)
Toynbee Hall 22, 44, 97
trade unions 20, 31, 34, 60, 76, 110, 139
Trades Union Congress (TUC) 60
Triple Alliance (trade unions) 139
Truro 145, 169
Tudor Walters Report 133
Tudor Walters, John 133

Unitarianism 61
Unwin, Raymond 6, 42-43, 46-47, 49,
    53, 58, 62, 66, 74, 79, 85, 87, 91, 94,
    97, 98, 112-113, 115, 123, 125, 133, 166
Upton Park 25

Vale of Leven Tenants 124, 160
Vauxhall 169
Vivian, Henry 31-32, 34-38, 46, 48,
    50-54, 57-61, 63, 66-69, 71-73,
    78-79, 82, 85, 88, 89, 92, 96, 98-99,
    100-102, 104-109, 118, 129-130, 146,
    154-155, 158, 167, 170
voting procedures in housing societies
    24, 59, 103-109, 157-158

Wakefield 10, 86
Wallhead, Muriel 86
Wallhead, Richard 85
Warrington 90, 91, 169
Warrington Tenants 90, 169
Waterlow, Sydney 115
Watford 14-15
Watts, Fred 49
Wavertree – see Liverpool Garden
    Suburb Tenants
Wayford (Norfolk) 75, 169
Webb, Beatrice 27-28, 50, 132
Webb, Catherine 112
Webb, Sidney 40, 50
Well Hall estate 17
Welsh Garden Cities Ltd 126, 160,
    163-165, 167, 169
Welsh Housing and Development
    Association 110
Welsh Town Planning and Housing
    Trust 75, 124-126, 130, 142-145,
    160-170
Welwyn Garden City 72, 140, 169
West Byfleet – see Byfleet
West Ham 25
Westerton 123, 130, 163, 169
Weston Rhyn Tenants 126, 130, 169
Wheatley, John 145
Whiteley, Edgar 85, 104
Wigton (Cumb.) 170
Wild, Harold 86
Wilford, J.S. 54
Williams, Aneurin 15, 44-46, 54, 56,
    105-106, 118, 119-120, 131, 146, 153,
    165

Williams, Bernard 15, 44-48, 54, 55, 59, 70, 105

Williams, Hall 144-145

Winchester 56, 170

Winfrey, Sir Richard 75

Wingland (Lincs.) 170

Winnington 118, 167, 170

Woking Co-operative Society 120, 170

Woking Garden Suburb 120, 170

Wolverhampton 63-64, 92, 95, 147, 163 (see also Fallings Park Tenants)

Women's Co-operative Guild 15, 84, 110-112

Women's Freedom League 86

women's participation 15, 54-55, 78, 81, 84, 85-86, 110-117, 128, 141

Woodworkers Ltd 101, 129

Wooler 3, 4

Woolwich 16-17, 27, 124

Worcester 118, 170

Workers Ltd (Malvern) 141

Worth Matravers 3

Wrexham Tenants 125, 170

Wrotham Tenants 170

Wythenshawe 133

Yerbury, John 29, 30, 54, 87, 101-102

Ynysybwl 170

York 43

Yorkshire 6, 8, 11, 13, 84, 163

Zetetical Society 40, 72